"For executives who think they have read all the right manuals and are following the rules but not getting the right results, this shrewd, witty guide to management techniques might be a godsend."
—*Publishers Weekly*

"So much more than the standard management manual . . . the art, not the science, of management."
—*Kirkus Reviews*

About the author

R.G.H. SIU brings an eclectic, yet deep, background to this study of the master manager. Among his previous positions are Research Associate at Harvard University, Chief Scientist and Technical Director of the Army Quartermaster Corps, Chairman of the Army Research Council, and Associate Law Enforcement Assistance Administrator of the Department of Justice. He has served as a member of the Army Science Board, as Technical Consultant to the Panel on the Peaceful Uses of Atomic Energy of the Joint Congressional Committee on Atomic Energy, and as Chairman of Members of the Academy for Contemporary Problems. He has lectured widely, before such audiences as IBM, DuPont, Yale University, and government, industrial, and academic groups in Warsaw, Taipei, and Buenos Aires. His books include THE CRAFT OF POWER, TRANSCENDING THE POWER GAME: THE WAY TO EXECUTIVE SERENITY, THE TAO OF SCIENCE, THE MAN OF MANY QUALITIES, and CH'I. Siu received his Ph.D. in Chemistry from the California Institute of Technology in 1943. Since 1969, he has been an independent consultant in corporate strategy, research and development management, and social problems.

THE MASTER MANAGER

BY
R.G.H. SIU

A MENTOR BOOK
NEW AMERICAN LIBRARY
TIMES MIRROR
NEW YORK AND SCARBOROUGH, ONTARIO

LIBRARY OF CONGRESS CATALOG CARD NO.: 81-85138

Siu, R. G. H.
The Master Manager.

New York : New American Library
224 p.
8201   811021

First Mentor Printing, January, 1982

2   3   4   5   6   7   8   9

To
Simon Ramo

PREFACE

THIS BOOK FOLLOWS two earlier volumes for readers interested in leadership and management. The first described the path to great personal power and the second, to executive serenity. We shall now address the intuitive artistry of the Master Manager and the kinds of real people with whom he or she must deal.

The important facets are delineated in the short basic text. These include the central art, 10 essential principles, 10 major pitfalls, and the hallmark of the Master. Three hundred sixty six mini case studies, illustrating these and other precepts associated with human interactions, are presented in a lengthier appendix. Finally, the salient points are recapitulated in the form of 100 proverbs in the second appendix.

With the completion of our trilogy on management (*The Craft of Power*, 1979; *Transcending the Power Game: The Way to Executive Serenity*, 1980; and *The Master Manager*, 1980—published by Wiley), we would like to express appreciation to our generous and understanding readers and to wish them well. May their lives become like the great deep river. Though gales churn violent waves and pelted rocks disrupting ripples, the great deep river keeps flowing steadily along.

R. G. H. Siu
Washington, D.C.
September 1980

CONTENTS

I
The Essential Art

THE GREAT MANAGER is born; so much of him is instinctive. But it is only later that he is made or destroyed. He is made by maturing the intuition through quickening art, or destroyed by smothering it under deadening technics.

At times the enabling artistry is expressed through the positive approach—by laying on, as in painting. At times it is expressed via the negative approach—by taking away, as in sculpturing. The various actions are dynamically blended into the singular characteristic of all great leaders and executives. Master it—not intellectually, but instinctively. Let it so become a part of you that you no longer hesitatingly analyze, but naturally act.

Before pointing it out, however, it might be useful by way of background to get our bearings about the kinds of situations in which executives find themselves. We cite 3 examples.

The first concerns written guarantees. Article V of the Constitution states that private property shall not "be taken for public use, without just compensation." Yet let us see what actually happens in practice. In 1962 New York and New Jersey state legislatures established the Port Authority. The Covenant specifically forbids the Port Authority from ever financing deficit-ridden mass-transit systems. With this and other understandings, many individuals and institutions bought its bonds. But came June 15, 1976, with a lot of bonds still outstanding, the 2 legislatures simply removed the restriction. The market price dropped significantly. There was no compensation.

The second example concerns international competition in air travel. During the early 1970s the transatlantic air carriers gradually decreased their respective fares based on close calculations of incremental gains in the fraction of total passenger business. The companies kept planning against each other and were beginning to reach some sort of equilibrium. Suddenly, Britain's Laker Airways appeared on the scene in late 1977 with a drastically reduced fare. The round-trip ticket for the no-frills, no-reservation travel between Los Angeles and London was less than half that charged by Trans World Airlines and British Airways. Overnight as it were, all the pricing schedules carefully formulated by the major carriers had to be tossed out the window.

The third concerns national politics. During the congressional debate on the energy bill in 1977 the President voiced his stiff opposition to the version being pushed by the Senate, whereupon several of his loyal Senators launched a vigorous campaign to defeat the Senate proposal. Just as their filibuster was succeeding, as everyone was being worn to a frazzle, the Vice President and the Majority Leader, with encouragement from the White House, abruptly pulled a parliamentary maneuver that resulted in the passage of the controversial bill. This left the erstwhile White House supporters, as the American vernacular would put it, "fit to be tied."

With these 3 examples of executive milieus before us, we can readily understand why it is that the unique art that sets all great leaders and executives apart from the rest is Chinese baseball, a game played almost exactly like American baseball—the same players, same field, same bats and balls, same method of keeping score, and so on. The batter stands in the batter's box, as usual. The pitcher stands on the pitcher's mound, as usual. He winds up, as usual, and zips the ball down the alley. There is one and only one difference. And it is this: after the ball leaves the pitcher's hand and as long as the ball is in the air, anyone can move any of the bases anywhere.

The polished manager therefore does not complain that people are not following the rules or are changing their minds while the program is underway. He does not expect that Nature is going to hold the Universe constant, while he goes about making up his plans and pursuing his projections. He recognizes that social dilemmas are not like mathematical problems, which can be solved for all times, like "2 plus 2 equals 4." There is no such thing as a "labor problem," for instance, which can be attacked and settled once and for all. There are only labor issues—never fully defined, gyrating in constant chameleonic flux and defying even semipermanent dispositions. Thus he is always "nimble of mind" and "fleet of foot."

So leave the scientific models, Occam's razor, and other simplifying temptations to the scholastic sirens to sing. But following Ulysses, let yourself be securely lashed to the mast of your own ship, lest you, too, like so many unhappy mariners, be impelled by the ravishing music to dive overboard into the perilous sea to your own destruction. Hearken instead to the eighteenth-century mystic poet William Blake, who prayed:

May God keep us
from single vision
and Newton's sleep.

II
Principles to Follow

MANAGERIAL TECHNIQUES THAT work in one kind of organization may not do so in another. The seasoned executive is not indiscriminately taken in by the hue and cry about bringing "sound business practices" into government or about putting universities on a management-by-objective routine. He is circumspect even about the application of uniform procedures across all parts of the same institution. Directing a production plant calls for different tactics from directing a research laboratory. He judiciously tailors the practices to the circumstances.

There are certain principles underlying the universal art of Chinese baseball, however, that govern across the spectrum—whether it be government, university, or industry; whether it be church, army, or syndicate; whether it be technical services, sales, or advertising. We shall list 10 of the most important and add a few hints about their respective features.

1.

ACT FROM AN INSTANTANEOUS APPREHENSION OF THE TOTALITY

WE START WITH a principle deeply inculcated in not only the greatest of executives, but also the wisest of people. And I invite your attention to the salient word, "apprehension," which stands in contrast to the word "comprehension." It is important to think things through with the mind, of course. But this, is not enough. Even though a person can give a logical explanation, he will never be a genius at action until he acquires an unerring intuitive sensitivity about things. Only then will he be able to reach into a mass of conflicting data and opinions and pull out the right thing to do and do it at the right time.

Experienced chief executives are clearheaded about the distinction between the *science* of management and the *art* of management. They recognize that the science of management is often decisive when it comes to the "small" decisions, but the art of management is always decisive when it comes to the "BIG" decisions. There was more art than science involved, for example, when International Telephone and Telegraph Corporation decided in the 1960s to engage in political activity toward overthrowing the Salvador Allende government in Chile, or when Harvard University decided in 1976 to shift emphasis from graduate research to undergraduate teaching; or when Japan decided in 1977 to move sluggishly toward reducing the $8.5 billion trade imbalance between itself and the United States, despite considerable American pressure. Mature executives do not commit the fatal mistake of overreliance on the scientific and intellectual arguments of experts to the suppression of their own gut feelings. They do

6

not let themselves be gored on the horns of rationality and logic.

The story comes to mind about the beautiful maiden who fell from her canoe into the hands of the King of the Alligators. The mother tearfully begged for her return. Being a good sport, the King offered the lady a fair proposition. "I will return your daughter," he declared, "if you can make one true statement." Without thinking, she exclaimed, "You're going to keep my daughter!"

Persistently, logical people frequently find themselves in the same fix as the King of the Alligators. If the statement that he is going to keep the girl is true, then he must release her. If the statement that he is going to keep the girl is false, then he must keep her. So he's damned if he does and damned if he doesn't. Scientists and romantics abhor such predicaments. But executives with any exposure at all are used to them as daily fare. The tragic heroes of Homer and other ancient Greek writers had long ago set the pattern. Agamemnon was faced with the choice of killing his daughter or betraying his military duty, Orestes with matricide or disobedience to Apollo, Antigone with being unfaithful to her dead brother or to her city.

For scientific arguments on the practical limitations of logic, we may examine some mathematical problems that arise in relatively simple events as in chess, checkers, and go. There are certain types of computational problems of this nature that can be solved in principle. But computer scientists at the IBM research center, Larry J. Stockmeyer and Ashok K. Chandra, disclosed in *Scientific American* in 1979 that ideal computers would be required as large as the universe operating at least as long as the age of the universe.

There is a more fundamental consideration. Rationality emerged relatively recently in the course of evolution. There is something else that we may refer to collectively as the intimate Self of the organism, which had been in existence eons before. We are still bound by this entrenched universal Self, this preintellect Self, this source of the intuitive and the emotional, of passion—in short, the Self that apprehends.

The second key word in this first management principle is "totality." We need not belabor the commonsense advice about getting the complete picture or the familiar moral behind the parable of the blind men and the elephant. But a comparison of the wholist strategy and the partist at resolving complicated issues may be of interest.

The wholist strategy encompasses the entire domain at all times. It takes all possible factors bearing on the subject into account at the very outset. The unessential elements are then successively removed from further consideration until a relatively pure answer is obtained. In the case of the wholist strategy therefore the tentative answers along the way are always correct but imprecise until the ultimate answer is reached.

The partist strategy, on the other hand, deals with only a part of the totality at any given time. It assumes a small number of factors at the beginning to be necessary and sufficient to explain the question at hand. If that assumption turns out to be false, it then moves on to the next combination. Successive formulations are tried and discarded until the ultimate answer is reached. In the case of the partist strategy therefore the tentative answers along the way are always precisely stated but incorrect until the correct one is finally found.

Preliminary studies have indicated that when time is of no consequence we can arrive at the optimal resolution via either route. But when time is of the essence, the wholist approach is much more dependable. The odds in its favor are increased dramatically when Chinese baseball comes into the picture.

Furthermore, as any aficionado of professional football knows so well, the BIG games are decided more often than not by the mistakes committed rather than the yardages gained. Although the wholist strategy may not make as much yardage in any one play or in any one game, it is relatively immune to fatal errors. In contract, although the partist strategy may make spectacular yardages in any one play or in any one game, it is invariably open to fatal mistakes during the interim period of trial and error.

The more proficient one becomes in wholist strategy, the more quick is he at eliminating irrelevant factors. The consummate expert arrives at the final answer in a single burst of apprehension. He is likened to the powerful Arabian sheik who lost one of his horses during a long desert journey. So he directed the requisition of another horse from the next town. When he arrived, two horses were brought to him for final selection. Since the owners did not want to lose their horses, each one exaggerated the age and weaknesses and how they would never meet the high standards of the sheik.

"Very well. Let's have a race," decreed the sheik. "I'll take the winner."

"Buy your Highness," whispered his aide. "This will not decide the better horse. The owners will not push the horses to their best."

"Ah, but they will, smiled the sheik. "Order each man to ride the other man's horse."

The greater the executive responsibility the more important it is to grasp the totality of the ramifications of one's policies and practices. In many cases the executive is capable of apprehending the situation in an abstract intellectual manner. But the pressures of day-to-day profits and expediences often shove the longer-term payments out of practical calculations. About a decade or so ago, the commanding general of one of the world's largest logistic operations told his technical director: "I appreciate the ultimate value of your basic research proposals in solving the problems of my successors. But let *them* pay you for solving *their* problems. *I'm* paying you to solve *my* problems. And they're *today's* problems."

The same narrow view appears to be a common trait. The current oil debate illustrates its universality. Basically, there is just so much oil in the ground. Yet here is what we observe: every individual, corporation, and nation is increasing the consumption of oil. Most are pressing for higher production to meet the insatiable appetite. Governments and corporations are riding the wave of consumption to generate greater taxes and profits. Instead of having alternative sources of energy on hand before increasing consumption of limited reserves, the policies of governments and corporations are actually driving the consumption skyward based on wishful thinking that in some fashion, like manna from heaven, the alternative source of energy will be fully developed at the time of critical need. But the day when the supply will be diminished to the point of scarcity all around is ineluctably approaching. Some estimate in several generations. Having depleted its own reserves several generations hence, will the United States then be forced into the position of imposing its spcial kind of relationship with oil- and gas-rich neighbors? Having depleted their own reserves in not many more generations, will the rich Arab countries go back to the drastic poverty of centuries back? Are there many in the present generation willing to forego their energy-consuming luxuries to conserve energy-consuming essentials for their great grandchildren? Are they not saying in effect, like the general, let *them* solve *their* problems?

Most executives are able to think through isolated segments of a problem in a logical fashion. There are relatively few who can apprehend the situation completely. Still fewer are those who can apprehend the situation completely and are able to implement the wholistic trade-offs. Be among this rare species.

2.

HEED THE CONTEXT

WHEN LOOKING AT a picture, human beings show a tendency of focusing on the figure in which they are interested and forgetting about the background. Executives have an analogous inclination of spotlighting the particular problem at hand and ignoring the context from which it sprang. They frequently forget the feature of change, sometimes referred to as "No-Balls." This is the dominance of the context in which social upheavals occur in contrast to the specific grievance or demand of the moment.

The game of No-Balls is derived from the incident involving a group of football rookies out for spring training. They were restless for action, as they stood around the field waiting for something to happen. One of the impatient youngsters could not stand it any longer and cried: "Let's scrimmage!" His teammate attempted to curb his eagerness. "But we don't have a ball, Joe." "The hell with the ball," Joe snapped back. "Let's get on with the game!"

Someone on the sidelines kept watching the boys lining up and thrashing about on the field. He became excited, ran into the locker room, got a ball, and joined the game, which then proceeded in earnest.

If the social climate within an organization or country is conducive, a conflict can be started with a phony complaint or none at all. A cause célèbre will emerge before long. This will then bring added reinforcements of people who genuinely believe in it. A strike, a riot, a revolution has the best chance for success not when there is a justifiable specific grievance but a condition of prevalent dissatisfaction. Under such circumstances, an enduring resolution of the conflict cannot be achieved by meeting an articulated claim or two. This might defuse the explosive assemblies of the moment. But it won't last. The context must be defulminated.

Many an executive feels that he needs not be bothered with what's going on around him. Since he has been able to overcome all obstacles to get to where he is so far, he is confident that he is equally equipped to take care of any that may arise. He is lord of his own destiny. Should you feel the same, disabuse yourself. The congenial context had much more to do with your good fortune so far, than you had to do with its prosperity. Georgi Plekhanov, the Russian Marxist philosopher, illuminated the relationship much clearer around the turn of the century. "If, owing to certain mechanical or physiological cause unconnected with the general course of the socio-political and intellectual development of Italy, Raphael, Michelangelo and Leonardo da Vinci had died in their infancy, Italian art would have been less perfect, but the general trend of its development in the period of the Renaissance would have remained the same. Raphael, Leonardo da Vinci and Michelangelo did not *create* this trend; they were merely its best representatives."

From the practical constraints of available time and energy, one obviously cannot be entangled with many peripheral events. To be detached in anxiety, however, is not necessarily to be unaware in vigilance. Passing aloofness is not to be equated with ignorance. The chief of an international institution, whether nation, church, or corporation, must constantly keep abreast of world politics and exert timely and permissible influence in his institution's own interest as the occasion compels.

During medieval times, capitalists were more directly enmeshed in political power plays. The Genoese Benedetto Zaccaria, who had cornered the alum of Phocaea, had his own navy to destroy the competitive commerce of Pisa. A group of exiled Florentines regained their status by financing the papal conquest of Sicily and creating the Guelf alliance with the King of Sicily, the Pope, and themselves as dominating bankers. Today, the giant multinational bodies are not as militaristic but equally astute.

In 1965, the Chairman of the Board of Chase Manhattan Bank delineated some of the ways in which it attends to the political forces enveloping the bank's business. "Last year, well over 100 legislators and other government officials were our guests at luncheons hosted by our senior officers," reported George Champion in *Nation's Business.* "In election year 1964, more than 1000 Chase Manhattan people performed meaningful work for their chosen parties. They served on their own time and in their own neighborhoods as political fund-raisers, canvassers, office workers and stump speakers. Some of them became candidates themselves—a practice we encourage by paying full salaries to employees who are elected to public office, and granting leaves to those who are elected or appointed to full-time posts. About 125 of our current staff members hold elected offices as mayors, village trustees, town councilmen and the like."

One of the most skillful of historical figures in triggering the context to his own purposes was Mahatma Gandhi. For millenia India had been a land of famine. People have known the pangs of hunger. They have witnessed slow painful death by starvation. Gandhi knew that they knew. So he resorted to self-inflicted hunger as a prime instrument of control over the masses. The great fast of 1924 was representative.

In his program of "purifying India," one of the first steps was the reconciliation of the Hindus and Moslems. He kept preaching the indispensability of harmony between the 2 groups. Despite his many speeches and exhortations in his weekly, *Young India,* the results were nil. Relations were actually deteriorating. Religious clashes grew worse. His own associates were disregarding his code of nonviolence. "Nothing evidently, which I say or write can bring the two communities together," he said in a statement on September 18. "I am therefore imposing on myself a 21-day fast from today and ending on Wednesday October 6th. . . . I respectfully invite the heads of all communities, including Englishmen, to meet and end this quarrel which is a disgrace to religion and to humanity. It seems as if God has been dethroned. Let us reinstate him in our hearts." Long before the fast ended, millions of Hindus and Moslems joined in the prayer and weepingly pledged to live peacefully together thereafter.

Should you aspire to become a major administrator in the American government, you need to develop a keen sensitivity about what makes the American people tick. Do not be guided by the ceremonial cliches and magnificent mouthings

that often magnetize the mass media. Be steered by the actu-
alities of societal transactions, rather than the hypothesized
traits of an ideal democracy.

To see us as we are, it is often more rewarding to listen to
a sympathetic outsider than to ourselves. Let us hear what the
well-liked British Ambassador James Bryce had to say in his
The American Commonwealth in 1868. The book had been
praised for over half a century as the most penetrating analysis in literature of American politics and society. In it, he
listed 4 conditions, under which American democracy was
forced to work:

"Firstly, a certain commonness of mind and tone, a want of
dignity and elevation in and about the conduct of public affairs, an insensibility to the nobler aspects and finer responsibilities of national life.

"Secondly, a certain apathy among the luxurious classes
and fastidious minds, who find themselves of no more account than the ordinary voter, and are disgusted by the superficial vulgarities of public life.

"Thirdly, a want of knowledge, tact, and judgment in the
details of legislation, as well as in administration, with an
inadequate recognition of the difficulty of these kinds of
work, and of the worth of special experience and skill in
dealing with them. Because it is incompetent, the multitude
will not feel its incompetence, and will not seek or defer to
the counsels of those who possess the requisite capacity.

"Fourthly, laxity in the management of public business.
The persons entrusted with such business being only average
men, thinking themselves and thought of by others as average
men, with a deficient sense of their high responsibilities, may
succumb to the temptations which the control of legislation
and the public funds present, in cases where persons of a
more enlarged view and with more of a social reputation to
support would remain incorruptible. To repress such derelic-
tions of duty is every citizen's duty, but for that reason it is
in large communities apt to be neglected. Thus the very cause
which implants the mischief favours its growth."

Much progress has been realized since Bryce's time. But
the general inclinations prevail. With each retreat by the enlightened and completely public-spirited, the power of
special-interest groups rises higher in the seat of government.
Although small in number, they have become so dominating

that they are being looked on by most politicians as the context that counts. Since what happens at the political centers reverberates in the corridors of management throughout the country, executives of institutions of any size must take the demands of these groups into account. "Today's chief executive [is] considerably more responsive to the concerns of the special-interest groups, recognizing that in our system the causes advanced by these groups do gain considerable public support and are of great moment to Congress," noted the Chairman of General Electric Company, Reginald H. Jones, in 1979. "Congress has certainly demonstrated that it is an overly responsive body. So the chief executive must recognize that he is going to be faced with legislation that will move from the area of voluntarism to requirements."

Failure to adapt to the environment and/or to adapt the environment to one's minimal necessities has led to the passing away of even entire civilizations. One of the earliest was the Magdalenian culture of France during the Old Stone Age. It was a hunting society, brilliant in its time, leaving impressive evidence in its Paleolithic art. The human and animal figures, some individually real and others generally impressionistic, rival many of the contemporary paintings in sheer beauty of form. When the last Ice Age gave way to warmer climates, the steppes and tundra receded before the invading forests. The herds of mammoths, bisons, horses, and reindeers were driven off and the Magdalenian hunters declined, for they were not as creative and adaptable as the succeeding Neolithic man, the food producer, who began the long technological revolution lasting to this very day.

The context of people, however, tends to equilibrate at the status quo over a significant fraction of one's executive life. To move it off dead center, as is one of the primary functions of management, often requires Herculean effort on the part of the leader. After a year or so as President of the large University of Cincinnati, Warren Bennis made the discovery that "I had become the victim of a vast, amorphous, unwitting, unconscious conspiracy to prevent me from doing anything whatever to change the university's status quo."

As some great microbiologist had said nearly a century ago. "The microbe is nothing; the terrain is everything."

3.

OPERATE IN PHASE WITH
THE YIN-YANG

THE YIN-YANG IS one of the oldest of Chinese generalizations. The Yin and the Yang represents opposite polarities. If Yin stands for softness, Yang stands for hardness. If Yin stands for darkness, Yang stands for light. If Yin stands for female, Yang stands for male, and so on.

The dictum of the Yin-Yang states: everything in the universe is made up of the Yin and the Yang. There is no Yin without the Yang. There is no Yang without the Yin. Everything is Yin-Yang.

This conceptualization is in direct opposition to the more commonly accepted one in the West, which has come down to us from Aristotle. This Law of the Excluded Middle affirms: *A* is *B* or *A* is not *B*. Things are right or wrong, white or black, good or bad.

The Yin-Yang view suggests that the Aristotelian precept obtains only in abstractions and not in reality. In real life, no person is absolutely right and another absolutely wrong; it depends on the circumstances. No one is 100% male or 100% female; he or she always has some hormones of the opposite sex. The chain of authority and power is never absolutely one-way, say, from the superintendent to laborer; there is always some flowing the other way. There is no 0 state in social realities.

Since there is no 0 state, one should expect the presence of a dormant seed for a resurgence of what may appear as a dead issue. Events are therefore naturally cyclical.

On a national scale, the Yin-Yang cycle is exemplified by the economic sequence in the United States over the past half century. Beginning in 1929, the country was in the throes of the Great Depression of economic hardships and domestic violence. Gradually, it worked itself out of the depths of despair. The economic machine picked up steam around 1939 and raced forward for the next 25 years. Filled with vitality and exuberance, it dominated the industrial world scene as no other power has ever done. By the late 1960s the Yin-Yang cycle began to turn downward. Within a decade the country was caught in a mesh of political scandal, high inflation, unemployment, energy shortage at home, and weakening of the dollar and American leadership abroad. Even self-confidence in its ability to solve the predicament began to ebb by the latter part of the 1970s.

On a company scale, the Yin-Yang cycle is exemplified by the rise and fall of Douglas Aircraft. Begun in the back of a Santa Monica, California, barbership, Douglas Aircraft built more planes in World War II than Japan and Germany combined. This company's DC-3 was the backbone of worldwide commercial aviation for a generation. But Douglas Aircraft began slipping with the coming of the jet age, as Boeing Company gained ascendancy toward controlling 60% of the commercial jet market by the late 1970s. Even after being taken over by McDonnell-Douglass, the company's fortunes continued to deteriorate as its giant commerical carrier, the DC-10, was grounded for over a month after a series of accidents in 1979.

On an item scale, the Yin-Yang cycle is exemplified by the commercial life cycle of durable goods. Following a difficult introductory phase with slow growth toward a break-even profit position, the product goes into a period of rapid climb in sales and profits, followed by the third phase of market saturation, intensive price competition, and customer services, and ending with the terminal phase of decline and phasing out of the inventory to be replaced by a product modification or an entirely new version.

On a human scale, the Yin-Yang cycle is exemplified by the taste of women, which varies in a rhythmic fashion—not only in the taste in fashions, but also in the taste of eggs.

Stay in consonance therefore with the cycles. Do not buck the strong trend unless essential at that point in time. Hold and forestall, if feasible; channel and retreat, if necessary. Instead of being "brave" and challenging the storm gathering into peak ferocity, adopt a holding posture and await a favorable turn.

Be particularly adept at sensing the approaching turning points. Lord Bolingbroke had noticed that few statesmen possess a precise perception of historical upturns and downturns. Because of this deficiency many leaders misjudge their competitors. They continue to dread an opponent who is no longer capable of hurting them. They fail to pay alert attention to one who is developing more formidable by the day on the verge of overtaking them. Many of the powerful refuse to recognize that they have long since gone past their own ability to control.

Successful executives are particularly keen in sensing impending upswings in the Yin-Yang cycles of their interest. Charles Revson of Revlon anticipated the women's increasing desires for beauty aids long before they did so themselves and prepared his company accordingly. Ralph T. Reed of American Express foresaw the post-World War II tourist boom, when he became President in 1944 and expanded his company from the 50 offices at the time to 378 when he retired in 1960, thereby overtaking the formerly first ranking Thomas Cook in the process.

An important corollary of the Yin-Yang is the Law of Reversal. "Reversal is the nature of the Tao," said the founder of Taoism, Lao Tzu, in the sixth century B.C. When something is stretched to the full, the opposite sets in. "To advance further and further means to reverse." The more one governs, the less one achieves.

The Law of Reversal goes the Law of Diminishing Returns one better. It attests to the inevitability that if you keep pushing in the same direction, not only will you eventually realize lesser and lesser returns per unit expenditure of energy, but also that after a certain point you will even lose what you had already gained up to then. People who keep nagging the boss for a raise soon find out.

The fate of hard bargainers in this respect is reflected in the experience of the newly elected Congressman who arrived in Washington and went around looking for a stable for his horse. The first place he came to was a beautiful farm just beyond the district line. He went up to the farmer and asked about the cost. The farmer replied: "A hundred and ninety dollars a month and I get to keep the manure."

That was too steep for the freshman Congressman. So he drove farther along the main pike. About 20 miles down the road, he stopped by a pretty good-looking farm. He went up to the farmer and asked the same question. The farmer replied. "A hundred dollars a month and I get to keep the manure."

That was still too high. So he decided to search along the side roads. After another hour or so, he came across a somewhat broken down place. But the barn did not look too bad. So he went up to the farmer and asked about stabling his horse. The farmer replied: "Forty dollars a month."

The Congressman felt he was within grasp of a terrific bargain. But he wanted to make doubly sure. "How about the manure?" The farmer replied: "Sir, at that price, there ain't gonna be no manure!"

The collapse of the 1975 strike by Local 6 of the International Printing & Graphic Communication Union against the *Washington Post* was an instance of disregarding both the Yin-Yang and the Law of Reversal. For years the pressmen held the upper hand in negotiations with newspapers throughout the country, having driven a number of them to fold. They did not take seriously the technological changes that were taking place, which enabled semiskilled typists to replace skilled typesetters in the composing room. In their refusal to recognize the downswing of their bargaining power, they pressed for the modification of work rules that required additional man power and allowed some of them to earn as much as $30,000 a year. This would have been much more than most professors were receiving at the time. When the contract expired and negotiations broke down, some pressmen went on a rampage and damaged the presses. One picket carried the sign: "Phil shot the wrong Graham"—alluding to the 1963 suicide of Philip L. Graham, the late husband of the current owner. The excesses drained the support of the public and other union locals. Katherine Graham was able to break the strike by hiring nonunion workers as replacements, who remained after the disruption was over.

The executive with a conformable temperament does not think in terms of "maximizing" but of "optimizing." The word "maximize" connotes at the expense of something else, while the word "optimize" connotes with the accommodation of all elements. The word maximize in such slogans as "Maximize profits" has a certain attraction for young and small companies, which are determined to expand at the fastest possible rate, even at extraordinary risk. Once a certain size or organizational complexity is reached, however, prudence calls for the philosophy of optimization to take over.

One of the main reasons for the changeover in emphasis from maximizing to optimizing is the vulnerability of large institutions to internal strategic imbalance. Once a large institution is internally unbalanced it takes considerable time to regain the smooth interaction of its parts. Instead of maximizing along any one line for a while, then trying to balance the mobile by maximizing along some other line for a while, and so on, as small institutions can do so well, large institutions should emphasize the optimizing at all instants of time on a continuing basis.

In the light of the Yin-Yang and the Law of Reversal, stop talking once you have made your point. Become progressively more moderate in your demands as you near a reasonable settlement. Do not shove anybody against the wall. Otherwise, the Law of Reversal will confront you with an obstinacy or counterattack that will surprise you in its intensity. Unless you are out to destroy your opposition, give him a way out.

Smile when things seem at their worst; be cautious when they seem at their best.

4.

SUBSUME YOURSELF
AND RESONATE

IF YOU WISH to find social meaning in your activities, make predictions about their future, and formulate fruitful plans for growth, you cannot find the answers by looking within. You must go outside. All the scientific analyses of the components of a clock and its workings, for example, cannot tell you it is a clock and that its purpose is to keep you on time for the next meeting. You must go beyond the clock itself to know this.

Predictions are not intrinsic to the present data. They are more like beliefs that the future will be the same as the present and therefore the pattern holding for today will be valid for the future. A direct extrapolation is then made. But to say that the future is the same as the present is to go outside the present for the statement.

Several steps are entailed in applying the principle of subsuming and resonating. The first is to determine the boundaries of your responsible operations and the relevant context in which they are to be imbedded. The next step is to sense the meaning of your operations by subsuming them in the larger context and looking at them from the perspective of the latter. The last step is to impart the broader-based meaningfulness from the subsuming context to your operations and extending the full benefit of your operations to the subsuming context by incessantly resonating one against the other and livening the resulting resonance through progressively adjusting your own operations and, where practical, modifying the subsuming context itself. At the same time, since you alone

21

are responsible for your operations, you must keep assuring the identity and vitality of your own organization.

We present 3 examples of how this principle can be used. The first involves the justification of rate increases before utility commissions. In this case, we subsume the corporation as a functional element into the community as the context. The accomplished utility executive understands that the decisive factor in granting the full-rate request is not the company's need for a higher revenue but the subsuming community's perception about where best to spend its limited monies. Being sensitive to the feelings of the people in the subsuming context, he does at least two things. At the time of his request for a rate increase, the executive presents his supporting arguments in such a way that there is an implicit answer in his favor in terms of the relative values of the subsuming community's interest as perceived by the people. But equally important, he keeps resonating his corporation's interest against the community's during the period between rate requests through sharply targeted public communications and collaborative projects. The closer the shared mutuality subsumes the anticipated request for the next round, the finer is the executive tuning his resonance.

The second example involves the development of a long-term thrust in the expansion of an electricity corporation. In this instance, we subsume the specialized technoeconomic operations of electricity into the broader field of energy. We then look at the long-term growth of the corporation from the viewpoint of the subsuming context of energy. No longer do we ask ourselves the question: What are the growth opportunities for the corporation as an electricity producer and supplier? Instead we now ask ourselves the question: What are the growth opportunities for the corporation as an energy producer and supplier? Having answered the subsuming question of possible growth opportunities as an energy producer and supplier, we would then resonate the realistic potential of the corporation against the subsuming possibilities. After going back and forth subsuming and resonating, we might finally evolve a series of feasible options as an energy producer and supplier, in addition to the electricity portfolio. One such option might be a joint venture on the production of gas from coal for local industrial customers—considering the fact that 41% of the energy to the industrial sector in 1975 came from gas, as compared to only 13% from electricity; considering the fact that a 14% decline in natural gas production for consumption by the United States is projected by the Bureau of Mines by the year 2000; and considering the fact that past experience has shown an increasing pressure to reserve a certain level of gas supply for residential purposes. On the other hand, we might well end up with the ongoing program limited to electricity as optimal for our own corporation. Until we have actually worked through a sequence of subsuming and resonating cycles, however, we can never be certain that we have explored the full potential of our corporation.

In this connection, it is interesting to note how the President of Heublein, Incorporated, in 1965 regarded his company, which was the fifth largest liquor producer in the United States. "Although liquor products [e.g., Smirnoff vodka] account for most of our sales at the present time, we consider ourselves in the consumer goods business, not the liquor business," said Ralph Hart. "Liquor is a consumer good just like toothpaste and is sold in the same way."

The third involves scientific research. The scientist is looked on by many people as allied with the forces of evil. To a considerable degree people feel this way because they think that the scientist just doesn't care about the human race. In other words, the scientist refuses to subsume himself into humankind and resonate in its humanness. He insists on experimenting on whatever fascinates him. He claims that he is after truth, that is, his kind of truth. As for the consequences to his fellow human beings, let them worry about it. He is too busy doing his own thing. This is a common perception about the scientist.

A typical research in question is the in vitro cultivation of human forms. The ethics has yet to be addressed with practical meaningfulness. Neither have the disposition of deformed bodies and mental monsters that are bound to arise, the legal ramifications of test-tube abortions of post-trimester fetuses, the doctrinal matter of when killing a life constitutes murdering an individual, and so on, been dealt with. Had the scientist subsumed himself into humankind, he would certainly have asked such questions of deepest human value of himself before pressing on.

But this is not the scientist's way. So human eggs are being fertilized in test tubes; emerging embryos are being implanted into human uteri; supporting tests are being conducted in animals toward the possibility of growing human beings outside the womb from eggs without even the need of sperms. The scientist will next rival God Himself as a creator of Man.

The widespread reluctance at subsuming and resonating among the intelligentsia had led to an anxious search for meaning in their own lives. But so long as they refuse to subsume and resonate and keep seeking within themselves, they will never find it. So long as they wish only to do their own little fun things, refuse to sacrifice now and then with the rest of their fellow beings, and undertake their share of the scut work of life, they will never subsume and resonate. They might want to observe William Faulkner when he used to go hunting and camping with his school seat-mate, a store clerk, a farmer, a concrete worker, and an ex-sheriff, Uncle Ike. Old Uncle Ike, who acted as camp boss, had warm recollections of the novelist: "I've never seen him shirk pickin' up the smutty end of a log."

Unfortunately, the intelligentsia and many others of talent are often diseased with the distemper of self-centeredness. Some executives are included. The more successful one is, the more infected with the virus. You see such types everywhere. Somehow he always manages to switch the conversation around to *his* topic of expertise, so that the social interest can revolve around him. Failing this, he acts like a child in the company of adults, coughing and choking to draw attention. He can never subsume himself and resonate. He craves others to subsume themselves in him.

The Secretary-General of the United Nations during the late 1950s felt otherwise. "From generations of soldiers and government officials on my father's side I inherited a belief that no life was more satisfactory than one of selfless service to your country—or humanity," Dag Hammarskjöld remarked over Edward Murrow's radio show in 1953. "This service requires a sacrifice of all personal interests, but likewise the courage to stand up unflinchingly for your convictions. . . . the explanation of how man should live a life of active social service in full harmony with himself as a member of the community of the spirit, I found in the writings of those great medieval mystics for whom 'self-surrender' had been the way to self-realization, and who in 'singleness of mind' and 'inwardness' had found strength to say Yes to every demand which the needs of their neighbors made them face, and to say Yes also to every fate life had in store for them."

Strangers remain strangers because of the failure of one or both parties to subsume and resonate. Where strangers exist, the miscarriage of aggression increases. Within a pack of house rats, for example, a genial tolerance prevails. Stronger members good-naturedly allow the smaller ones to take food away from them. There is no biting in their occasional fights, only boxing with the forepaws and kicking with the hind ones. But let a stranger rat wander into their territory. A shrill cry is sent out by the observer. The sharp sound is taken up by all within earshot. Their eyes bulge and their hairs stand on end as they take up the hunt. The poor stranger is soon tracked down and shredded to pieces. There is no subsuming among rats of different packs into "ratkind."

The same deficit of charity seems to hold for people of different nations. National leaders have yet to subsume themselves and their citizens into humankind. As Joshua trumpeted to the Israelites of Biblical times, "Hereby ye shall know that the living God is among you, and that he will without fail drive out before you the Canaanites, and the Hittites, and the Hivites, and the Perizzites, and the Girgashites, and the Amorites, and the Jebusites." So human history remains a chronology of wars.

The difference in miscarried aggression between rat packs and man packs is that in the latter case the strangers are blown to pieces rather than bitten to pieces. The genesis is the same: strangers share no love.

5.

LEAD THROUGH
VECTOR MENTALITY

ONE OF THE reasons for the creeping paralysis in some large organizations is the scalar mentality of its management. A scalar number is just a magnitude, say, 3. A vector is one with a direction, say, $+3$. We may divide managers in an analogous fashion, namely, scalar managers and vector managers.

The average scalar manager is forever groping as in the initial canto of Dante Alighieri's *Divine Comedy*:

> *In the middle of journey of this our mortal life, I came to myself in a dark wood where the straight way was lost.*

A capable scalar manager is one who carries out a program as prescribed. A capable vector manager is one who not only does so, but also assumes a readiness posture toward something better at the same time.

A scalar vision goes from day to day, year to year—targeting on just one stipulated objective at a time. A vector vision sights not only on the stipulated objective, but also on the subsequent direction and growth of his group. There is a swing and a follow-through. Instead of keeping the customers happy, as a polished scalar manager would, the polished vector manager keeps them happy in such a way that they would tell others about it.

The average vector manager is unidimensional along a single line of extrapolation. But the sagacious vector manager is multidimensional. His vision is omnidirectional, whereby he

26

couples movement along the quantitative extension of present lines with qualitative initiations for new differentiations of progress.

The growth curve of an institution guided by scalar vision usually takes the form of the S-curve of biological organisms. There is a lag phase, followed by a steep growth phase, then a tapering off at maturation. The growth curve of an institution guided by vector vision, however, is more like a succession of overlapping S-curves. Before the steep part of one curve begins to taper, the steep part of the succeeding curve has begun to exhibit itself, resulting from a series of anticipatory actions taken some time back.

In other words, the scalar personality is a static producer fluttering about the same market position. The single vector personality is more likely to produce greater growth trends along more or less the same general commodity and service lines. The multivector personality is more likely not only to increase growth along the same general lines, but also to create new trends as well. Pioneering ventures are activated from time to time to replace the ones that age and pass off the scene. There is no treadmilling, no backward glance, but ever the forward look.

The vector mentality imparts the resolution behind snowballing triumphs. "Knowing what to do with money once you have it," the management author Auren Uris quoted a top businessman in *The Executive Breakthrough*, "that's the knack that separates the millionaire from the man who cuddles a nest-egg." He displayed the quality in Jeno Paulucci, the son of Italian immigrants, who made a mint of money producing and selling Chinese food in, of all places, northern Minnesota. Paulucci started with bean sprouts, added mushrooms, then exotic dishes for American supermarkets, and even sold his used-up topsoil. By the time he was forty-eight years old, he was President and sole owner of the Chun King Corporation.

In effect, vector mentality paves the way for a second-order management by objectives. It gears up to attain the immediate objectives and at the same time preserves that nebulous insistency toward the subsequent as yet unspecified objectives falling within the broad strategic push of the enterprise. It is this moving 3-point trajectory that provides a smoothness to one's style of management, in contrast to the usual 2-point conventions connecting the present with the approved annual objectives. Once you develop such an orientation, you will always be one jump ahead of your subordinates, busily filling out those reams of paper on management by objectives, which you yourself had sent streaming down the corridors.

The difference between scalar and vector mentalities can be observed in every profession, ranging from academic scholars in the laboratories to revolutionaries in the streets. In the latter arena, those who participate as political adventurers are more scalar in mentality. Those who think deeply and act responsibly in a long progression of attempts to improve the political and social condition of the people are more vector.

One of the better exemplars of vector revolutionaries is the founder of Czechoslovakia. Thomas Garrique Masaryk had been a philosopher for years and served in the government under Hapsburg rule. He had been a pacifist against the dismemberment of the Austrian Empire. But he had also been dedicated to freedom and justice. This was the committed vector in his life. He first operated within the established political structure. "One must speak to the public at meetings and in parliament, through the newspapers and books; for it is necessary to have explored all peaceful and constitutional ways of bringing about the necessary reform," he recalled in a conversation with the biographer Emil Ludwig in 1933. But he was forced to the conclusion: "It is no use. I must bring the necessary reform by revolutionary means." For 4 bloody years, 1914 to 1918, Masaryk led the secession from Austria. Even so, he had never forsaken the vector of moral justice. "Revolution is not morally justified by success alone but, as in the case of every other deed, it will be judged according to the motives; and not merely as a whole, for each single act is subject to the same moral verdict," he emphasized. "In a revolution single acts may be entirely reprehensible. They must be branded as crimes, as the murderous act of the anarchist."

The vector mentality also filters out the superfluous from competing with the essentials for attention and resources. It is not cumbered with irrelevant details and peripheral attractions. Concentration is the secret. A wise banker once said to young Thomas Buxton: "If I were to listen to all the projects proposed to me, I shall ruin myself very soon. Stick to one business, young man. Stick to your brewery and you will be a great brewer of London. Be brewer, and banker, and merchant, and manufacturer, and you will soon be in the gazette."

When the chief executive is able to imbue the common vector not only among the top management, but also among the members, the organization is destined to flourish. An impressive example over the last thousand years is the dedicated missionizing arm of the Christian Church. As the Reverend Godfrey Phillips of England expounded, "It will greatly ease the missionary situation, and lift a burden from not a few consciences if it is firmly established that it is *our* God who is dimly perceived by the fetish-worshippers, *our* God who hears prayers on the trembling lips of the non-Christian fatherless and widow, *our* God who receives psalms of faith addressed in ignorant society to different beings."

You yourself may also be entrained by the vector of personal power to a greater or lesser degree. Otherwise, you might not have gotten to where you are now in the hierarchy. But our present discussion is not aligned to this particular vector. This has been covered in our previous book, *The Craft of Power.*

What is being highlighted here is the vector of social responsibility in your position, that of organizational progress as expected of your role as a manager, executive, or leader, that of corporate and public good without considering the aggrandizement of personal power and personal gains in particular. This kind of vector mentality is the voice of conscience in executive duty. Nurture it as the source of your unique perspective of the organization. Infuse the same vector into your cadre. Unless you succeed in this, your once-vector management will before long become de facto scalar in effect.

6.

IMPART ADAPTIVE
CENTRALITY

THERE IS A natural tendency for organizations to drift into the state depicted in Ivan Andreevich Krylov's fable of the swan, the crayfish, and the pike:

> Once swan, crayfish, and pike
> Undertook to pull a loaded wagon
> With all three harnessed together as one;
> Though straining themselves out of their skin, yet moves the wagon no farther!
> For them the load would have seem light:
> But swan toward the cloud takes flight,
> Crayfish claws backward, pike tugs toward the water.
> Who among them is to be blamed or not—for us is not to judge;
> But to this very day the wagon does not budge.

The executive is beset with complex multiallegiances, few of which he can completely sever. Each of them is tied up with people of varying motivations, competences, and importance. At times, essential knowhow and resources are alloyed with the highly questionable aims of expedient allies. At times, lofty high-mindedness is inextricably bound with the impracticability of the idealist. At times, valuable backing is fused with the incorrigibility of the patron. All these and other centrifugal forces are to be unified amid the vicissitudes of change into a positive organizational expression. Only when the members are pulled together into a critical psychological mass can the leader breathe inspiration into the organization, which can then carry on as a self-sustaining chain reaction. To control the process, the executive must be in the center of things. "Maintain the mean of centrality so as to touch the four corners of the universe," enunciated the classical Chinese advice to statesmen.

Adaptive centrality does not mean conformity on your part. Conformity is being conditioned by others, as in keeping up with the Joneses. Exercising adaptive centrality means drawing others into the organizational center of gravity, where you are situated, so that the entirety can move as an integrated activity and adapt to the contingencies of the environment. It means your being in nonconformity to deviant individuals. You are the one who is nudging others, not toward functional conformity or uniformity, but toward functional complementarity. Your achievement is not measured by making everybody behave alike but as best suited to their respective proper roles in a concerted drive.

Three qualities are called for in the exercise of this kind of actively adaptive centrality. These are (1) leadership, (2) centripetal force on the personnel, and (3) blending into the organization.

With respect to leadership, the executive should at all times significantly influence the direction of movement of the mass, as well as its mode of operation. He cannot afford for long to keep boxing himself into situations like the one that occurred during the 1848 upheaval in Paris. As narrated by the late President of Harvard University, A. Lawrence Lowell, a man saw his friend marching after a crowd heading for the barricades. Knowing that the troops behind the ramparts were well seasoned and well armed and that the mob would certainly be slaughtered, the man urged his friend to leave. "I must follow them," his friend persisted. "I am their leader."

With respect to attracting personnel to the executive center, 2 things are essential. The first is a conduct based on a familiarity of human desires and behavior, enabling him to maintain the requisite ties.

The Chairman of Bendix Corporation, W. Michael Blumenthal, made it a practice of meeting over luncheon and dinners with field personnel whenever he traveled to the 100 or so field elements of the company. At the headquarters in Southfield, Michigan, he would personally hand-deliver memoranda he drafted to lower-level executives. "It's a nice way to stay in touch," he explained. "I like to see where a guy works, what his desk looks like, and so on. It kind of rounds out my picture of the guy."

Ivy Lee was nationally respected as the great public relations figure that he was because of his intimate sensitivity to the reactions of human beings across the spectrum of social status. One little incident is indicative. He had been retained by the most exclusive Waldorf-Astoria Hotel in New York City as counsel during its construction in the late 1920s and early 1930s. When he heard about the fancy fittings being planned, he objected to the President Lucius Boomer. "I for one hope that gold-plated door knobs will not be used, and even if found wise to use them, I hope they won't be called gold-plated. A thing of that kind gives the impression of unnecessary luxury—luxury that gives no comfort but is simply something to talk about."

One of the most adept at interfacing with people was Lyndon B. Johnson. He was especially skillful with media representatives. "You learn that Stewart Alsop cares a lot about appearing to be an intellectual and a historian—he strives to match his brother's intellectual attainments—so whenever you talk to him, play down the gold cuff links which you play up with *Time* magazine, and to him emphasize your relationship with FDR and your roots in Texas, so much so that even when it doesn't fit the conversation you bring in maxims from your father and stories from the Old West," the President reminisced. "You learn that Evans and Novak love to traffic in backroom politics and political intrigue, so that when you're with them you make sure you bring in lots of details and colorful descriptions of personality. You learn that Mary McCrory likes dominant personalities and Doris Fleeson cares only about issues, so that when you're with McCrory you come on strong and with Fleeson you make yourself sound like some impractical red-hot liberal."

The second thing needed to sustain your cadre's vibrant attraction to you is showing them off in their best light whenever they are with you. It commences with the excitation of interest in the possibilities of their self-development and advancement under your aegis, with an experience of satisfying results, felt proof of their expanding worth. In this way, you are joined with your associates by a zest toward achievement.

There is an imaginative transformation of what is a mechanical implementation of directives in the hands of other executives into an energizing opportunity for personal growth in stature. Their gravitating to you would become pleasingly natural to themselves. As the scholar Chang Chao of the seventeenth century observed, flowers invite the butterflies and a pond invites duck weed.

With respect to blending into the organization, you cannot be apart from the members and yet lead. If you try, you merely strut about like a comic hero. Your associates may admire you and even accord you the accolade of a hero. But they will not identify with you like they would with a tragic hero. They will laugh at you as the butt of their jokes or envy you as the sink of their own shortcomings. The poet W. H. Auden delineated 2 prototypes of the comic hero. One is Don Quixote, who refuses to accept the values of the people around him. The other is Falstaff, who refuses to pretend to accept one set of values and live another, like the others.

This does not mean that your comportment is to ape the masses. There needs to be a higher dignity and worthiness about your demeanor, qualities in which your associates may be deficient but are glad to witness in you, with whom they for that additional reason would like to identify. Do not, on this account, ever condone vulgarity in your presence. Acquire what Maxim Gorki referred to as "the art of hitting upon and setting off vulgarity everywhere, an art which is accessible only to a man who makes high demands of life, which is created only through a fervent desire to see men simple, beautiful, harmonious." There is nothing more debilitating to your organization than having the poison of vulgarity coursing through its channels.

True leadership then rests on a judicious melding of the leader and the members in organizational life. "In fact," wrote Crawford H. Greenwald, the President of Dupont Company, the *The Uncommon Man*, "the more effective an executive, the more his own identity and personality blend into the background of his organization. Here is a queer paradox. The more able the man, the less he stands out, the greater his relative anonymity outside his own immediate circle." He repeated an ancient observation. The old Chinese books have told us over two thousand years ago that when people speak about a good emperor, they would say: "He has done this and he has done that." But when they speak of a superior emperor, they would say: "We have done it all ourselves."

7.

ORCHESTRATE THE
VIRTUAL PRESENCES

VIRTUAL PRESENCES ARE unique to the human species among animals. They are essences that are not real in the space-time sense, yet exert practical effects as if they are. An example in mathematics is the square root of minus 1. There is no such thing even by its own rules. It cannot be plus 1, because plus 1 times plus 1 equals plus 1—not minus 1. It cannot be minus 1, because minus 1 times minus 1 equals plus 1—not minus 1. Yet this purely imaginary number is used very effectively in calculations involving real events, producing very worthwhile and practical answers that cannot be obtained in any other way. There would not have been modern physics and engineering in the sense that we know them today had not the virtual presence of the square root of minus 1 been invented.

Our social activities revolve around virtual presences. There would not have been the great religions had not all kinds of gods and devils been conjured up and disseminated. Few of the presidents and congressmen would have been elected, had not shaped and manicured public images been projected to the voters. The operas, concert halls, and publishing houses would not have lasted, had not the capacity of imagination been involved. Wars would not have been as plentiful and fierce, had not inspiring myths been inbred into the people; the Vikings of the Norse sagas would not have been the courageous fighters they were, had they not been led to believe that the maidens of Odin, the Valkyries, would carry the brave warriors slain in battle to Valhalla, where they would feast and sport in eternity.

Life for the individual without virtual presence would go back to the animal pattern. There would be no more spiritual heightening of the pious, no more hallucinations of the schizophrenic, no more sin and pornography in sex, no more phantom pain where the amputated limb once was, no more placebos that work, no more trials of faith, no more fantasies, no more symbols, and no more images.

The philosopher Ernst Cassirer would argue that the human intellect "is in need of symbols." His confrere Immanuel Kant would say it "is in need of images." Whether we speculate that man cannot think without symbols or without images, the fact is that the very thinking process itself revolves around virtual presences.

In the field of business, the stock market would crash without dreams of riches. The Ponzi schemers and investment swindlers would starve. Advertising agencies would fold. Elaborating on the point, an expert on public relations testified before a congressional committee during the 1960s that "our entire social structure depends on the mass production of psychologically satisfying products as much as the individual depends on these products in fulfilling his emotional needs." He argued for the continued classification of "giant," "colossal," and "mammoth," rather than "small," "medium," and "large," for olives and prunes. Words like 'colossal" and "mammoth" mean much more than "large" or even "very large." In summary, he insisted: "Customers do not want small prunes at any price!"

Not only are individuals making profitable livelihoods creating and spreading virtual presences, many others are doing equally well in countering and regulating these virtual presences. Regarding virtual presences in "false advertisement," the Federal Trade Commission found it necessary to warn that the departure from the real presence may not be unreasonably great. In discussing the related "substantiation program," a representative of the Commission's Bureau of Consumer Protection, Robert A. Skitol, stated in a speech in 1972: "It's clear that permissible puffing covers less territory today than it did a few years ago. In reviewing new campaigns and preparing substantiation before dissemination, advertisers and agencies would be well advised to take a narrow view of the puffing concept, to resolve all doubts in favor of insisting that adequate substantiation exists to support a new representation."

The impression left by the advertisement as well as the legal accuracy of the wording are to be judged as relevant. "The buying public does not weigh each word in an advertisement or a representation," the Commission had ruled. "It is important to ascertain the impression that is likely to be created upon the prospective purchaser." In 1977, the Commission instructed a leading mouthwash company to include the statement in its next $10 million's worth of advertising: "Contrary to prior advertising, ——— will not help prevent colds or sore throats or lessen their severity."

What something may be called therefore may not be what it is. This is a perfectly human thing to do, even without ulterior motives. There is the old saw among zoologists that the guinea pig has been so named because it is neither a pig nor is it from Guinea.

In this connection, one of the more prevalent deficiencies among the inexperienced and the so-called "strong" superintendents is the disdain with which they view ceremonies. They regard them as a waste of time. They rely on straight talk and direct action. As a consequence life for them is more often than not a continuous struggle, filled with managerial friction.

A gracious person is naturally ceremonial without thinking about it. But those who seem to get much done with relatively little resources are equally gifted in the use of awards, committees, and other ceremonial devices. They also understand the meaning behind the Confucian admonition to the effect that all life is a ceremony and if the ceremonies are properly conducted, the social order will proceed smoothly. For example, the ancient philosophical text, *Li Chi*, advised: "In our relations with the dead, treating them simply as being really dead would signify a lack of affection and hence should not be done. But treating them simply as being really alive would signify a lack of wisdom and hence should not be done." The superior person follows the middle way of treating them both as we know and as we hope. This is treating them *as if* they are alive.

Tact, after all, is being able to give your subordinate a shot in the arm without his feeling the needle. Persons of great power are particularly proficient, for they know all too well

that ceremonies constitute the lubricant of social processes
and the seal of community approval. They are creatively
facile in the use of ceremonial stratagems.

Even the most inconspicuous president of the littlest of
universities and companies practice that universal ceremony
known as boards of trustees or directors, as the case may be.
The ritual assures the public and the stockholders that their
interests are protected. To live up to this image, members are
selected with prestigious titles to fulfill the expectation that
they are persons who speak their convictions. In actual fact,
of course, if they do too much of it, they would not last long.
For their real presence is a ceremonial shield for the chief executive officer. The directors of one of the American oil companies once were even required to submit signed letters of
resignation in advance. Only when open crises occur, such as
in the case of the Penn Central some years back, are the
boards of directors painfully compelled to do what is expected of them on behalf of the stockholders. There are exceptional cases. But the ensuing turbulence becomes unbecoming
and the conflicts eventually resolve themselves into the standard mold. In any case, no chief executive, weak or strong,
can afford to forego the appropriate minuet in the conduct of
this particular ceremony.

From many observations of these kinds has come the realization that the continuing creation and transformation of virtual presences and their use have exerted as great an effect on
the evolution of human behavior as biological mutation and
adaptation have in the evolution of human anatomy and
physiology. The metabolism of the substance of virtual
presences is as intrinsically a part of human beings as the metabolism of the substance of physical mass. We therefore arrive at the basic axiom of social dynamics: the fashioning
and controlling of virtual presences is the leverage of power.

8.

BE PROPITIOUS

PRECISE TIMING IS the key to dramatic effects and smooth efficiency. We can learn much in this respect from the music-hall comedian. He knows exactly how long it takes for the audience to warm up to his jokes. Some are fired off in rapid succession; others are delivered only after the listeners are suitably prepared for the subtleties. The pace of the patter is adjusted so that the peak receptivity of the audience coincides with the delivery of the punch line.

The lack of good timing is widespread in everyday life. The Greek philosopher of the third century B.C., Theophrastus, spoke about the ill timing of the tactless person. As translated by J. M. Edmonds, he "will accost a busy friend and ask his advice, or serenade his sweetheart when he is sick of fever. He will . . . come to bear witness after the verdict is given. Should you bid him to a wedding, he will inveigh against womankind. Should you be but now returned from a long journey, he will invite you to a walk. He is given to bringing you one that will pay more when the bargain is struck . . . At the flogging of your servant he will stand by and tell how a boy of his hanged himself after just such a flogging as this . . ."

The complexing of perfect timing with glorious surprise is one of the leading talents of polished politicians. The following incident was detailed by Arthur Krock in his *Memoirs*. The Washington correspondent from the *Louisville Courier-Journal* was asked by Kentucky Congressman A. O. Stanley to inquire of Theodore Roosevelt about the latter's willingness to testify before his Congressional Committee investigating the

United States Steel Corporation. While President, T. R. had opposed U.S. Steel's acquisition of Tennessee Coal and Iron as part of his Administration's trust-busting policy. T.R.'s appearance before the hearings would be of great importance. In the telephone conversation, Krock proposed that he come over to Roosevelt's residence on Long Island to discuss the matter.

Roosevelt, however, did not want the reporters hanging around the house to deduce what was happening. So he proposed an alternative. Krock was to follow him the next morning, without any sign of mutual recognition, as he boarded the Hudson River ferryboat at nine forty-five from Twenty-third Street to the Jersey terminal and thence to his compartment on a West Coast train. There the conversation could take place.

In the session, Roosevelt consented to testify on the proviso that there be no advance publicity of any kind and that his stipulated scenario be played. Congressman Stanley was to assemble his committee in the City Hall in New York on a certain day the following week. A witness was to be on the stand prior to ten that morning, when Roosevelt would enter the committee room through the double doors. On recognizing him, Congressman Stanley was to ask the witness to step down temporarily and invite Roosevelt to testify. The Colonel's program was accepted.

"I explained to Stanley that there must be no leak of any kind because obviously T. R. wanted to make a dramatic appearance," Krock recounted the episode. "He was already running for the Republican nomination in 1912, and this was to be the formal overture. It was bound to get enormous publicity on the first page all over the United States and it did."

On occasions, you should be immediate in response, as Nahum Ish Gamzu had learned much to his sorrow. "I was once traveling to the house of my father-in-law, taking with me 3 donkey-loads of food and drink," he retold the sad experience, as recorded in the *Talmud*. "A starving man asked me for food. I answered that I would give him some when I unloaded, but before I could do so, he fell dead. I greatly grieved over his death, and prayed that the Lord send sufferings upon me in expiation for my sin. I should not have delayed my help, but should have cut through the load and given him food at once."

An example of prompt executive decision in modern times is that of General Mills in 1978. One day after its toy subsidiary Parker Brothers was officially notified of the second death, 10 months after the first, of a child, who choked on a rubber rivet in the very profitable Riviton Kit, it suspended shipments forthwith and mounted a massive publicity campaign to recall those outstanding. The decision to recall was made despite the fact that the kit had passed all government safety requirements. It was purely voluntary on the part of Parker Brothers. The exercise wiped out the year's profits of the company. But company President Randolph G. Barton put it simply: "Were we supposed to sit back and wait for death number three?"

If certain kinds of critical questions require rapid decisions, the organizational structure should be modified to insure the essential propitiousness. Do not let the conventional notions of span of control delay the transmittal of data and/or recommendations to your level of decision making in disregard of critical timing. Flatten out the echelons or insert shunts for the special cases, if necessary. It is not communication per se that matters most in managerial networks but actionable communication. Communications that are too late are not actionable.

Large bureaucracies are especially frustrating in this responsiveness. A not-too-unusual exhibit of government sluggishness is President Gerald Ford's establishment of a Commission on Federal Paperwork in December 1974. The Commission's purpose was to analyze the 15 billion federal forms printed during the year and what to do about reducing the load. The General Accounting Office had estimated that about $18 billion were being spent by American businesses a year in filling them out. After 6 months had passed and 7.5 billion more forms printed, the Chairman had yet to be appointed.

On other occasions, you should bide your time. The moral is contained in the legend told King Bahrām Gūr by one of his 7 wives. A visiting prince in China inquired of his host why all the men in town wore black. The host remained silent, took him to the foot of an abandoned tower in ruins, and hoisted him up in a basket. When he reached the top he found a fairy land. The beautiful queen welcomed him royally. He fell violently in love with her. The queen pleaded for postponement of their pleasure for a while. But he could not restrain himself. Suddenly, everything vanished and he found himself at the bottom of the tower again. The prince's host then informed him that all the men had gone through the same experience and wore black in mourning.

On still other occasions, you should best do nothing directly. "The talented person knows the art of doing something," said the Sage. "But only the wisest knows the art of doing nothing." In *The Managerial Mind*, Professor David W. Ewing cites a contemporary example of the effectiveness of doing nothing decisive, such as by the management of Lincoln Electric Company during the 1940s. The plant workers were gambling during the lunch hour. Although management recognized the freedom of the workers to spend their money and lunch hour as they please, it was concerned over the eventual morale of the place. Yet it was reluctant to jeopardize the good relations between the men and their foremen and guards by expecting the latter two groups to enforce a prohibition against gambling. So the company's President discussed the affair with the plant-wide representatives on the advisory board. The board took the matter under advisement but made no recommendations for a while. When word of the concern leaked out, the workers themselves put pressure on the gambling ringleaders to stop. There was no need for top management to disrupt anything to attain its objective.

The problem went away on its own. When feasible, this is always the best way. It leaves no scars.

9.

PRESERVE FLEXIBILITY

INSTITUTIONS WITH THE flexibility to give, enabling them to leap over and skirt around unyielding obstacles and hazards, and flow with the irresistible tides of the times usually outlast those without it. Blind consistency may be courageous but not necessarily enduring. Given this understanding, scholars should not find it difficult, as some of them do, for example, to explain how it is that Catholicism could have developed from what was written in the synoptic Gospels and how Mahayana Buddhism could have grown from what was said in the early Buddhist texts. Institutional survival and prosperity have always taken precedence over precedents. From a practical assessment of the "secrets of success" of movements that continue to grow over millenia, one of them must certainly have been flexibility.

There is a considerable amount of faith in the normal conduct of social activities. Faith in turn is associated with an equivocalness in expectations and an ambiguity in outcomes. This is especially true with political interactions. As the Puritan Governor of the Massachusetts Colony John Winthrop described the distinction, "When you agree with a workman to build you a ship or house, etc., he undertakes as well for his skill as for his faithfulness, for it is his profession, and you pay him for both. But when you call one to be a magistrate, he doth not profess nor undertake to have sufficient skill for that office, nor can you furnish him with gifts, etc.; therefore you must run the hazard of his skill and ability."

One needs be resilient in confronting the unexpected through a keenness in observing the perpetually changing scene, a tentativeness with which ideas are held, a reasonableness with which contrary opinions are treated, and a responsive spontaneity. Effective flexibility, however, is not that pictured in Basho's haiku of the seventeenth century:

With every gust of the wind,
The butterfly changes its place
On the willow.

True flexibility calls for a steadfast self-discipline. It is kept in line by a continuous boresighting on the objective, despite considerable buffeting about, like an airplane heading for home base through rainstorm and high winds. This is to be distinguished from vacillation, which is more akin to the aimless Brownian movement of pollen grains being jerkily bumped this way and that by random microforces. It is leashed by courage in meeting the convulsion without panic, insightfulness that penetrates beyond the smokescreens, creativity that quickens with each new roadblock, and patience in guiding the whole matter through to its fruitful termination.

It is expected that some apparent inconsistency may arise in one's successive actions. "That is not an evil, but rather the avoidance of an evil," said the author Havelock Ellis in *The Dance of Life.* "We cannot remain consistent with the world save by growing inconsistent with our past selves. The man who consistently—as he fondly supposes 'logically'—clings to an unchanging opinion is suspended from a hook which has ceased to exist." The inconsistency in managerial flexibility relates to hypothetical situations that no longer exist. It is actually a consistency relative to the existing realities.

Perhaps the most insidious glue of bondage for the chief executive is the layer of aides and intervening echelons between him and the point of action. Be ever on guard against being imprisoned in a walnut-paneled cell by your own cordon of courtiers. "If something bothers me," said the Chief Executive Officer of Xerox Corporation, C. Peter McColough, "I don't rely on the reports or what other top executives may want to tell me. I'll go down very deep in the organization."

The flexibility of the skillful manager is therefore manifold. Not only does he have multiple tactical targets to achieve a given strategic purpose, but also multiple means of bypassing obstacles to a specific tactical target. This can be illustrated through the analogy of the force parallelograms of physics. The same resultant effect can be obtained through an infinite combination of efforts. In the 2-dimensional diagram of Figure 1, any combination of appropriate vector forces *OB* and *OC*, of which only 2 pair are shown, would lead to the same resultant vector force *OA*. In other words, should you want the system moved from position *O* in the direction of *A* by applying a force corresponding to the length of the line represented by *OA* but are prohibited from doing so because of something standing in the direct path, you can do it by any number of combination of other forces. Of these, two are shown. One is to simultaneously pull at *O* in the direction of B′ with a force corresponding to the length of the line OB′ and in the direction of C′ corresponding to the length of the line OC′. The other is to simultaneously pull in the direction of B″ and C″ in a corresponding fashion.

No greater flexibility in overcoming obstacles has been exhibited than by learned missionaries. The Dominican Bishop of Antioch in the thirteenth century asked Thomas Aquinas for assistance with "moral and philosophical arguments, to which the Saracens give a hearing." The theologian came up with his missionary handbook of 1270 in which he counseled that the usual intellectual reasoning based on provable categories is not productive in converting Moslems and showed how Christian evangelists can lead from the Moslem's own values and insights.

You should be particularly flexible during a phase change. The style, orientation, techniques, and staff that have worked in acquiring a position of power are not necessarily appropriate for governing from that position. When Ogotai succeeded his father Genghis Khan as head of the Mongol Empire in the thirteenth century, his advisor urged him to build a permanent capital at Karakorum and adopt the budgetary and other administrative procedures of the Chinese. "The empire has indeed been conquered on horseback," Ch'i-tan Yeh-lü Ch'u-t'sai counseled. "But it cannot be governed on horseback."

Flexibility in your personal Self alone does not necessarily mean effective flexibility in your role as an executive. Since your organization is part of your extended executive Self, executive flexibility hinges on a commensurate delegated flex-

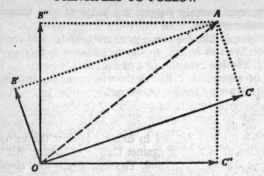

Figure 1. Force Parallelograms.

ibility in your subordinates as well. Do not therefore immobilize your organization with regulations. To impose discipline is not to induce paralysis. To insure your own operative flexibility is to give flexibility to your subordinates. Otherwise, the fossilization of old age creeps in. "When a state is about to perish," noted Duke Chao in 536 B.C., "many new laws will be found in it."

If at all possible, do not surrender all your flexibility by submitting to compulsory arbitration, especially to an arbiter much stronger than you. The lesson was taught in W. H. McGuffy's *Reader* of 1857:

"Two hungry cats, having stolen some cheese, could not agree on how to divide it. So they called in a monkey to decide the case.

'Let me see,' said the monkey with an arched look, 'this slice weighs more than the other.' With that, he bit off a large piece, in order, as he said, to make them balance.

The other scale was now too heavy. This gave the upright judge a fine pretense to take a second mouthful.

'Hold! Hold!' cried the two cats. 'Give each of us his share of the rest, and we will be content.'

'If you are content,' said the monkey, 'justice is not. The law, my friends, must have its course.'

So he nibbled first one piece, and then the other. The poor cats, seeing their cheese in a fair way to be eaten up, most humbly begged the judge to give himself no further trouble.

'Not so fast, I beseech you, my friends,' said the monkey. 'We owe justice to ourselves as well as to you. What is left is due to me in right of my office.'

So saying, he crammed the whole into his mouth, and very gravely dismissed the court."

Perhaps the greatest poison to dynamic pragmatism on the part of an official is vanity. Many of the fastest rising protégés are trapped not in bidding against the value of the objective at stake but against their own vanity. All sensible options are blindly ignored. The initiative is lost, since vanity can only be satisfied by the praises of others, who, of course, are gaining lucratively in return. Since vanity feeds on itself, the escalation goes on unceasingly until the day of rude reckoning beckons. It is for this reason that prophets never tire in preaching: "Pride goeth before a fall."

10.

HUMANIZE WITHIN
ELASTIC LIMITS

THE EXECUTIVE IN the West has become the focal point of a kind of repressed moral crisis of the age. The secular and humanist tradition of the Occident reached an eddying stage in the mid-twentieth century. Having been carried by the political waves of liberalism and Marxism for decades, the intellectual spearhead, represented by such thinkers as Max Weber, foundered in trying to establish a clear basis for decision. Subsequent sociologists began deserting the difficult value concerns of society in its human wholeness and retreating into the academic fortress of neutral facts.

Although leaders in society never weary from declaiming their determination to protect and enhance the freedom of the individual, they are actually, perhaps unintentionally, constantly draining it away with each pumping of institutional progress. "The liberty of the individual is not a benefit of culture," asserted Sigmund Freud in *Civilization and Its Discontents*. "Liberty has undergone restrictions through the evolution of civilization and justice demands that these restrictions apply to all." Much effort is exerted toward perfecting various expediences in reconciling individual claims and institutional demands. The basic irreconcilability can never be dissolved. But it can be reasonably attenuated through continual awareness and caring.

During the last century, the dehumanization of workers took a great spurt. With the perfection of the assembly line, came the phrase "man-machine system." Managers were driven by this question: How can we raise the efficiency of the man-machine combine so that material production can be maximized? One of the prerequisites is compatibility between man and the machine. Since we cannot manufacture machines to feel like man, we will have to make man behave like machines.

Resistance to the introduction of the machine gradually crumbled since the armed attack of 200 Luddites against William Cartwright's textile mill at Rawfolds in Yorkshire was crushed in 1812. The movement to stem the use of the gig mills, the shearing frames, and other machines from destroying the clothworkers' traditional way of life fizzled.

Since then man has become so well fitted into the man-machine complex that he is becoming more and more a social module instead of a human being. The more efficient the organization, the more depersonalized the worker became. The greater the greed for profit and power, the more dehumanized he became. It has fallen on the executive to act as the chief depersonalizer and chief dehumanizer on behalf of our technological society.

A quandary arises. As a human being, the executive cannot help but sense the resonating oneness with fellow human beings—subordinates though they may be on the organization chart. Yet he must be tough or so he tells himself, as he suppresses the natural empathy within. He too is becoming naught but a social module. Still he does not quite feel comfortable. Somehow he must find a way out. This is not easy. But it is not too hard.

The 2 poles of the humanizing-dehumanizing spectrum have been contrasted by Bertrand Russell in *A History of Western Philosophy*. He imagined Gautama Buddha and Friedrich Nietzsche appearing before God, as in the first chapter of *Job*, with advice about the kind of world that He should create.

Buddha would begin by referring to "the lepers, outcast and miserable; the poor, toiling with aching limbs and barely kept alive by scanty nourishment; the wounded in battle, dying in slow agony; the orphans ill-treated by cruel guardians; and even the most successful haunted by the thought of failure and death." He would pray for salvation from this "load of sorrow," which "can only come through love."

"Good heavens, man, you must learn to be of tougher fibre," Nietzsche would interrupt. "Why go about snivelling because trivial people suffer? Or for that matter, because great men suffer? Trivial people suffer trivially, great men suffer greatly, and great sufferings are not to be regreted, because they are noble." He would scoff at the negative ideals of Buddha's, completely attainable only through nonexistence. He would extol the positive ideals. Nietzche's heroes are men like Alcibiades and Frederick the Great. "For the sake of such men, any misery is worthwhile," he would emphasize, as he appealed to the Lord not to curb His artistic impulses "by the degenerate fear-ridden maunderings of this wretched psychopath."

You may wish to determine what general segment of this wide range of executive behavior is permitted in your particular position in its exercise of authority and discretion. Within that latitude, you can then decide the center of gravity for your own doings.

Although the task may appear too nebulous for precise demarcation, a reasonable judgment is not too difficult, given a modicum of perception and sincerity. A soldier following orders from his commander to carry out an immoral act can still be acting morally on a personal basis. We should not fault him for not going beyond the elastic limits of a position, which he could not resign.

This is quite different from the American officer shooting defenseless women and children cowering in a trench during the Vietnam War.

The decision on the part of an executive is usually more complicated than such more or less straightforward choices of personal morality and charity. The executive is encumbered by the oath of office to insure the survival and progress of his organization. As a division commander on the eve of battle, the general can hardly be expected to humanize his soldiers to the point of seeing them individually as a mother's son. He is tightly delimited by the dictates of his post to look aside and order them to a high probability of pain and death. After the battle is won, however, the margin of elasticity is much wider. Many a commander has wept openly at the sight of the wounded. Others have been understanding even to deserters. As an executive he must know when and how to save the lives of his men and when and how to expend them. The margin of elasticity is progressively wider as one rises in the ranks.

There are military commanders like William Sherman, who

not infrequently made life-wasting frontal assaults. But there are also generals like George H. Thomas, who have completely different reputations. Never has it been said that he wasted his men in useless battle. Once he was even relieved from command for refusing to battle before he was ready. Yet he is honored today as a great general, for it was he who was mainly responsible for the military security of the middle states during the Civil War.

There are limits therefore to how far an executive can actually go in letting individual preferences of his subordinates jeopardize the health of the institution and still remain chief. In 1979, John Paul II made it explicitly clear that he was not going to look favorably as a rule on requests from priests for a release from their vows to return to secular life. Since the number of applications for the ministry had been declining for some years, the decision made good managerial sense at that particular point in time.

In general, executives tend to cluster toward the hard-hearted pole of the permissible range rather than the soft-hearted. This follows a long history. In the sixth century B.C., Heraclitus had said: "Every beast is driven to pasture with blows." A century later Protagoras tried to negate his influence by propounding: "Man is the measure of all things." In recent decades many industrial executives have twisted the statement the other way around: "Things are the measure of man."

The disadvantages to leaning toward the human pole of the elastic range are several. One is the handicap given the competitor operating at the machine pole. The differential has been widened by the gamesmanship and upmanship that have so captured the imagination of the more aggressive occupants of the executive suite. These executives engage in such practices even needlessly to the corporate objectives at hand or those of their own. The manipulation of people as things become to them a thrilling sport of virtuosity in leadership.

An even more natural inhibitor to humanizing lies in the very personality of individuals who rise into executive ranks. It seems that the psychological traits that fit people for high executive posts might have been determined early in life. Studies suggest an independence from the mother and identification with a strong father image; intense drive toward achievement, with a compulsive need for repeated self-assurance in this respect; suppressed imaginative introspection; and positive self-directedness. After empirical reinforcements along the ladder of success the executive tends to become a person who is grim, without play, and continually enveloped in an atmosphere of uncertainty in the work place.

Robert Endleman surmised the presence of considerable anxiety behind the compulsion in the activity drive. The sociologist posed the problem in *Personality and Social Life*. "Does the denial of helpless dependence on the mother . . . cover a deeper persistence on such dependency which must be constantly disproved by the decisive marks of manly independent adulthood? Is the almost total lack of empathy or emotional identification with subordinates a compelling buttress for denial of such weakness in oneself?" So the executive takes pride in being hardhearted. He has become this way "by suppressing, even repressing, major parts of his self, or at least his potential self, and that at some level it is these that he is constantly battling against, and never quite sure he can 'make it.' Hence the draining uncertainty and ever-renewed efforts to overcome them."

The dehumanizing of subordinates then appears to have begun with the dehumanizing of oneself. To undo one is to undo both.

Much of the loneliness and emptiness that disturb executives in the midst of a large company of people is a function of the degree to which they have dehumanized their associates and subordinates. The greater the dehumanizing, the lesser the actual human environment. When the ramrodding executive treats people around him as flesh-and-bloodless instrumentalities and machines, he is lonely. There are no human beings around him—only walking-talking-doing machines.

Yet the executive presses on, not only dehumanizing his subordinates at work, but also members of his family at home to a greater or lesser extent—usually greater the higher the office. They are taken for granted—and one can only take machines for granted—when it comes to their accommodating to his work habits. The president summons the aide out on a family picnic for consultation. The aide's family is supposed to take the disruption without fuss. The children are not supposed to protest. They are expected to act like machines when the switch is turned off.

The more the executive dehumanizes members of the family, the more lonely and empty his family life becomes. Like at the factory, the other people are only part human and part machine. Home life too becomes a little more lonely and empty with each racheting of executive claims.

There are many executives who remain alienated to the bitter end. Such was the case with King Aurangzeb of India of the seventeenth century. He had dethroned his father by capturing him in a rebellion and imprisoning him in the Fort of Agra for 9 years without ever paying him a visit. He tried to destroy the Hindu and Christian faiths as a Moslem King. In a single year he razed 123 temples at Udaipur alone. The people were terrified by his despotism and bled by his tax collectors. One of his deathbed letters read: "I know not who I am, where I shall go, or what will happen to this sinner full of sins. . . . My years have gone by profitless. God has been in my heart, yet my darkened eyes have not recognized his light. . . . There is no hope for me in the future. The fever is gone but only the skin is left. . . . I have greatly sinned, and know not what torments await me. . . . May the peace of God be upon you."

But there have been many others who have been active near the humane end of executive discretion and succeeded impressively according to any objective measure of management that can be applied. They recognize that as executives their purpose is to get things done most efficiently, repeatedly in their absence as well as in their presence. It is not to disgrace someone, hurt him, or demean him. Engaging in the latter kinds of activities is only wasting their precious time and energy at best. It makes attaining the institutional goals much more difficult. They do not injure beyond necessity.

This behavior in benevolent self-interest is exhibited in many animals and has even been labeled as "altruism." When male fiddler crabs fight over a burrow, for example, they are never known to kill, even though their enlarged claws are sufficiently powerful to crush the opponent's abdomen.

Ruthlessness and other inhuman acts have been shown over and over again to be ineffective tools of management, even in warfare. "They [the German authorities during World War I] defend the burning of Louvain, the shooting of hostages, the bombardment of undefended towns, and . . . the proposal to torpedo merchant ships and send their crews to the bottom, not as acts of national hatred, but as the only means of terrorizing the Allies into submission," commented Robert Lynd. "One would imagine that, if ruthlessness has been found ineffective as a means of suppressing badly armed and badly equipped criminals, it must be found still more ineffective as a means of suppressing well-armed and well-equipped nations."

Two illustrative incidents in the lives of executives who have been internationally acknowledged as the finest in their respective lines of work would suffice to make the point.

The first involves one of China's greatest emperors. T'ai Tsung of the T'ang dynasty during the seventh century visited the jails of Ch'ang-an one day and met 290 men who had been condemned to death. He ordered them out to till the fields with the understanding that on their word of honor alone they would return. Everyone did. The Emperor was so pleased that he set them all free.

The second involves one of the most well-known general managers in the recent world of music. During the 1960s the General Manager of the Metropolitan Opera House of New York City, Rudolf Bing, sent the following memorandum to the house manager: "At least ten days ago I asked that a little stool be placed in the new elevator as I see no reason at all why the old man running it should be expected to stand all the time. I consider this very bad employment tactics to force an employee to completely unnecessary strain and I would like this situation to be remedied at once."

All this goes to show that you need not have ice water in your veins to achieve greatness as an executive. On the contrary, warm blood and a human heart make the accomplishments all the more complete for everyone around you. Furthermore, in the redounding humanizing of your own Self in the process, life for you too becomes more complete.

Take that step forward and discover for yourself how it feels to be on the very threshold of nobility in management.

III
Pitfalls to Avoid

GIVEN THE ART of Chinese baseball and an intuitive grasp of the 10 major underlying management principles, you are well on your way to avoiding the pitfalls that commonly entrap your less-gifted colleagues. We shall touch on 10 of the more prevalent.

1.

LACKING REALISM

"EVERYTHING THAT DECEIVES," noted Plato 24 centuries ago, "may be said to enchant."

So it is that many of the standards of behavior and associated assumptions in human society are largely garlands of illusions and delusions. The folklore and most revered faiths of the world are filled with things that just are not so. We can easily point to the figments in other cultures and religions. With equal rigor, they can easily point to figments in our own. "Individual, group or nation-state, we cannot judge our own cause," the author Raynard West stressed in *Conscience and Society*. "And if we try to do so, we shall be reduced again and again to fighting for a supposed 'right' against a supposed 'wrong,' for one set of illusions against another." Yet as demonstrated so frequently, men will battle to the death not for the right of living the illusions but for the belief of their being realities. Self-critical acumen is a rare trait.

We discuss 3 of the most common managerial deficiencies as far as realism is concerned. These are (1) planning, (2) assessing personnel, and (3) evaluating ideas.

With respect to planning, I have seldom seen planners, including those at the highest levels, who are totally untainted by wishful thinking. Fortunately, in most cases, someone else in the group was sufficiently clear-eyed on that particular issue to save the day. There are many instances, however, in which the deluded person also turned out to be the most convincing among the conferees and his emotional appeal tilted the decision to the euphoric side of the ledger. Wayward inspiration carries the day.

Planners get infected with the exhilaration of the big boss to "think big." I am reminded of the rooster who saw an ostrich egg rolling down the slope and resting against the fence. He cackled his hens together. "I don't want to complain about the quality of our production here," he crowed out a shrill exhortation. "But I'd just like to point out what's going on elsewhere"

As a result, the targets are set out of realistic range; the difficulties are minimized; the time frames are impossible. After 1 or 2 cycles of this kind, plans are tacitly accepted as an incentive to greater productivity. We are not claiming that the carrot on a stick does not have salutary effects. What we are emphasizing is that it is not a plan formulated by a craftsman of depth.

A plan is meant to be realized in implementation. It is to be plausible and highly probable of attainment by your organization under the actual conditions it will find itself in the future. The boundary conditions are clearly spelled out, such as those imposed by higher echelons, functional areas reserved for other divisions of the institution, technical state of the art, inflationary and rising labor cost trends, growth trends and options of competitors, in-house financial resources, in-house talent, and so on. Of course, it is not to be expected that the first couple of tries will hit it right on the nose. But the successive editions should come increasingly closer.

You might feel insulted by being exposed to what appears to be a set of sophomoric admonitions. But even some of the most well-known executives have let unrealistic hopes lead them downhill on the tobaggon slide and out of control. During the 1960s, one of the largest American corporations nearly succumbed from just such a disaster. As R. A. Smith summed up the case in *Fortune*: "One is led to conclude that the top management failed to recognize that the new age of advanced technology demands advanced management techniques. It failed to establish intelligence systems that would have given accurate and timely warning of danger. It failed to limit divisional programs to those that would not imperil the whole enterprise and failed to call a halt on one such program even when it appeared to be in grave danger. Instead it pursued a 'double-or-nothing' policy, risking greater and greater losses in the hope that one more commitment would square all accounts. This, in short, is the story of a great corporation that got out of control."

Leaders who naturally have an enormous gift of persuasion need be fastidiously careful. They may succeed for a while, even spectacularly so. But unless reined realistically, things eventually catch up. A striking case was the famous American realtor of the 1950s. He became a folk hero of sorts following a string of exciting developments. He was able to talk people into putting large sums of money into his ambitious building projects. But his financial backers dried up after a while, even at offers of 24% interest. By 1966 his company had gone into bankruptcy and he personally did the same.

With respect to sizing up people, experience has revealed how frequently even the most astute executives can be off the mark. This occurs especially in the appointment of successors to strong leaders. The successors to Pat Patterson of United Airlines, Juan Trippe of Pan American, and C. R. Smith of American Airlines all stumbled on the job and were finally relieved by the respective boards of directors.

Being unrealistic about human behavior is even more universal a deficiency than being unrealistic about things. That part of us that is idealistic would like to believe that grasping power-hungry people are nonexistent among our friends and close associates. Or that petty pluckers are rare and innocuous. "Can you imagine a petty person as a high official?" Confucius warned us long ago. "After he gains the position, he is anxious about losing it. When he becomes anxious about losing it, there is nothing he will not do to keep it." Or that large institutions are administered by morality. After 11 years of governing for the Church during the sixteenth century, Francesco Guicciardini reflected, as translated by Ninian Hill Thomson: "States cannot be established by conforming to the moral law. For if you look at their beginnings, all will be seen to have had their origin in violence; save only the authority of commonwealths within the limits of their own territory, and not beyond. Nor do I except the Emperor himself from this rule, and still less the priests, which last use a twofold violence against us, constraining us at once with weapons spiritual and temporal."

That part of us which is attracted to devotion and good intentions tends to overlook ineptness on the part of individuals whom we are considering promoting. When they foul things up afterwards we feel worse in having to replace them, because they are such nice people. There is the model of the good samaritan who bumped into a staggeringly drunk man leaning against the doorway of a small beaten-up apartment building. "Do you want me to help you upstairs?" queried the good samaritan. "Yup," came the reply.

With great difficulty, he half-dragged the drooping figure up the stairway to the second floor, "Is this the floor you live on?" "Yup," came the reply.

The corridor was rather dark and all he could see was one tiny door at the far end. He tried it and it was unlocked. So he shoved the limp fellow through it and came downstairs.

Just as he did so, he came across a second fellow, who was even worse off than the first. The same sequence of questions and answers occurred and the good samaritan pushed him through the same door on the second floor.

As he groped his way down the dark stairs into the vestibule, he walked into a man for the third time—much worse off than the other two. He was just about to offer assistance when the man took one look at him, let out a loud shriek, lurched out into the street, and threw himself into the arms of a passing policeman. "Off'shur! Off'shur!" he gasped. "Protec' me from dat man. He ain't done nuttin' all night long but dragged me upstairs and throw me down de elevator shaft!"

With respect to evaluating ideas, the executive needs be alert in these times of articulate expertise. After the Bay of Pigs fiasco, President John F. Kennedy ruefully confessed: "All my life I've known better than to depend on the experts. How could I have been so stupid to let them go ahead?" Beware of bogus erudition.

You should be critical when research economists, psychologists, and others advance practical recommendations based solely on theoretical models and laboratory data. Much of the contemporary economic research on underdeveloped countries carried out by economists in wealthy countries, for example, are biased by the respective political interests. Such research, in the words of Gunnar Myrdal in *The Challenge of World Poverty*, "tends to become 'diplomatic,' forebearing and generally overoptimistic: bypassing facts that raise awkward problems, concealing them in an unduly technical terminology or treating them in an excusing and 'understanding' way." The paradigms and hypotheses based on economic concepts as employment, savings, output, demand, supply, and prices, which provide valid inferences in the developed countries, do not in the undeveloped countries. "The assumed aggregates of the 'economic' terms mentioned above (and many others) cannot be carried out when markets are nonexistent or grossly imperfect." The forced analysis becomes "irrelevant and grossly faulty."

Let us examine the degree of confidence that should be placed in a typical psychological experiment. If an academic psychologist is conducting an investigation on incentives in increasing productivity, using college juniors in a controlled protocol with excuse from a term paper as reward, and if that is the full extent of his interest, without anything else on his mind, then this immediate experimental concern also becomes his ultimate concern. The professor then has no need to look further than the conventional probability of significance for meaningfulness in his results.

But if the psychologist is interested in the research as leading to a proposal on bonuses in a company, then something else is needed. The conventional probability of significance alone does not provide real meaning of the kind he is now interested in. This probability of chance, which may designate as P_c, only gives the probability that the difference found is due to chance. Another probability of significance is required. This we have called the "probability of irrelevancy," P_i. This is the probability that the entire experimental protocol is nonrepresentative of the real-life situation in which the practical application is to be made and therefore irrelevant. Most of the published psychological experiments of this kind would probably have significant $P_c < 0.05$, but nonsignificant $P_i >>> 0.05$.

Pending the time when an actual method is developed and accepted to calculate a semiquantitative P_i, we will have to be satisfied with adjectival ratings of high, medium, and low significance. It is conceivable that, as an interim measure, some procedure might be devised toward a 9-point scale, as calibrated against certain agreed-on standards for the respective fields of inquiry.

To increase the relevancy of research toward practical application in management, the development of P_i would appear to be both timely and essential as a complement to P_c.

Should psychologists, sociologists, economists, and other investigators make practical recommendations to you based on theoretical or laboratory results, may I suggest you put this question to them: What is the probability of irrelevancy, P_i, of your experiment?

Another small plug for realism!

2.

ASSUMING ONE HAS
THE FACTS

THIS PITFALL IS commonplace in large organizations. The sheer size makes complete availability of information for any one person physically impossible. Were this the case, the executive's own filing cabinet would be as large as that of the organization's. What actually happens is that each echelon boils the data it receives down to a small enough volume for relay to the next higher echelon, which, in turn, summarizes its own raw data into still briefer statements for further transmittal. And this process happens continuously until the data get to the senior officials. Many factual details and significant nuances are thereby sifted out at each stage. What might be considered of major importance by a particular senior official for a given decision might not have been foreseen by the intermediary junior official in the latter's handling of the routine information and thereby eliminated unwittingly in the process.

Human shortcomings compound the problem of accurate and timely communication of information. The temptation always exists of delaying the reporting of bad news to the boss, hoping it would go away or be resolved before long, or of beveling the sharp edges, so that the problem does not cut as badly as it actually might. Another temptation is to exaggerate the good news, especially favorable to one's own performance, so that it sounds better than it actually is.

The problem of factual data faced by chief executives was delineated by Tsou Chi to King Wei of Tsi during the time of the Warring States around the fourth century B.C. "Sire," he went on. "I am not unhandsome. But I heard of a Mr. Shu in the north who is reputed to be very handsome. As I stood looking at myself in the mirror one day, I asked my wife, 'Who is more handsome, Shu or me?' She said, 'You are, of course.' I put the same question to my concubine the next day and she gave me the same answer. Then to a guest with the same response. It so happened that Mr. Shu himself came to see me. It was clear to me that he was much more handsome than I. As I lay in bed I thought to myself: My wife says I'm more handsome because she's partial to me, my concubine because she's afraid of me, my guest because he wants something from me. Your Majesty, all the people within the palace are partial to you. All the courtiers are afraid of you. All the people want something from you. It must indeed be difficult for you to get the truth."

Therefore, the higher in the hierarchy you are perched, the more you should expect an informational obeisance to your strongly voiced feelings. You may wish to bear in mind the instructive piece about the viziers of Nushirvan in the *Gulistan* by the Persian author Saadi of the thirteenth century. The viziers were invited by the King to give their opinions about an important matter of state. Each advanced his own analysis of the problem and recommendation. Barzachumihr, however, concurred with the King's opinion. After the latter left, the others expressed astonishment that their colleague could have possibly agreed with the King's ill-informed conclusion. "Since the outcome cannot be known at this time and depends upon the will of God, it is better to be on the side of the King," disclosed Barzachumihr. "If this actually turns out wrong, we would on that account not be blamed. To go contrary to the King's views is to wash one's hands in one's own blood. As a matter of prudence, if the King in plain day say it is night, it is meet to shout: 'Lo, the moon and the Pleides!' "

Even if your lieutenants try to be scrupulously exact in conveying the factual data to you, there is always a question concerning the accuracy and completeness of the data coming to them for digestion and transmittal. History confirms this to be an even worse deficiency. "Businessmen tell the hard truths about their doings only to the extent required by law," reported a former editor of *Life* and *Time*, Thomas Griffith, in *How True*. "Governments lie. Politicians dissemble. Trial lawyers, when they can't challenge the facts, plant doubts.

Whole industries live on pretense, by flattering your self-importance in exchange for your money, by rearranging reality."

Unreliable information can be passed on by even the most respected segments of the most respected corporations. One of the most profitable pharmaceutical houses was accused officially in 1977 by the Food and Drug Administration for "numerous and substantial errors" in the safety petition submitted on leading antihypertensive and oral contraceptive drugs. Measurements were recorded on animals that cannot be located. Other animals have been sprayed with insecticides, thereby making the data undependable. Still others were mixed up with each other as far as the particular dose administered was concerned. As a result, the government agency stated that it could not rely "upon the integrity of the basic safety data" in the company's submissions.

Factual inaccuracies on a grander scale are exemplified by the public admission by the Federal Reserve System in October 1979 that it had overestimated the American money supply by $3.7 billion for two consecutive weeks. This was traced, in large measure, to mistakes submitted in the weekly reports to the Federal Reserve by one of the large New York banks. The erroneous figures had been processed, refined, and weighted by the central government staff as an indicator of the state of the banking system, leading thereby to the great miscalculation of the money stock.

Then there are the intentional subterfuges of facts by the opposition in any competitive arena. The well-practiced cunning goes as far back as man's first discovery of speech. We need cite just the one example leading to the destruction of the Persian fleet. After King Xerxes won at Thermopylae in the fifth century B.C. and sacked Athens, all the Greeks had left was a fleet one-fourth the size of the Persians. The Athenian admiral Themistocles chose Salamis as the only place where his small fleet had a chance to win. The restricted approach protected it against a flank attack, while taking full advantage of the greater maneuverability of the Greek ships with powerful bronze-sheathed rams. The problem facing the admiral was how to lure the Persian navy into the bottleneck. So he dispatched a servant to spread the tale surrepititiously that the Greeks were completely demoralized, quarreling among themselves and planning to slip out of the channel and race for safety. On hearing this, Xerxes decided to attack the Greeks before they had a chance to escape. The ruse worked. The Persians lost 200 ships and 20,000 men. Greece was saved.

Suppose there are no intentional prevarications, how trustworthy would reports then be? About 70 years ago, A. von Gennep rendered an account of an experiment conducted at a conference of psychologists in Göttingen. A masked ball was going on. Suddenly, the door was swung open. In rushed a clown pursued by a black man with a revolver. The pair fought in the middle of the room. The clown fell and the black jumped on him and fired. Both then fled out of the room. The Chairman of the Conference asked those present to write an immediate report of what they saw, since a judicial inquiry was certain to happen. Only 1 of the 40 reports submitted had less than 20 mistakes with respect to the main facts. Fourteen had 20 to 40% errors, 12 had 40 to 50%, and 13 had more than 50%. Twenty-four accounts fabricated 10% of the details and 10 an even higher proportion. Only 6 of the 40 reports could have been acceptable as approximating factual evidence.

Acknowledge therefore that neither you nor your competitor has all the facts. You will have to feel at home with data distortions and deficits. Do not look for answers to gnawing questions only where brightly lit facts are available in this age of, to use C. Wright Mills' phrase, "fact fetishism." Do not be reluctant about delving in the darkness. The message has been charmingly conveyed in the Polynesian myth of Nganaoa.

One day Nganaoa was out in his tiny canoe in the great ocean, when suddenly a great whale came swimming toward him with its huge jaws wide open. The lower jaw was already under the boat and the upper one was above it, when Nganaoa sprang into action. He broke his spear in two, and just as the jaws were about to close, he stuck the 2 pieces between them, so that they were unable to close. Then our hero leaped into the mouth of the whale and peered into the dark. And what did he see? There sat his parents, his father Tairitokerau and his mother Vaiaroa, who had been swallowed by the monster when they were out fishing. Nganaoa then took 1 of the 2 sticks from the whale's mouth—the other was sufficient to hold the jaws open—and broke it. He told his father to hold 1 piece firmly below, while he himself manipulated the other until the fire began to smolder. Blowing it into a flame, he began to burn the fatty parts inside the belly. Writhing with pain, the monster sought relief by swimming to shore. As soon as it reached the sandbank, the hero and his father and his mother stepped out safe and sound.

The symbolic moral is clear enough. It is in the dark that a person gains enlightenment. To find what he is seeking, the creative executive must plunge into the darkness of the depths. As was mentioned in the Bible, it was in the belly of the whale that Jonah saw the "mighty mysteries."

People in general, however, have always been fearful of the darkness of the unknown. They have always felt much more comfortable in following the well-trodden path littered with facts from clanging bandwagons. It is also understandable why many executives, being all too human, also reflect the same fears and preferences.

But we are not writing for most people but for a special group of select ones. These are the individuals who listen to Herman Melville the novelist, who said: "I like all men who dive. Any fish can swim near the surface, but it takes a great whale to go down five miles or more." These are the individuals who understand Charles A. Beard, the historian who said: "When it is dark enough, you can see the stars." These are the individuals who agree with J. H. Farbre, the entomologist, who said: "The darkness is light enough."

3.

SHYING AWAY FROM
THREATS AND CRISES

ANIMALS IN THE wild have good reason to be fearful. So prevalent are the predators. Yet there are brave souls among them. Against the timid water turtle sliding off the floating log at the first sight of an approaching man, we can point to the fearless land turtle slowly trudging along. Against the snatching-and-running squirrel, we can point to the courageous coon standing his ground against attacking dogs.

We see the same spread of valor among executives in the asphalt jungle. All sing a brave tune. But some are feebly timid underneath. The first appearance of a possible threat unsettles them. They are the type that gets nervous on hearing that a pair of ling fish produces 28 million eggs. What if a substantial proportion of them hatch? The ocean soon will be nothing but a sea of ling. They do not stop long enough in their trepidation to learn that in actuality only 2 or 3 ling survive from each batch.

Do not hide your head in the sand just because you do not like the view. Face problems squarely when they show up. Do not bury them. Do not run away. Encounter them. Size them up for what they are. And deal with them.

If you do this at the propitious moment, you will inevitably find that they are not as bad as they might be imagined. There is no need for consternation from extrapolations ad absurdum. You will be able to handle them forthrightly although with some complications and even considerable personal embarassment. But these are rarely professionally fatal.

On the other hand, if you try to flee from looming threats

and crises, they will continue to grow sub-rosa and catch up with you later in a much more violent form at a time when you are least prepared. The point was well made in an old Mohammedan anecdote.

One day while the Sultan was sitting in his palace in Damascus, his favorite youth rushed into the room. The boy was shaking like a leaf, sobbing that he must escape to Baghdad and begged the Sultan for his swiftest horse. When the Sultan asked the reason, the youth responded: "Death is after me! As I walked through the garden just now, he was there. When he saw me, he stretched out his arms as if to grab hold of me. I must not lose any time in getting away." The Sultan let the boy have the horse and the boy left in a hurry.

The Sultan dashed out into the garden. Finding Death still there, he cried out: "How dare you threaten my favorite in my own palace?"

But Death was surprised at the accusation. "I assure Your Excellency," Death apologized, "I did not threaten him. I only threw up my arms because I was astonished to find him here in Damascus. You see, I am supposed to pick him up tonight in Baghdad."

Threats often come in constellations of damned-if-you-do and damned-if-you-don't. Many executives tend to handle one threat at a time, while ignoring the others or retreat from the whole affair, because "you can't win anyway." In some ways this is reminiscent of Britain's original reactions to the European Economic Community (EEC) some time back. It seemed clear that with its empire gone and trying to export a third of its production, Britain would have to arrange for some economic union of some kind beyond the island boundary for replenishing its declining fortunes. This meant participation in something like the EEC. But the threat of being out-competed in a tariff-free relationship with Germany with a production per man exceeding Britain's by 50% was unpalatable. At the same time the alternative threat of Germany moving closer toward Russia was unacceptable. So Britain remained immobile for a number of years.

Therefore, when your turn comes, face the crises without resenting or blaming. Do not waste energy venting your resentment or shifting blame—expending energy that can better be spent toward resolving the situation. The temptation to cast blame is nonetheless widespread and hard to resist.

A senior domestic policy advisor wrote a memorandum to the President in July 1979 urging him to blame the Organization of Petroleum Exporting Countries' (OPEC) raising of oil prices for the inflation and energy crisis at home. The fact that Japan and Germany, without the American domestic oil production, paid the same prices with nowhere as great an inflation would have made such accusation simplistically unconvincing for thinking individuals. But the advisor felt it was necessary to "shift the cause for inflation and energy to OPEC, to gain credibility with the American people . . . to regain our political losses."

Shifting blame may work once but seldom twice in the same post. Such had been the experience of the executive vice president, who had sought the counsel of the beleaguered president, who was retiring ahead of time and whom he was to succeed. He was especially interested in the weathering of crises. The retiring president gave him two sealed envelopes. The vice president was to open the envelope marked #1 when he faced the first great crisis of his presidency, for which he was at wit's end, and the one marked #2 for the second. Three months later the first major crisis occurred and the new president opened the first envelope and read: "Blame your predecessor." He did and the crisis blew over as the company absorbed the losses. Nine months later, the second great crisis occurred. He then opened the second envelope and read: "Write two pieces of advice."

4.

TAKING CONSTITUENTS LIGHTLY

FROM A THEORETICAL standpoint, every human being has been accorded certain rights. Some of them have been termed "inalienable;" others are contingent on special understandings and conditions. These rights are not realizable from within the individual possessing them but through those with corresponding obligations. A direct linkage is thereby established between the executive and his constituents. The obligation on the part of the executive effectuates tangible rights in the claim of the constituents. Without this active bond, neither executives nor constituents would exist. For an executive to take his constituents lightly therefore is to take his own Self lightly.

From a practical standpoint, no one can retain power for long without keeping the constituency happy by providing a satisfactory net service of some kind. By "net service" is meant the amount of benefit actually experienced by the constituency from all that is believed to be available less that used up in the leader's exercise of power. If the constituency is convinced that they are receiving more as subjects of a given leader than they would otherwise, they would gladly overlook his occasional excesses, personal accretions, and even authoritarian behavior.

The type of service expected varies, depending on the setting. The prototype for political leaders was announced 4000 years ago in the Prologue to the Code of Hammurabi: " . . . Anu and Bel [Lord of Heaven and Earth] called me, Hammurabi, the exalted prince, the worshipper of the gods, to cause justice to prevail in the land, to destroy the wicked and the evil, *to prevent the strong from oppressing the weak . . . to enlighten the land to further the welfare of the people. . . .* Hammurabi, the governor named by Bel, am I, who brought about plenty and abundance; who made everything for Nippur and Durilu complete, . . . who gave life to the city of Uruk; who supplied water in abundance to its own inhabitants . . . who made the city of Borshipa beautiful . . . who stored up grain for the mighty Urash; . . . who helped his people in time of need; who established in security their property in Babylon; the governor of the people, *the servant,* whose deeds are pleasing to Annunit."

In modern business, department stores are particularly sensitive to the feelings of the cutomers. Marshall Field of Marshall Field & Company of Chicago left an impressive example. As he was walking one day in the new palatial quarters on State Street in 1868, he overheard a clerk arguing with a lady. He stopped and asked the young fellow what was going on. "I'm settling a complaint," replied the salesman. "Oh, no, you're not," snapped Field. "Give the lady what she wants."

The same solicitous policy was announced by the Nieman-Marcus Company in a full-page advertisement in the *Dallas News* in 1907 on the opening of "the South's finest and only exclusive ready-to-wear shop." It assured the clientele that "we will miss a sale rather than have a garment leave the establishment which is not a perfect fit."

For a firm hold on the constituency it is necessary that services be provided over and beyond that normally associated with what you might be doing in any case. It is that extra something that conveys the conviction to your constituents that you care about them. A contemporary demonstration is that of Sears Roebuck and Company. Noting that 15% of the homeowner policies in Chicago was insured by its Allstate Insurance, the company made a $1 million grant to the Chicago branch of the Neighborhood Housing Services in 1979. It had previously pledged $200,000 to the nonprofit organization engaged in stimulating urban renewal. An official called the gesture "a serious investment in the cities where we have been doing business."

Going far back into history we may compare 2 contrasting ways in which a King treated his people as far as religious preferences are concerned. In the case of the Hittites in the second millenium B.C., when a conquered people was incorporated into the Empire, the King worshipped each year at all the religious centers, including those in which the previous gods continued to be adored.

Ikhnaton, who ascended the Egyptian throne in the fourteenth century B.C., did not confer the same consideration. He decided that since his ancestors had unified the Mediterranean world under Egypt, his own god should be the god of all. Not content to let his novel doctrine of monotheism gradually gain acceptance, he ordered that reference to all gods other than Aton be removed from all public monuments, declared other religions illegal, and closed their temples. Powerful priests and many craftsmen dependent on the polytheist faiths became resentful and plotted against him. When he ordered the word Amon chiseled from his own father's name, Amenhotep III, on 100 monuments, the public was shocked by the sacrilegious act. He died a broken failure at age 30.

Should circumstances not permit largesse to your constituency on your part, the very least you must do is to refrain from ever humiliating, doing wrong to, or breaking faith with the least of them. This is the essential line of demarcation to bear in mind. Transgressing it is to take your constituents inexcusably too lightly. A billowing resistance follows in its wake. It has been observed that wolves cache their prey and call their fellows to join the feast. Should they arrive and find no food on digging, they would instantly pounce on their erstwhile host and tear him to pieces.

But one needs go further than rest at ground zero. He should take his constituents seriously, seriously as human beings and seriously as professional associates. There is to be a welcoming open-mindedness to listen to what the constituents have to say and a reasonableness to what you intend to give. There is to be a sense of humor through it all, not of buffoonery, but of a sense of proportion about not taking things too seriously, which serves no good purpose but often leads to absurd frictions.

Just because you feel you are treating your constituents better than your neighboring chiefs does not necessarily mean you are not taking them lightly. Taking them lightly or seriously is not a comparative affair. If you think so, you should examine the situation more deeply.

When King Hui mentioned to Mencius in the third century

B.C. that he was puzzled over the fact that the population of the neighboring kingdom did not seem to be decreasing and his not increasing, despite the fact that he took much better care of his citizens, the philosopher resorted to a soldiering analogy.

" 'The drum sounds with a loud noise. Weapons are engaged. Suddenly the soldiers broke ranks and ran, discarding their helmets and weapons right and left. Some retreated 100 paces before they stopped to look back. Others 50 paces. Suppose those who stopped after 50 paces laughed at those who stopped after 100 paces and called them cowards. What would you say?'

" 'They're not entitled to do so,' answered the King. 'They may have run away less than 100 paces. But they ran just the same.'

" 'Since that is what you think, Your Majesty should not expect an increase in the number of your subjects at the expense of the neighboring kingdoms.' "

In the provision of goods and services to constituents, it is important that practically all of them are reasonably cared for, relative to available resources. When there is an insufficiency of one item to go around, it is judicious to arrange matters such that those left empty-handed are compensated for that lack in the distribution of the next kind of goods and services in limited supply. You may and should, of course, reward the contributors more generously than others. But do not begin with such lavishness that you run out of things to pass out even to contributors. Goods and services should be metered carefully from the very beginning.

The unifier and first King of Norway showed how resources can be husbanded. The edict put out by Harald Fairhair in the tenth century controlled the parceling of land thusly: "No one is to take more land than he and his crew can circumnavigate with fire in one day. He is *to light a fire when the sun is in the east*. The other smoke fires are to be lit, so that one fire can be seen from the other. But the fires that were lit when the sun was in the east are to burn until nightfall. *Then he is to walk until the sun is in the west*, and again light a fire." In this way, he succeeded in having enough land left over for everyone. There were no have-nots in this regard among his constituents.

As someone had once said, "The well-managed orchard produces enough fruit to be eaten, enough to be stolen, enough to be enjoyed by the birds, and enough to be left rotting on the ground."

5.

ALLOWING DISTRUST
TO FESTER

LIKE OTHER SOCIAL animals, the aggressiveness of the individual in competing for survival, growth, and reproduction is moderated by various societal mechanisms, such as dominance hierarchy and territoriality. Although much of the individual aggressiveness is thereby reduced and channeled, it is nonetheless always present. Each person feels it within himself and feels it in others. There is a basic distrust among individuals, especially within an avowedly competitive environment.

The distrust toward each other among human beings is of a higher order of seething than exists among animals. This is largely due to imagination. Man can imagine as well as react like animals to a specific action directed against him. A large part of his distrust then is engendered by imagined nonexistent intentions on the part of others. The cleverer the person the more he uses his imagination. Since executives are by and large the empirically proven cleverest among the lot, they tend to be more distrustful of each other. They become even self-righteous in their counterdistrust of imagined distrust by others.

"The latent causes of faction are thus sown in the nature of man," opined James Madison in *The Federalist*. "So strong is the propensity of mankind to fall into mutual animosities, that where no substantial occasion presents itself, the most frivolous and fanciful distinctions have been sufficient to kindle their unfriendly passions, and excite their most violent conflicts."

The higher distrust among human beings is also reinforced

by constant displays of the severity of actual harm being inflicted by people. Romantic suicide, armed robbery, racial extermination, torture of heretics, and ruthless wars have no general counterpart in the animal kingdom.

The higher the stratosphere of power the rarer is the atmosphere of trust. The English poet Edmund Spenser chronicled the rivalries in the great palaces of Windsor, Hampton Court, and Whitehall during the sixteenth century in these words:

> *For sooth to say, it is no sort of life*
> *For shepheard fit to lead in that same place,*
> *Where each one seeks with malice and with strife,*
> *To thrust downe other in foule disgrace,*
> *Himself to raise.*

The distrust among people seems to flow in every direction. There is a higher distrust by the people of executives as compared to other professional groups. Julian B. Rotten published results of relevant psychological research in 1970. Of 20 occupations, clergymen ranked first in altruism and dentists sixth. Executives of large corporations stood eighteenth in altruism and fourteenth in truthfulness.

Another study was completed in the mid-1970s on academic governance by J. Victor Baldridge. This study revealed that about a third of the faculty of elite liberal colleges and half of that of community colleges do not have a high degree of trust in the university administration.

The wariness of each other among executives is fanned by many forces. Beginning with the 1950s the commitment of top executives to their organizations gradually but noticeably declined. This was indicated in the practice of hopping companies in bidding up one's own remuneration. Before World War II the annual turnover among policy-level executives, except for retirement, was relatively negligible. In 1975 it was about one-seventh of the 130,000 executives in American industry. A 2-way suspicion is fomented by this shifting. The corporation is distrustful of even loyal employees, suspecting that they too are marking time for more attractive opportunities. In 1979 the Presidential Chief of Staff ordered all senior officials in the government up to and including deputy secretaries be rated on this score of loyalty. The relevant question read: "To what extent is this person focused on accomplishing the Administration's goals (———) percent: personal goals (————). Total: 100 percent." Conversely, the employee is suspicious of the organization's top management as solely interested in bleeding him dry. The final effect is an insipid bidirectional rankling.

Since many individuals in high positions got there because they are both ambitious and shrewd, the incumbents are presumed to be potentially dangerous to their superiors as well. The fact that a subordinate of this character had taken an oath of loyalty has often seemed immaterial. Iyeyasu represents a case in point. Before Emperor Hideyoshi died in 1598, he exacted a promise from the Shogun to recognize the Emperor's son Hideyori as heir to the Regency. But Iyeyasu proceeded to eliminate his rivals, captured the Castle of Osaka as Hideyori committed suicide, and completed his seizure of national power by slaughtering all of Hideyori's legitimate and illegitimate children. Iyeyasu brushed aside his oath to the former Emperor as invalid, because he had sworn on blood drawn from a scratch behind his ear rather than from his finger or gums, as required by the code of the Samurai.

And the fact that the superior had been a strong champion of the subordinate does not necessarily count for much against the latter's rising against the patron-boss. The Executive Vice President of one of the largest semiconductor companies provides a not-too-uncommon standard. He went over the President's head to the Chairman of the Board and threatened to resign unless he took over the presidency. The fact that the President had been his backer, having been his chief at their former company and having brought him along to the new company and promoted and groomed him, did not deter this aggressive man in his thirties. He was not willing to wait. The Chairman felt he could not afford to lose the very capable executive. So the successfully competitive executive got the job of his erstwhile promoter.

Some misgivings are often traceable to the very rules set up by management to spur performance and competitions. In 1970 Dave Meggysey exposed some of his experience as a linebacker in American football in *Out of Their League*. He had been paid in proportion to the number of defensive plays in which he actually participated during the regular season. "So, where I was able to pick up a particular tip on the opposition, I was confronted with the dilemma of whether or not to share it with the other linebackers. Coaches constantly talk about team spirit but I've always wondered how the hell there can be team spirit if I know that the more the other linebackers screw up, the more I'll be able to play and the more I play, the more money I make." Suspicions naturally ran high. "Rumors began to spread around the league during the 1969 season that receivers who had bonus clauses for the number of passes they caught were paying kickbacks to the quarterbacks."

Although the specifics may be new to many readers, the general state of affairs is probably not. A certain degree of distrust is part of life itself. We need not talk about animals preying on each other nor about international intrigues. Neither do we need recount the scandal after scandal from Washington that covers the front pages of newspapers month after month nor even about the tough competition within institutions. All these appear fairly normal and anyone who has been around understands such occurrences very well.

But anyone who has been around also understands that there is a limit to the amount of distrust that can be tolerated beyond which everybody suffers. The particular amount of distrust that can be condoned varies from one kind of activity to another. In the case of international politics, the intensity can be quite high, within which nations can still live in peace and carry on mutually beneficial trade and cultural exchange. In the case of a corporation, however, the amount of distrust between supervisors and subordinates or between company and community cannot be more than a rather low minimum without ruinous consequences. There is no more important a responsibility of line managers than to insure that this level of mutual confidence and trust involving their own operations is kept well above that essential for efficient teamwork and healthy rapport.

To receive trust from one's associates and subordinates, a person must not only be deserving of trust, but also be believed by others to be so. To gain this status, he must be convincing through things he actually does in dealing with people. The desirable condition can only be achieved by consistent conduct over a long period of time without letdown. As long as this is maintained, the rest will follow.

But once distrust is allowed to set in or once a breach of faith is surfaced, the output of the unit will drop precipitously. It is well on its way to becoming as unproductive as the team of 2 large turtles and a little one that went to a bar one day to quench their thirst with a mug of sarsaparilla. Just after they poured it into 3 glasses, they noticed that it had begun to rain. After a lively discussion, it was decided that the little turtle should go home and get their umbrella. The little turtle objected, saying that if he went, the big turtles would drink his sarsaparilla. But they convinced the little fellow that they would leave his sarsaparilla alone. So he started toward the door.

Three weeks passed. Finally, one of the big turtles said to the other. "You know I don't think the little guy is ever coming back. Let's drink his sarsaparilla." "I was thinking the same thing," said the other big turtle. "Let's do it."

Suddenly, a shrill voice cried out from the far end of the bar near the door. "If you do, I won't go after the umbrella!"

6.

OUTWITTING ONESELF

HISTORY IS STUDDED with distorted views of man. Always one facet of man is blown out of context, only to give way to another facet equally overstated. Rarely is man presented in his wholeness. The poet kept egging us on.

During the dawn of the Graeco-Roman culture, the poet celebrated the heroic quality in man. The hero was likened to the Olympian gods. We believed the poet, so flattered were we, that we attempted to live beyond the limitations of mortal flesh.

During the Middle Ages, the poet glorified the free will in man that he shared with God Himself. But man chose selfish sin. We believed the poet and let guilt infuse our conscience.

During the neoclassical period, the poet praised the reason in man that lifted him above the beasts. We believed him and alienated ourselves from Nature by walling ourselves in the Polis of Rationality.

Then came the poet of the eighteenth century, proclaiming self-consciousness as our prime excellence. We believed him and kept repeating "I" and "I" over and again.

Today, the "I" has taken over and refuses to be dislodged. Especially is it entrenched within those who feel themselves a superior "I" to those immediately around them. These are the leaders and executives—no longer just the romantic "I," the noble "I," but the doing "I," the bossing "I." And so it has become that the most successful hoodwinker of yourself is you. We shall now discuss some of the tricks of the folly.

Most executives outwit themselves by thinking they are mightier than they actually are, so feverishly conditioned by the circle of sycophants. They forget the many things, some of the littlest dimensions, beyond their influence. They act like the praying mantis raising its arms to stop the approaching carriage. They overlook numerous other things that lie even beyond the power of institutions to attain, such as matters of personal transmittal and cellular enrichment. "None of the institutions, measures, or means of education established for the masses and the need of men in the aggregate, whatever shape or form they may take, serve to advance human culture," asserted the Swiss educator Johann Pestalozzi. "In the vast majority of cases, they are completely worthless for the purpose or directly opposed to it. Our race develops its human qualities in essence only from face to face, from heart to heart."

Another common way of outwitting oneself is the naturalistic fallacy. Caution against this entrapment had been raised two centuries ago. It had been shown that one cannot logically pass from "is" or "is not" to "ought" or "ought not." Just because in one's zeal for toughness in management he fired a vice president at nine in the morning without warning, telling him to vacate the premises by noon does not necessarily mean that it ought to be. But a number of prominent executives think so.

Just because there is gambling going on does not necessarily mean that it ought to be legalized. But New York City and Atlantic City officials recently argued that while gambling was morally reprehensible before, it no longer is today because people still seem to like it and do it and therefore gambling ought to be legalized. Besides the governments need the tax-money which used to fall into the hands of bookies. In any case, income supersedes logic.

A third way of outwitting oneself is in guessing what the competitor is going to do. Many individuals would write off certain courses of action on the following bases: (1) The competitor won't do that, because he's not *that* crazy. (2) The competitor won't do it, since *we* wouldn't do it if we were in *his* shoes. Based on such reasoning, the strategists would then brush off preparations against those particular contingencies. This is risky business. First, the competitor is not you. Second, he does not have your outlook and data and you do not have his.

A more secure choice of an optimal strategy for a large organization is one that will lead to at least the minimum goals, no matter *what* the competitor does. Another version of this approach is embodied in the old adage: in situations of great import involving great uncertainties, select that alternative which if in error would result in the least damage.

We tend to forget that other people do not necessarily believe or behave the same way we do even under similar circumstances. We transfer our own ego to them. This ego transference is illustrated in the episode involving the retired army Colonel who married a demure damsel from the quad cities in the Midwest. She had been fascinated with royalty but had never left that part of the country. So the Colonel took her to Europe for the honeymoon to look at some castles. As they were registering at the George V Hotel in Paris, in walked a gorgeous blonde, exquisitely dressed. The wife nudged the Colonel and whispered adoringly: "John, there's a princess!"

"Nah, Mary," the Colonel muttered. "She's just a prostitute."

But Mary had read a lot about princesses and insisted that the blonde was a least a duchess. The argument persisted through supper to when they were just about to retire for the night. So the Colonel finally decided to end the discussion. He said to his wife: "Okay, honey. I'll prove it to you. You get into the closet when I tell you and listen for the evidence."

He lifted the phone and asked the desk to send the blonde up to the room. A knock was soon heard. He motioned to the wife to get into the closet. She did and he opened the door. The blonde walked in and the Colonel promptly said, "I'm a man of few words. How much for the whole night?"

"Three hundred dollars," came the reply. "Three hundred dollars!" blurted the Colonel. "I thought it's only 30 bucks!"

The blonde felt insulted and left in a huff. The wife came out and acknowledged that the husband was right. They went to bed and got up for an early breakfast downstairs.

Just as the Colonel was about to sip his coffee, he felt a tap on his shoulder. He looked up and there was the blonde standing over him. She looked down at him, then at his wife, then back at him, and said, "You see, honey, what you get for 30 bucks!"

Allied to this ignoring of disastrous possibilities is the failure of many planners in overlooking potential technological breakthroughs. With today's great emphasis on science and technology, unexpected innovations should be counted on as normal rather than exceptional over a ten-year period. The case of the Lloyds of London is worth remembering.

In 1973 Lloyds began insuring contracts between computer leasing companies and their customers. Most of the cost of the computers were paid through borrowed monies. Should the customer exercise the right to terminate the lease before the loan was paid off, the old equipment might not cover the outstanding loan. This was the risk being covered. The critical question that had to be faced at the time was this: What if a new line of computers suddenly appeared on the market with major improvements in price and performance? Apparently, Lloyds gambled that improved performance of future machines would be accompanied by higher costs, as had been the case in the past. A relatively low premium was therefore charged. It so happened, however, that a new series of commercial computers did appear with significant improvements per dollar. As a result, there was considerable incentive on the part of the customers to break their leases. They did. By July 1979, Lloyds was faced with a collection of suits. The total might sum up to be the costliest settlement in its history, amounting to a possible $225 million.

Throughout the competitive maneuverings one should always bear in mind the meaning of winning. One should not outwit himself by thinking he has won when he has actually lost. Winning is not beating the competitor as such. Winning is increasing oneself in those values considered worthwhile to oneself. This may or may not be what the competitor is primarily after. For this reason clarity of the values at issue should be maintained at all times.

Negotiations toward conflict resolution should be based on this clear point of reference. The natural leader always optimizes his own values. He is always on guard against sacrificing a strategic value of his own for a tactical gain by adopting someone else's standards. public image notwithstanding. When the situation involves nonmutually exclusive factors, there is much room for accommodation and avoidance of reciprocally destructive behavior. More often than not, there is every reason for common benefit. One of the secrets of success in these instances is not only clarity of perception regarding the primary values of oneself, but also that of both parties in their individual and interacting points of view. It frequently happens that the competitor himself is confused in his own interests in the heat of the game and becomes entangled in the pursuit of the wrong objective. Once the competitor is subtly led around to realizing his misplaced focus, the negotiations proceed much smoother after that.

When everything's said and done, many executives stop short of being great because they fail to be themselves. They try to be someone else. The net result is phony. Being phony, they behave in a phony fashion. Having lost their complete integrity, they no longer possess that essential compass of being true to themselves. The hoodwinking goes on and on.

7.

BEING FEW-SIDED
IN EFFICIENCY

WHEN FIELDING A basketball team, the coach simply dreads signs of weakness in even a single position. The same should hold for venturing into any other form of competition. The entire enterprise can come tumbling down on the side of the weak pillars, no matter how powerful the others.

Professors Joel E. Ross and Michael J. Kami analyzed one such debacle in the computer field in *Corporate Management in Crisis*. Beginning in the late 1950s over a period of 15 years, Radio Corporation of America (RCA) launched into a frontal competition against the International Business Machines Corporation (IBM) in the computer field, especially against the IBM Series/360. RCA's strength was in the lower price and higher capacity of its design. But its marketing staff was relatively weak. So was its technical service. One strength alone could not make up for the other weaknesses. The final outcome was an overall loss of about half a billion dollars when the company got out of the contention in 1971.

Grand efficiency is extremely difficult to determine even on a subjective basis. One can numerically assess the efficiency of the more pedestrian aspects of his operations. By following the indices in several critical areas on a continuing basis and the rest on a spot basis, the executive usually hopes to gain a reasonable feel of the overall progress of his unit.

The task is complex even in restricted aspects, such as the allocation of resources to various needs. As pointed out by James W. McKie in his presidential address before the Southern Economic Association in 1971, "Many elements in the total allocation of resources in the society simply do not have satisfactory price equivalents. . . . [and] cannot be measured or expressed in a continuum of numbers." The much-publicized "quality of life" is a catchall for many of them. "Economists (and businessmen) of late have been often bemused by the fact that a long and continuous increase in all the indices that are supposed to measure (or at least indicate) economic progress has not brought with it a corresponding increase in the public well-being, certainly not in the conception that many people have of their own welfare. Something seems to have escaped and lost itself in urban decay, overpopulation, the breakdown of public amenities and of public order, in congestion, uglification and the ennui that follows excessive consumption artifically induced."

All of us have seen how vaporous are the "authentic evaluations" of the "state of health" of institutions. How quickly has many a highly touted "growth" company dropped in earnings into the loss column. How suddenly has many a corporation, just rated "excellently managed" by leading evaluators on Wall Street, declined.

When measures of efficiency cannot be expressed in numbers, executives tend to be callous in matching their allocation of rewards and resources to their avowed goals. University presidents preach eloquently about raising the quality of teaching. Yet the academic system overwhelmingly rewards research accomplishments, as determined by number of publications, and promotional competence, as determined by the amount of grant money raised.

These mensural dilemmas had been anticipated 2000 years ago by Augustine, who confessed: "For so it is, oh Lord my God, I measure it. But what it is I measure, I know not."

Most executives are few-sided by nature. Financial raiders pursue short-term profit at the expense of long-term health of the institution. Many directors of research and development emphasize applied investigations, as compared to more pioneering research, only to lose technical leadership to competitors within a decade. Other directors overemphasize basic research, as compared to the more immediately applied investigations, only to lose the near-term markets to competitors.

An example of a more historical misallocation of emphasis is the thirteenth-century King of Castile, Alfonso X. He was famed for marshaling the intellectual and artistic talents of

Christians, Moslems, and Jews in Spain into a brilliant burst of cultural attainments. Rightly deserved was his reputation as the first Renaissance Man of the Middle Ages. But he left his domestic economic and political situation in shambles. In the words of a later historian, "He studied the heavens and watched the stars, while losing the earth and his kingdom."

There are certain executive positions, in which it is humanly impossible for the incumbent to be anything but few-sided in efficiency. Perhaps one of the outstanding examples is the Chief of Police. As Chief in a small town with a handful of officers, his department cannot even keep up with the thousands of laws that have been and are being passed by federal and state authorities, let alone enforce them. In a large metropolis, the bulk of the Chief's force is assigned to routine chores, such as traffic control. The criminal side of law enforcement becomes less efficiently pursued. Within the area of criminal offenses, those that are uppermost in the minds of the citizenry at a particular point in time receive the most attention, such as mugging in wealthier parts of the city. White-collar crimes are generally overlooked.

Some communities signal their preferences for the maintenance of order rather than the enforcement of laws as their prime expectation. The watchman style then becomes the police department ethos. "To the extent that the administrator can influence the discretion of his men, he does so by allowing them to ignore many common minor violations, especially traffic and juvenile offenses, to tolerate, though gradually less so, a certain amount of vice and gambling, to use the law more as a means of maintaining order than of regulating conduct, and to judge the requirements of order differently depending on the character of the group in which the infraction occurs," observed Professor James Q. Wilson in *Varieties of Police Behavior* in 1968. Juveniles and blacks are "expected" to deviate from the law and their infractions, unless serious or offensive to those affected, are overlooked. Blacks offending blacks are not as quickly arrested as blacks offending whites. Motorists are usually left alone unless their driving is endangering or annoying others or their demeanor is insulting to police authority. "Vice and gambling are crimes only because the laws says they are; they become problems only when the currently accepted standards of public order are violated . . . And disputes that are a normal business risk, such as getting a bad check, should be handled by civil procedures if possible. With exceptions to be noted, the watchman style is displayed in Albany, Amsterdam, and Newburgh."

Because of a limitation in resources, the Chief of Police is necessarily few-sided in efficiency. For this, he should not be criticized. However, he should be at all times clear about the skewness of his performance and the specific aspects of his responsibilities that are being short-changed. The overall pattern should not be shaped by the usual passive equilibrium resulting from the squeaky wheel getting the grease. It should be formulated in the light of the philosophy and priorities of the people and/or organization he serves, the resources made available to him, and his professional estimate of the situation. In this way, although he may be few-sided in efficiency on an absolute criterion, he is not on a responsive criterion. He is doing the best and the most prudent that can be expected. Failure in impossibilities requires no excuse.

Therefore, not being few-sided does not necessarily mean being efficient in every conceivable aspect of things. It means not being few-sided relevant to the issue and requirements at hand. This contrast is seen in the episode involving the learned professor who stopped on a country road and looked about the countryside in confusion. He noticed a farmhand leaning on a fence nearby. So he called out to him, "Hey, how far is it to Ames?"

The farmhand thought for a while and replied, "Don't know."

"Well, then, what's the best way of getting there?"

Again, the farmhand thought and said, "Don't know."

"Where's the nearest gas station where I can pick up a map?"

The farmhand thought quite a long time at this question. Finally, he answered, "Don't know."

The professor sneered at him in contempt, "You don't know much, do you?"

The farmhand slowly drawled, "But I'm not the fella who's lost."

8.

DISREGARDING
HIGHER-ORDER EFFECTS

EVERY MEDICINE HAS its side effects. Every drinking party leaves its hangovers. Some of the inevitable unplanned-for higher-order effects to what we do may be desirable; others, not so. "If you kill German soldiers in order to save France and then at the end of a certain time you acquire a taste for assassinating human beings, it is clearly an evil thing," according to the sensitive French analyst of modern life, Simone Weil, in *The Need for Roots*. "If, in order to save France, you offer your assistance to workmen avoiding transportation to Germany and then at the end of a certain time you acquire a taste for helping those in misfortune, it is clearly a good thing."

Higher-order effects on a cultural level seem to have an inexorableness of their own. The higher-order progressions attending the technological advancements of an energy-based society is a case at hand. The discovery of directing the flow of energy from the wind to the sail in ships enabled the bringing of food to people living where there is timber but no food and of timber to people living where there is food but no timber. New social relationships and dependencies resulted. As societies became more high-energy in character, technical specialization increased. The extended family of former days is no longer capable of providing the minimum skills for earning a livelihood. The head of the family is unable to assign roles and responsibilities. He is inadequate as the font of essential knowledge and can no longer assume the role of respected teacher. The members now look elsewhere for expertise. The conjugal units move under the attraction of the high-energy processors. The further decline of the family's power, function, and centrality is an inevitable higher-order symptom of the high-energy society.

Those in charge of research and creative enterprises should be especially perspicacious about unanticipated higher-order effects. They should not be so carried away by their prowess that the product of their genius becomes a threat to themselves and humankind. Let knowledge and sophistication propose but let judgment and common sense decide. The moral is contained in the fable of the lion-makers in *The Panchantantra*, written around 200 B.C. in Kashmir. As condensed from the translation by Arthur W. Ryder, the fable goes as follows:

There once lived four Brahmans as close friends in a certain town. Three were erudite scholars; the fourth had only common sense. One day they decided to travel afar to seek the fortune that would come from their collective learning. Along the way they came across the bones of a dead animal. "A good opportunity to test the ripeness of our scholarship," said one of the scholars. "Here lies some kind of creature, dead. Let us bring it to life by means of the scholarship we have honestly won."

The first offered to assemble the skeleton; the second, to supply skin, flesh, and blood; the third, to infuse life itself. As the Brahman with common sense observed how the first succeeded, then the second, he interrupted the third. "This is a lion," he advised against completion of the project. "If you bring him to life, he will kill everyone of us."

"You simpleton!" exclaimed the third scholar. "It is not I who will reduce scholarship to a nullity."

"In that case," requested the Brahman with common sense, "wait a moment, while I climb this convenient tree."

He did and the three scholars brought the dead lion back to life, whereupon the lion jumped up and devoured all of them. After the lion left, the Brahman with common sense climbed down and went back home.

The trade-offs between the first-order gains of one party versus the higher-order payments by another are matters of continuing controversy. Whether the factory owners, making larger profits because they do not have to pay the social cost of the harmful smoke being breathed by the neighboring inhabitants, should be permitted to continue is now a topic of hot debate. In 1967 the British government decided to build an airport in the beautiful Essex countryside, north of London. The *Daily Mail* objected strongly: "What is the point of Technology if it is going to make life faster but also uglier, drabber, dirtier, noisier? Is it right to create slums near London so that jumbo loads of passengers from New York can get to Piccadilly a few hours earlier?"

The order of higher-order effects to which a person should be alert depends on his executive responsibility. If he is the head of state or church, the *n* should be rather high. The current concern over inflation in America has raised the option of wage and price control as a remedial measure. The Roman Empire around the end of the third century had been plagued with the same social problem. Prices were going up "not only year by year, month by month, day by day," bemoaned Emperor Diocletian, "but almost hour by hour and minute by minute." In the year 301 A.D. the Emperor imposed a price ceiling for every item and service. This worked for a while. Black marketing and hoarding became established. So the new laws required taxes to be paid in commodities. The small farmers then left their poor farms in search of greener pastures to meet the higher taxes. So more laws were promulgated, tying the tenant farmers to their particular land. One bounce of the legal ball led to a rebound in higher-order effects, which called for ensuing cycles of the same, until the final solution became a rigid and all-pervasive totalitarian state. Whether such an experience would necessarily repeat itself on the American scene is difficult to say.

The rippling effect of government aid toward the gradual weakening of the free-enterprise system in the United States is often overlooked as a matter of personal urgency and collective expediences. This end would seem logical on the part of individuals who feel that the free-enterprise form of American democracy of the early 1900s has outlived its usefulness and should be replaced by a socialized form of government with comprehensive planning and centralized social direction. But some of the avid pursuers of government assistance have been among the most fervent believers in the free-enterprise system. In 1967 the troubled American Motors obtained congressional help in changing tax-loss provisions for the specific purpose of bailing out the company. In 1974 ailing Lockheed Corporation received a $250-million loan guarantee from the federal government. In August 1979 Chrysler Corporation, faced with a quarterly loss of hundreds of millions of dollars and possible bankruptcy, appealed for similar financial aid totaling $1.5 billion from the same source.

Many argued that the country could not afford to jeopardize the jobs of the company's 250,000 employees. Besides, everybody else seems to be subsidized in one form or another by the federal government anyway. So why not Chrysler?

Others were strongly opposed. In the opinion of the Chairman of General Motors, it "presents a basic challenge to the philosophy of America." The free-enterprise system is endangered. "If you say, 'O.K., if somebody fails in the competitive race, then we're going to bail them out someway,' I don't think that's in accordance with what really made this country great," said Thomas A. Murphy. "It removes and compromises that discipline in the marketplace. . . . Competition is inherent in our American system and competition is what got us where we are."

Increasingly, the American government has been loading higher-order goals onto its first-order purposes in its procurement of goods and services. The $100 billion outlay and subsidies in 1980 have been used as a weapon to extend racial desegregation, wage-and-price guidelines to fight inflation, support to minority business, relief of local unemployment, assistance to handicapped persons, humane slaughtering standards, prod to geographical distribution of doctors, and so on. In many cases, the first-order objective of the actual goods and services procured are downgraded in importance and sacrificed to attain the ostensibly higher-order effect. In 1979 30 such socioeconomic provisions were included in the impact on what may appear to be a purely internal management practice. As elucidated by Robert S. Holzman in *Dun & Bradstreet's Handbook of Executive Tax Management* in 1974, "The Commissioner of Internal Revenue has the authority to reallocate items of income or expense among corporations under common control where there are intercompany transactions at less than arms' length. . . . if a corporation has to pay more taxes because of managerial ignorance than otherwise would be payable, stockholders may compel the offending directors or officers to reimburse the company from their own pocketbooks."

Following the qualitative introduction of a given higher-order effect, a quantitative expansion ensues until it meets another higher-order effect, expanding in a contrary direction. During the 1950s the individual right of privacy protected the preferences of the members of private social clubs regarding where, how, and with whom they would like to fraternize. By the early 1970s the Civil Rights movement against racial discrimination in public places spilled over into the provinces of private clubs. The public pressure all but eliminated selective membership in these organizations based on race. In 1976 the President insisted that all appointees to his cabinet resign from private clubs that are exclusively male in membership. In 1979 the Attorney General nominee stressed at his confirmation hearing that he intends to urge all judges to resign from clubs limited to a single sex. It may well be that private social clubs will next be opened with respect to religious affiliation. Race, sex, and religion have been so closely linked together in antidiscrimination proclamations that the same sentiments may also engulf the religious affiliation.

Very few individuals are gifted with the clairvoyance to foretell the vicissitudinous chain of events arising from what may appear to be a well-circumscribed act. Even the most respected and experienced stub and stumble. The more mortal among us need therefore exercise that much greater care before acting. We may cite a relatively recent episode. Under pressure by the Chairman of one of America's largest banks with the widest of global connections and a former Secretary of State highly regarded for his sensitivity to the subtle intricacies of international joustings, the President admitted the deposed Shah of Iran for medical treatment in New York in October 1979 over the expressed objections of that country. Little did they dream of the enormous perturbations and lasting damage that unraveled.

Iranian students invaded the American embassy in Teheran and held about 60 American hostages for the return of the Shah for trial. A tit led to a tat, back to an escalating tit for tat. Within 3 weeks, the American-Iranian relations on the mend for months completely fell apart. The official Iranian government collapsed, giving way to a more anti-American one. The flow of Iranian oil to the United States, comprising 9% of America's oil import, halted. Disruption of the oil supply pattern spread anxieties over allies like Japan, heavily dependent on Iranian oil. Billions of Iranian dollars in

American banks were frozen by the President, raising uneasiness among the international financial centers regarding the longstanding assurance that such deposits would not be disturbed for political purposes. Half a billion were seized by several American banks to offset outstanding loans to the Iranian government. Apprehensions over the impact of these actions on the international monetary system spread. There was talk about the reduction of vulnerable deposits in American banks by petroleum producing countries and saving their national wealth by leaving more of it in the ground as oil instead. This would mean a cutback in petroleum output, something dreaded by the western nations and Japan in particular. Iranian students in America were ordered to prove their legal immigration status; 150 were ordered to leave the country from New Jersey and Connecticut alone. Americans clamored for more forceful actions: withholding food shipments to starve the Iranians into submission, even though the government was asking other nations to rush food to the starving Cambodians. Talk spread about sending the Central Intelligence Agency back into Iran, this time to overthrow the Khomeini government, and about severe reprisals after the hostages were freed. After releasing 13 women and blacks, Khomeini stated the others would be tried for espionage. In response, the White House threatened the possibility of military action. In turn, Iranian students stated that the hostages would be killed at the first sign of such military action. Within hours the conflict spread. The Grand Mosque in Saudi Arabia was seized and retaken after a gun battle. American buildings were burnt in several cities in Pakistan and the embassy attacked at the capital, killing 2 Americans. Two other American embassies were also disturbed in Turkey and Bangladesh. American aircraft carriers and guided missile ships were ordered into Persian waters. Khomeini ordered the Iranian navy to station themselves in readiness and declared that the state of affairs amounts to a war between Moslems and pagans. In less than 3 weeks—we end our narrative at this point—hopes of regaining strong American presence and influence in a geopolitically critical region vanished for the near future. The entire world was thrown into political, economic, and religious fear.

The question before powerful people is not only whether the first-order direct purpose is desirable, or even humanitarian, but also whether the higher-order ramifications have been reasonably foreseen and weighed and the decision taken on the basis of judicious executive trade-offs among an array of options to gain the first-order objective, assuming it to be necessary. It may be that measures other than the immediate one at hand may prove more prudent and humanitarian in the totality of effects.

The interconnectedness of successive cause and effects into a polyorder reticulum recalls the Englishman in his spanking new Jaguar. He was speeding along one day on a gradually rising country road. Nobody was in sight. So he pressed the accelerator to the floorboard. Just as he sped over the top of the hill, a circus train was crossing the road. A column of elephants, each one hanging with its trunk onto the tail of the one ahead, was meandering along. At the end of the passing line was a tiny baby elephant. It too was hanging onto the mother's tail.

The driver slammed on the brakes and swerved to the right, but too late. He crashed into the baby elephant, landing both elephant and car into the side ditch.

As he crawled out from under the wreckage, the circus manager strode up to him and said, "Son, you owe me a 100,000 pounds."

"A hundred thousand pounds?" gasped the Englishman. "For just 1 tiny baby elephant?"

"Hell no!" replied the circus manager. "You've just yanked the tails off 20 large elephants!"

9.

FOSTERING DISCONTINUITIES

ALL KINDS OF discontinuities are inevitable in a large organization. These result from conflicts of interest, personality clashes, sheer lapses in communication, and other sources. For enduring productivity these discontinuities must not be permitted to expand into major unbridgeable gaps in the operationally integrated network.

Our first example is actually fashionable in many quarters. It is the practice of segregating long-range planning from current operations. Many people tend to compartmentalize long-range planning and short-range operations. They would establish independent long-range-planning offices. The rationale for the isolation is understandable. Unless long-range planning is kept apart from immediate concerns, the long-range thinking will be cramped by day-to-day attentions.

We are not questioning the wisdom of a dedicated long-range planning office. Some top managements make the mistake, however, of disjoining long-range planning and current operations psychologically and philosophically. It confuses the essential input of relevant thinking from all sources with the domination of planning by shortsighted views. Once this splintering habit takes hold, long-range planning loses much of its sharpness in practical relevance.

"The history of economic activity thus exemplified the moral consequences of the separation of present activity and future 'ends' from each other," concluded the philosopher John Dewey in *Human Nature and Conduct*. "For the professed idealist and the hard-hearted materialist, or 'practical,' man have conspired together to sustain this situation. The 'idealist' sets up as the ideal not fullness of meaning of the present but a remote goal. Hence the present is evacuated of meaning. . . . Meantime the practical man wants something definite, tangible and presumably obtainable for which to work. He is looking after a 'good thing' as the average man is looking after a 'good time,' that natural caricature of an intrinsically significant activity. . . . He empties present activity of meaning by making it a mere instrumentality."

A more fruitful conceptualization of corporate planning is that of a continuum embracing future anticipations and current actions with a constant iterative relationship among all the parts. The corporate plan would then consist of a single moving portfolio of current actions by all elements of the organization related to given projects. Each action is part of a sequence leading to practical returns at stipulated dates to meet cumulative corporate goals. As far as the more serious plans are concerned, no matter how far out in the future lie the targets of first returns, there exists at all times at least a theoretically possible thread linking the here of present operations to the there of the gleam in the planner's eyes.

We may diagram the moving portfolio as shown in Figure 2. Let p be the date at which the initial return is expected from a continuum of antecedent actions, X_p represents the action in the X series to be taken at the date of expected initial

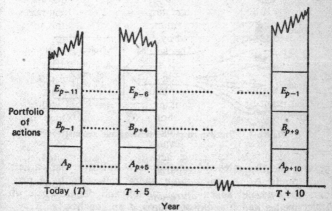

Figure 2. Moving portfolio of current actions.

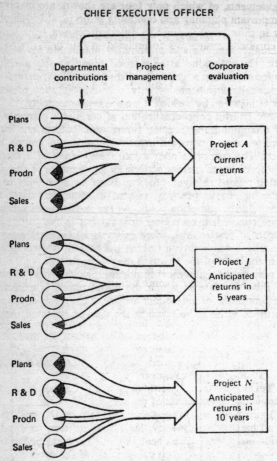

Figure 3. Unity of corporate strategy and actions.

return, X_{p-1} an antecedent action to be taken a year earlier, and so on. At the same time, there must also be a progressively greater specificity of action and definitiveness of objective, as the initial day of returns, p, approaches.

In this way, as indicated in Figure 3, all planning and operating elements, of which only four are shown, are involved in all important planning and operating projects, although obviously in different ways and to different degrees over time. When corporate strategy is formulated in this light, there is an intimate unity between ongoing operations and future planning. Present actions shape the future plans coming into fruition and future plans being made determine the present portfolio of actions. All are one.

Another not uncommon uncoupling is that between plans and the implementing capacity. Often, fine-sounding plans are completed without taking the executive agents fully into account. The subordinate echelons might have been overloaded at the moment, deficient in the essential know-how, or uncooperative with any endeavor not initiated by itself. Outside consultants often commit the error of recommending courses of actions without having any idea about who is going to carry them out. This is inviting trouble.

The mismatch between plans and implementation can be seen in the story of the Texan who wanted to be an Alaskan. When Alaska was admitted as a state, the Texan moved to Alaska, so that he could still be living in the largest state of the Union. After spending some time there, however, he was yet to be accepted as a real Sourdough by the natives. As he was crying in his beer in a saloon one day, the bartender took pity on the Texan and told him the secret requirements. "What you have to do to be accepted as one of us are 3 things," the bartender whispered. "First, drink this fifth of whiskey in one swiggle. Second, make love to an Eskimo gal. And third, shoot an Alaskan bear."

The Texan grabbed the bottle of whiskey, downed it in one long gurgle, then stalked out of the saloon.

Six hours later, he came staggering through the swinging doors, all battered and bloody, his clothes all torn to shreds, but still undaunted. He beat his chest and bellowed: "Naow—where's that Eskimo gal ah'm s'posed to shoot?"

A third example of discontinuity is the breakdown of social order by the conflict between classes. Within the capitalist countries, workers have been urged for years by Mikhail Bakunin, Ferdinand Joachim Lassalle, and other social activists to look on the rich and the powerful—which in their minds include contemporary top executives—as exploiting rivals to be "brought down to size" before the workers' welfare can be assured. In the Communist countries the people are being bombarded by outside exhortations to look on their own leaders as oppressive tyrants to be weakened in their control before their human rights can be assured.

Your behavior in any executive post should be such as to respond constructively to the challenges posed by these forces of cleavage. You should foster adaptive change on the part of the social establishment to meet new social contingencies and conditions toward its preservation. While the preservation of the prevailing social order is not a direct responsibility of any one executive, it is nonetheless a collective one. This is consistent with your oath of office. Toward this end, you should realize that the hatred aroused by the leader of one group against another is often an overflow of the hatred within himself. Not to exacerbate discontinuities between classes begins with not exacerbating the neurotic tendencies toward hatred within the leaders—yourself included.

"Seek the roots of disastrous conflicts between nations and classes and sects, and invariably you find a man, often gifted and resourceful, who has failed to master his own inner turmoil—a neurotic, perhaps, or an epileptic, a slave of sensuality or of pride—who diffuses the bitterness and desperation of his tortured soul among masses and classes and vitiates the clean air with the psychic poisons of suspicion and hatred and vindictiveness," discerned the writer Francis Meehan in *The Temple of the Spirit.* "We allow such men to rise, we retain them in places in influence, and then we wonder why rational human beings cannot live together in amity. Men are at war with one another because each man is at war with himself."

The fourth example involves scuffling and splitting apart within one's own jurisdiction. Two contrasting national policies can be presented regarding the treatment of "outsiders." The ancient Egyptian, Babylonian, Phoenician, and Greek nations extracted a treaty of submission by the "barbarians." In contrast, Rome invited the neighboring Latin tribes to join them as full citizens in their common "res publica" or commonwealth. In return for the privilege they were expected to fight for the strongly fortified city in time of danger. There were no first- and no second-class citizens. All were equal.

Incipient breaks should be continually ameliorated. Adjustments are not to be restricted to specific progress review points but are to be made at all moments of action along the way. An incident involving the Columbia Broadcasting System (CBS) anchorman Walter Cronkite is apropos.

In 1967 Cassius Clay announced that he was changing his name to Mohammed Ali and asked that he be henceforth known by his new Black Muslim identity. A writer on Cronkite's show, John Merriman, used the new name as requested in composing the newscast about the champion's refusal to be drafted for the Vietnam War. Cronkite not only asked that the name be changed back to Cassius Clay but admonished Merriman for being taken by Clay's publicity stunt to evade military service. The quarrel heated up.

As reported by Gary Paul Gates in *Air Time*, "Merriman, incensed, speculated on how wonderful it must be to be a big and important TV anchorman and play God by telling black athletes how uppity they were for changing their names." Things went from bad to worse. Cronkite told Merriman that Cronkite's the boss of the program and Merriman better take orders. But when the show went on the air and Cronkite looked at the prompter with the words "Cassius Clay." he drew a deep breath and said, "The heavyweight champion Mohammed Ali today . . ."

10

LOSING ONE'S COOL

WHOSOEVER LOSES HIS temper has also lost the argument. He has admitted in fact that he has nothing better to offer than anger. If he has not lost the argument, he will soon lose the game, for he has already lost control of his wits.

As a point of departure, one should never get unduly excited just because there is a lot of noise. He should first ascertain who is causing the commotion. In these days of professional organizers of "spontaneous demonstrations," pressure groups without followers, and bull-horn messiahs, the number of decibels does not necessarily correlate with the degree of importance.

"Because half a-dozen grasshoppers under a fern make the field ring with importunate chink, whilst thousands of great cattle, reposed beneath the shadow of the British oak, chew the cud and are silent," the British statesman Edmund Burke prompted us almost 2 centuries ago, "pray do not imagine that those who make the noise are the only inhabitants of the field; that of course they are many in number; or that, after all, that they are other than the little shrivelled, meagre, hopping, though loud and troublesome insects of the hour."

When difficulties appear intractable, one should not become frustrated. The reverse causal relationship is often closer to the truth. The difficulties appear increasingly intractable over time because the person has become increasingly frustrated. Had he not so become, they might not have gotten intractable. At the least he would have reached a draw, which is another way of resolution. In effect, a draw means that one has accepted the situation as chronic. He then adopts it as a given in his equation of life. And he goes on from there. "The greatest art in theoretical and practical life consists in changing the problem into a postulate," as some German author had noted over a century ago. "That way one succeeds."

The most important single transformation of problem into postulate for anyone aspiring to become a great manager concerns the problem of being fired—of professional death, as it were. Once that possibility is accepted as a given and no further thought is accorded it, the major obstacle to greatness has been removed. The essence was well brought out in a passage in the *Hagakure*. As retold by the Zen Buddhist philosopher Daisetz T. Suzuki in *Zen and Japanese Culture*, it goes like this:

One day a personal guard of Shogun Tokugawa Iyemitsu came to the swordsmaster Tajima no kami Munemori for lessons in swordplay. "As I observe," the master said to him, "you seem to be a master of the art yourself; pray tell me to what school you belong, before we enter into the relationship of teacher and pupil?"

The guard modestly stated that he had never learned the art. But the teacher of the Shogun refused to believe it. The guard stuck to his claim. So the master finally gave in, saying that while he could not figure it out, there must be something of which the guard is a master. The guard told him about how he had been grappling since childhood, as a Samurai, over the problem of death. But now he is a complete master over it and the question has entirely stopped worrying him in the least. "May this be what you are hinting at?"

"Exactly!" exclaimed Tajima no kami. "That is what I mean. I am glad I made no mistake on my judgment. For the ultimate secrets of swordsmanship also lie in being released from the thought of death. I have trained ever so many hundreds of my pupils along this line, but so far none of them really deserve the final certificate for swordsmanship. You need no technical training. You are already a master."

Now that we have established the essential baseline, let us take up some of the finishing détails to round out the picture.

Do not be one of those easily vexed, scowling cursers at subordinates. There may be many reasons other than their incompetence or laziness for the messed-up situation. One or more of the following might well be the principal cause: (1) You had not exercised good judgment in assigning the task to him in the first place. (2) You had not given sufficiently clear instructions. (3) You had not provided adequate time and/or resources for the job at hand. (4) You do not understand the total picture and extenuating circumstances. (5) You are mean-spirited. Before cursing someone else, therefore, look first at yourself. Even if you should feel you are not at fault, consider the probability that your cursing at your subordinate will almost certainly dampen whatever enthusiasm he might have had for voluntarily exerting himself on your behalf beyond the call of duty. It does not make selfish sense to curse at people. Rectify yourself and be civil.

"I consider my ability to arouse enthusiasm among the men the greatest asset that I possess, and the way to develop the best that is in a man is by appreciation and encouragement," contended Charles Schwab, who had been paid $1 million a year as a steel executive over half a century ago. "There is nothing else that so kills the ambitions of a man as criticism from his superiors. I never criticize anyone. I believe in giving a man incentive to work. So I am anxious to praise but loath to find fault. If I like anything, I am hearty in my approbation and lavish in my praise."

Do not even waste time castigating yourself. This does not ameliorate any misfortune. Who said that you are expected to be superhuman anyway? Rather than beat your own breast in self-flagellation, doing something good or constructive serves a better purpose.

In these days of persistent inquiries by government agents, congressional committees, newsmen, consumer representatives, and so on, keeping one's self-control under cross-examination needs become second nature. Since such questionings are often not motivated by the gentle probing for information, but by the adversarial jabbing for proving a preconceived position or eliciting some "newsworthy" remark, it is difficult not to become annoyed, to say the least. No matter how intense your inner irritation, however, you should never let it so waggle your tongue that you find yourself saying something you will regret later on. One of the more famous remarks of this kind was made by William H. Vanderbilt, whose New York Central Railroad was engaged in a rate war with Pennsylvania Railroad in 1882. The industrial tycoon explained to the reporters in a news conference that Central could not make a profit on the $15 fare from New York to

Chicago. Were it not for the fact that Pennsylvania was charging that price, "we would abandon it [the route]." A free-lance writer interrupted and wanted to know: "But don't you run the train for public benefit?" Vanderbilt retorted: "The public be damned!" He never lived that remark down.

It may also be well to remember that maxim about a person being as big as that which irritates him. So do not react heatedly at someone falsely accusing you for some mishap. What he says does not alter what you are. So why bother? It may mean one or more of the following: (1) He is envious of your good luck. (2) He is misinformed. (3) He is trying to cover up his own inadequacies. Sympathizing with the accuser's pitiable state does you greater credit.

This advice, however, is not easy to follow. The response of the leader of the Knights of Labor in the latter part of the nineteenth century is more normal. The more he was criticized, the more viciously he counterattacked. "We are more sincerely desirous of aiding the movement," blasted Terence V. Powderley to Tom O'Reilley in 1889, "than a lot of damn gin guzzling, pot-bellied, red-nosed, scab-faced, dirty shirted, unwashed, leather assed, empty headed, two faced, rattle-headed, itch palmed scavengers in the field of labor reform." Largely as a result of his abrasiveness even his closest associates eventually deserted him. The Order deteriorated and Powderley departed hated and poor.

No matter what the trying circumstances, losing your equanimity means expending energy for nonproductive purposes and letting others determine the quality of your inner life. It beclouds your vision of reality and precludes creative inspirations from entering your agitated mind. You have lost your integrated Self, in sum, you have become a less competent manager and you are broadcasting the fact to the world.

As exasperation and anger being to creep over you, remember the little monkey in the Russian story. He was carrying two handfuls of peas. One fell out. In trying to pick it up, he spilled 20 more. In trying to pick up the 20, he dropped them all. Then he lost his temper, scattered the peas every which way, and scampered off.

IV
The Mark of the Master

So FAR, WE have discussed the central artistry of Chinese baseball, 10 underlying principles to be followed, and 10 damaging pitfalls to be avoided.

It may be well to note that these categories have been singled out only for purpose of deliberation. It seems that we can talk about things only in a serial fashion. This is not the way, of course, how events occur in Nature. Events do not stand still for our slow-witted thinking. Even a relatively incomplete list of significant organizational and societal factors influencing corporate strategy would produce a trillion-trillion combinatorial situations that are continually changing in kind and intensity. How can you possibly conceive of "thinking it through?"

To be effective in our actions, we must catch the instant on the wing in agglomerate fitness. That is why we presented as our first managerial principle: act from an instantaneous apprehension of the totality. Like your knocking on your associate's door, the sound does not wait for the completion of the knock before issuing forth. Knock and sound, cause and effect, theory and practice, plans and operations, means and end, executive and person—all merge in the instant of action.

That ineffable agglomerant is the hallmark of The Authentic Master. May it be yours as well.

Appendices

1.

366 MINI CASE STUDIES

WHEN EVERYTHING IS said and done, leaders and managers deal primarily with people. They need to feel at home with them, sense what makes them tick, and intuit how best to influence them this way and that. At bottom, this is what leadership and management is all about.

This first appendix presents a representative sampling of the kinds of personalities and behaviors you are likely to meet in your own work and play. Over 500 actual characters from all walks of life in many lands over thousands of years are portrayed in a calendar of anniversary sketches. Each of the brief narratives is capped with a proverb, a decision-making rule as valid in these times as in Aesop's.

As you reflect and chuckle over the humanness of people at large, you might recognize much of yourself in others and much of others in yourself—and no wonder.

As the Chinese proverb puts it:

Within the four seas, all men are brothers.

JANUARY 1

On this day in the year 1900, James Buchanan Brady again impressed his chief executive at the 11-month-old Pressed Car Steel Company of New Jersey by accumulating a backlog of orders amounting to $16,596,863.

Had it not been for a chance label, however, the head salesman would have gone down anonymously into history like so many other successful businessmen. Early in life, he had developed a fondness for diamonds. He would stop at every pawnshop he could and drive a hard bargain with the broker, leaving the latter with only a narrow margin of profit. Before long, his collection rivaled those of European royalties. He mounted a 3-carat diamond in the ferrule of his cane and a 25-carat emerald in his stickpin. "If you're going to make money," he used to say, "you must look money." One day he and others had arranged to get together for a poker game in a Cincinnati hotel. After waiting for the rest to show up, one of them by the name of Mackie Morrell asked: "Has anyone seen Diamond Jim?" "Y'mean Jim Brady, the big fat guy who doesn't drink?" "Yep, that's the fellow," said Morrell, "Diamond Jim Brady!" With that, 28-year-old Diamond Jim Brady was on his way to becoming a household phrase and an American legend.

As the Thonga proverb puts it:

The little bird becomes known by its feathers.

JANUARY 2

On this day in the year 1935, Fred L. Siegling accused Samuel W. King of having "bought" the election just completed for the delegate from Hawaii to the United States Congress.

The Chairman of the territorial Democratic central committee sent a letter to the Clerk of the House of Representatives charging excessive campaign expenditures by the Republican. He strongly supported the allegations of the incumbent Democratic delegate Lincoln L. McCandless who was contesting the election. King was accused of spending $1500 for hula girls alone and over $2000 for free beer and food for a total exceeding $51,000. King defended himself by listing his total expenditures as being only $4864.57.

As the Hebrew proverb puts it:

Attend no auction if thou hast no money.

JANUARY 3

On this day in the year 1973, Mihajlo Mihajlov was informed by Belgrade authorities that he must serve another prison term for violation of the publication ban.

The Yugoslavian social critic had refused to be silenced. He criticized the Yugoslavian system of worker participation in enterprise management in the article "For Utopian Only," released a month before. Several months before that he had published another article in an American newspaper, critical of the Communist way of doing things. This was only 7 months after he had served three-and-a-half years in jail for disseminating such writings abroad. As far back as 1965, his "Moscow Summer" had aroused a political storm. His appeal to the Supreme Court of Vojvodina was turned down.

As the Latin proverb puts it:

Be careful how you irritate the wasps.

JANUARY 4

On this day in the year 1941, Charles Chaplin declined the New York Film Critics Award for his performance in *The Great Dictator*.

The English comedian said he sought "only to please the public." Accepting the honor would be tantamount, in his eyes, to admitting "that actors are competing with each other." The fact of the matter was that while other actors do compete with each other for fame and limelight on the marquee, there was none to compete with Chaplin. As writer, composer, director, producer, and star, he was unique. His inimitably amusing and endearing "little fellow" was in a class all by himself, as he shuffled his way through *The Tramp* in 1915, *Easy Street* in 1917, *Shoulder Arms* in 1924, *The Kid* in 1924, *The Gold Rush* in 1925, *City Lights* in 1931, *Modern Times* in 1936, and *The Great Dictator* in 1940.

As the Chinese proverb puts it:

A good drum does not require hard beating.

JANUARY 5

On this day in the year 1757, Robert Francois Damiens darted from a crowd in the Versailles Palace and stabbed Louis XV with a penknife.

The King lived but Damiens was sentenced to the standard punishment for violating the King's person. There was a preliminary session of methodical crushing of legs by progressive tightening of wooden "shoes" with repeated revivals from faintings by attendant physicians and intermittent offers of confession-hearings by chanting priests. At two in the afternoon, Damiens was flanked by praying monks and marched to the square in front of the Notre Dame Cathedral. A large gathering had filled the area and adjoining windows and roofs. Silence. Burning sulphur poured on hands. Cries. Silence. Bits of flesh plucked from legs, thighs, arms, and chest with sharp iron pincers. Screams. Silence. Tight ropes tied to arms and legs. Ends hitched to four horses. Sixty times, horses surged in opposing directions. No limbs torn off. Two horses added, one to each leg. Horses again tugged. Screams. More tuggings under whip. Still no torn limbs. Surgeons consulted. Thigh muscles and tendons cut. Six more lunges by horses. Limbs jerked off. Applause from crowd. Torso left twitching.

As the Armenian proverb puts it:

The wolf with education becomes no lamb.

JANUARY 6

On this day in the year 1495, Yan Yur'evich Zaberezinsky and a party of distinguished Lithuanians arrived in Moscow to escort the royal bride Elena, daughter of Tsar Ivan III, for her wedding to their Grand Prince Alexander.

In his eagerness to consummate the negotiations successfully, Zaberezinsky agreed to all the Russian demands related to the Greek Orthodox faith of the bride. No attempts were to be made of any kind toward her conversion to Catholicism. She was to worship only at Orthodox churches. She was not to enter a Catholic church. An Orthodox church was to be built for her use. A large Russian entourage was to remain with her until she became accustomed to her new life. Any constraint whatsoever on the Princess in religious matters would be regarded as a breach of treaty. After receiving solemn reaffirmation on these and other contractual details, the Tsar and his boyars permitted the Princess to leave a week later. But subsequent deeds never caught up with the promises. The wedding took place in a Roman church with Roman rites. No Orthodox church was built. Princess Elena's

Russian companions were sent home early. The Prince, released from his vow to the Tsar by Pope Alexander VI, pressed Elena to become a Catholic.

As the Chinese proverb puts it:

Out of ten matchmakers, only nine will lie.

JANUARY 7

On this day in the year 1934, Alexandre Stavisky shot himself in a villa at Chamonix in the shadows of Mont Blanc.

Having twice been imprisoned for fraud under his real name Serge, Stavisky sought new opportunities under the identity of Alexandre and became very wealthy. He had set up the Crédit Municipale de Bayonne in 1931. With the public endorsement of the Minister of Commerce Albert Dalimier, the firm sold 200 million francs of bonds. In 1933, however, the authorities discovered them to be forgeries. Stavisky disappeared. The police closed in on him in his hideaway and reported a suicide. Mme. Stavisky claimed her husband was murdered. The Chautemps government floundered. Politicians hurled accusations and counteraccusations. A magistrate of the Court of Appeals, who knew a lot about the affair, was mangled. The police said he choked himself. Mme. Stavisky was jailed for refusing to hand over her husband's records. His body was twice exhumed for autopsy but the medical results were suppressed. Rioting broke out. Controversy raged on. When the final report of the official commission of inquiry was released, nobody believed it.

As the Russian proverb puts it:

Politics—a rotten egg; it stinks when cracked open.

JANUARY 8

On this day in the year 1723, Jonathan Swift advised John Gay on the technique of getting favors from well-placed persons.

The English satirist wrote to his poet-friend, "I have been considering why poets have such ill success in making their court, since they are allowed to be the greatest and best of all flatterers. The defect is, that they flatter only in print or in writing, but not by word of mouth. . . . Besides, they are too libertine to haunt antechambers, too poor to bribe porters and footmen, and too proud to cringe to second-hand favorites in a great family." Then Swift recounted in passing that "I left you in a good way both for the late Court and the successors; and by the force of too much honesty or too little sublunary wisdom, you fell between the two stools."

As the Chinese proverb puts it:

If you bow at all, bow low.

JANUARY 9

On this day in the year 1931, Alfred P. Sloan, Jr. directed the members of the Operations Committee at General Motors Corporation to conduct a searching analysis of its problems in the face of the economic depression.

One of the points emphasized in the Chief Executive Officer's memorandum was that, "notwithstanding that we have the reputation of a fact-finding organization, we do not get the facts, even now, as completely as we should. We sit around and discuss things without the facts." Another was that "we become too superficial . . . Problems are crowding in on us; time is limited; the meetings are some times long and we naturally get tired. These circumstances and many others lead us to make mistakes without adequate consideration and mistakes are bound to occur. It is easier not to do it at all than to do it haphazardly or without due consideration and even if we lose an opportunity it will come up again sooner or later and in the long run we will gain by more thoughtful dealing with our problems."

As the Czech proverb puts it:

Measure twice; cut once.

JANUARY 10

On this day in the year 1810, W. C. C. Claiborne expressed concern to the President over his difficulties in maintaining order in New Orleans.

The territorial Governor was frustrated over the problem of creating harmony between the Creoles and the Americans, who have come to settle there. "The credulity of the people is only equalled by their ignorance; and a virtuous magistrate, resting entirely for support on the suffrage and good will of his fellow citizens in this quarter, would at any time be exposed to immediate ruin by the machinations of a few base individuals, who with some exertion and address might make the people think and act against their interests." In addition, there were the immigrants from Nova Scotia, the Canary Islands, and Málaga, as well as thousands of imported slaves. "The population is composed of so heterogeneous a mass," he went on in another letter to the President, "such prejudices exist, and there are so many interests to reconcile, that I fear no administration or form of government can give general satisfaction."

As the Slovak proverb puts it:

Even God does not satisfy all the people.

JANUARY 11

On this day in the year 630, Mohammed conquered Mecca.

Mohammed's forces had been routed 5 years before by the Meccans, who attacked his stronghold at Medina and his career appeared nipped in the bud. But a special revelation came just in time. He was told by Allah that the defeat was just punishment because the soldiers were fighting in their hearts for worldly gains instead of Allah's glory. Mohammed informed the soldiers of the divine message and assured them that there was a way to recoup their good graces with Allah through inspired fighting. At the same time, he relieved the incompetent commanders, disciplined others, and subjected the soldiers to rigorous training, as he enlarged his army to 10,000. There was no stopping the Prophet after that.

As the Telugu proverb puts it:

Pretend to condole when you cauterize.

JANUARY 12

On this day in the year 1910, Baroness Rosen asked William Howard Taft for a cigarette at a White House dinner.

The President borrowed one from a member of the band and lit it for the wife of the Russian ambassador. This caused a diplomatic scandal, resulting in the blackballing of the

Baroness by high society. Well-bred women in 1910, at least in America, were simply not supposed to smoke at all. One had been arrested the week before doing just that on Fifth Avenue in New York City. None had ever done so at an official function. The men would always gather separately after dinner in the drawing room, so that the indecent odor of their smoke would not foul the delicate nostrils of the fairer sex.

As the Chinese proverb puts it:

When you enter a country, first inquire what is forbidden there.

JANUARY 13

On this day in the year 1864, Stephen Foster was found deathly ill in his dirty room in a run-down hotel in New York City.

He had been composing songs since he was a youth: *Camptown Races, Old Kentucky Home, Massa's in de Cold, Cold Ground, Jeannie with the Light Brown Hair, Old Black Joe,* and 190 others. His *Oh! Susanna!* cheered the soul of many a lonely California miner during the gold rush of 1849. His *Old Folks at Home* issued in 1851, became a national favorite. Yet when the ambulance came for the 38-year-old genius, who had brought so much joy to his fellow human beings, all he had left to his own name was 35 cents and a slip of paper in his pocket with the words "Dear friends and gentle hearts." He died 3 days later in the municipal Bellevue Hospital.

As the Polish proverb puts it:

The lemon, having been squeezed dry, is thrown away.

JANUARY 14

On this day in the year 1794, Jesse Bennett performed a Caesarean operation on Mrs. Bennett at Edom, Kanawha Valley, Virginia.

Bennett asked a fellow doctor for assistance. The associate refused because of the very high risk involved. So Bennett went ahead with the help of two blacks. The patient was held on 2 planks placed on top of a couple of barrels. Instead of an anesthetic, laudanum was administered. The procedure proved to be the first successful one of its kind.

As the Japanese proverb puts it:

The good calligrapher is not fussy over his brushes.

JANUARY 15

On this day in the year 69, Marcus Salvius Otho had Servius Sulpicius Galba and Piso Licinanus murdered.

Galba had displaced Nero as Emperor of Rome the year before. After a short reign, he named Licinanus as his successor. These events were not to the liking of Nero's friend Otho, who had gained the support of the Praetorian guard. After the elimination of Galba and Licinanus, Otho was recognized as Emperor by the Senate. But this was not to the liking of the Roman legate in lower Germany, Aulus Vitellius, who then defeated Otho's army in the first battle of Bedriacum on April 19. With the ensuing suicide of Otho, Vitellius was recognized as Emperor. This, in turn, was not to the liking of the legate in Judea, Titus Flavius Vespasianus, whose supporter Antonius Primus defeated the forces of Vitellius in the second battle of Bedriacum. With the slaying of Vitellius on December 20, Vespasianus was recognized as Emperor.

As the Chinese proverb puts it:

The shrike hunting the locust is unaware of the hawk hunting him.

JANUARY 16

On this day in the year 1908, R. L. Lynch reported to the Washington newspapers his experimental demonstration of the feasibility of wrapping bread when it is taken from the oven, so that it can be distributed to the consumer without contamination as was expected from the then-current unwrapped distribution.

The local bakers had stood adamantly against the recommended procedure. They insisted that wrapping bread in this manner would significantly degrade the palatability and digestibility. The government chemist undertook a series of tests to prove his point. Loaves of bread fresh from the oven were wrapped in 10-pound onion skin paper, light wax paper, and unsized 32-pound newspaper, respectively. It was shown that when unsized paper was used, the bread was as good or even better after 24 hours than the unwrapped bread and was equal in condition to a freshly baked loaf. The bakers remained unmoved in their determination to continue the old practice.

As the Bihari proverb puts it:

Fish or no fish, the blind heron sticks to his pond.

JANUARY 17

On this day in the year 1950, Anthony Pino and his associates robbed the Brinks North Terminal Garage in Boston of $1.25 million.

It was almost the perfect crime. Eleven professional criminals worked meticulously and surreptitiously for 18 months in the planning. As they padded about in stockinged feet, they mapped out exactly where the money was to be held and precisely how each door operated. Every lock was removed, keys made, and then replaced without anyone else the wiser. Even the alarm company that installed the Brink system was burglarized for a detailed study. Came the night of the action, seven of the robbers wearing gloves and masks stealthily walked the appointed route and surprised the five guards, held them up, and escaped with the loot. Although the police suspected the identity of some of the bandits, they had no evidence. As they were about to give up the case, one of the gang got angry for being cheated, so he felt, out of $63,000 and turned informer. The rest were arrested within days, tried, and given long sentences.

As the Yiddish proverb puts it:

A friend remains a friend up to his pockets.

JANUARY 18

On this day in the year 1876, Henry James sent another one of his letters from Paris to the New York *Tribune* about local politics.

"The intensity of political discussions is sharper in France than it is anywhere else—which is the case, indeed, with every sort of difference of opinion," wrote the American author. "There are more camps and coteries and 'sets' than among the Anglo-Saxons, and the gulf which divides each group from every other is more hopelessly and fatally impassable. Nothing is more striking to a foreigner, even after he thinks he has grown used to such things, than the definiteness with which people here are classed and ticketed. The ticket reads so or so, of course, according to your point of view; but to the man who wears another ticket it always reads villainously. You ask a writer whose productions you admire some questions about any other writer, for whose works you have also a relish. 'Oh, he is of the School of This or That; he is of the *queue* of So and So,' he answers. 'We think nothing of him; you mustn't talk of him here; for he doesn't exist.' . . . It is simply the old story that, either in politics or in literature, Frenchmen are ignorant of the precious art of compromise."

As the Greek proverb puts it:

Meat is sold with bones.

JANUARY 19

On this day in the year 1160, Yoshitomo raided the Sanjo Palace in Kyoto and kidnapped the retired Emperor Go-Shirakawa.

Yoshitomo of the Mimamoto military clan had been recruited by the incumbent Emperor Nijo in his struggle against the retired Emperor, who insisted on retaining the power of government. But no sooner did Yoshitomo succeed when the opposing Tiara military henchmen led by Kiyomori launched a counterraid against the Nijo Imperial Palace and after several more battles in the Heiji War, killed Yoshitomo and his 2 eldest sons. After his victory, Kiyomori immersed himself in the life of the Court, had his daughter wedded to the Emperor, and saw his own grandson ascend the throne in 1180. In his overconfidence, he ignored the forces building up around Yoshitomo's third son. The latter rapidly grew in strength, seized the capital, and drove the Tiaras into the Inland Sea.

As the Japanese proverb puts it:

Having conquered, tighten the thongs of your helmet.

JANUARY 20

On this day in the year 1775, Samuel Johnson hurled defiance at James Macpherson, who demanded a retraction of his statement that the Ossianic lays "discovered" by Macpherson were phony.

"You want me to retract? What shall I retract? I thought your book an imposture from the very beginning. I think it upon yet surer reasons an imposture still. For this opinion I give the public reasons which I dare you to refute." Johnson retreated not one inch in his reply. "But however I may despise you, I reverence truth and if you can prove the genuiness of the work I will confess it. Your rage I defy, your abilities since your Homer are not so formidable, and what I have heard of your morals disposes me to pay regard not to what you shall say but to what you can prove."

As the Swedish proverb puts it:

He who wants to wrestle with wolves should have claws of bears.

JANUARY 21

On this day in the year 1769, Junius began his series of letters to discredit the British ministries of the Duke of Grafton and Lord North and unite the opposition.

A steady barrage of merciless invectives and bitter sarcasms was leveled by the author behind the pseudonym at those he had considered politically and personally despicable. Over 60 communiques were published over a 3-year period in Henry Sampson Woodfall's *Public Advertiser*. But the widely read denunciations made no practical impact at all on the political scheme of things. Junius eventually became discouraged and gave up.

As the Indian proverb puts it:

Cattle do not cry from the curse of a crow.

JANUARY 22

On this day in the year 1922, Kuo Mo-jo wrote the preface for his translation of Johann von Goethe's *The Sorrows of Young Werther*.

The Chinese intellectual reacted enthusiastically to the permeating themes in the young German author's novel, such as the forgetting of the self in action within the context of pantheism, the love of nature, and the admiration of the positive life. Reason was seen as the means to discovery which everyone can follow in the same way with the same effect. But it is the heart rather than the mind that is the unique source of individuality. A person therefore is not to analyze the universe through the reason of the mind, but embrace it through the emotion of the heart. In so doing, he is able to create heaven wherever he happens to be.

As the Swedish proverb puts it:

The wise man has his tongue in his heart.

JANUARY 23

On this day in the year 1913, Ford Maddox Ford sent Lucy Masterman his opinion of her block of poems.

"My dear lady, your poems in the future must not be written in that pleasant and sheltered verandah with the grey sea and grey sky and all the chastened romance of it. That is holiday time." The English poet criticized the same deficiency in the contemporary verses. They are "too much practised in temples and too little in motorbuses—LITERARY! LITERARY! Now that is the last thing that verse should ever be, for the moment a medium becomes literary it is remote from the life of the people, it is dulled, languishing, moribund, and at last dead." He then proceeded to suggest that she should "sit down to write, metaphorically speaking, in a railway waiting room, or in a wet street, or in your kitchen . . . or in the lobby of the House of Commons . . . for what the poet ought to do is to write his own mind in the language of the day."

As the Spanish proverb puts it:

He who does not mingle with the crowd knows nothing.

JANUARY 24

On this day in the year 1818, Ramsay Crooks wrote a long letter from Mackinac to his chief, John Jacob Astor, in New

York, urging specific actions to correct the business losses of the prior years.

The first recommendation from the local manager of the American Fur Company was to have the government's Indian agent for the area, Major William Puthuff, fired for his licensing of foreign competitors. The second was to make an example of the Commander of the American Garrison, Colonel Talbot Chambers, so that succeeding military officers would be less inclined to interfere with its trading activities. Puthuff was quickly transferred through pressures in Washington and a lawsuit was brought against Chambers. The Governor of Michigan himself joined the chorus, as he insisted that officers like Chambers who usurp the law "ought to be taught a practical lesson, no less wholesome to himself than to those disposed to approve his conduct and imitate his example."

As the Argentinan proverb puts it:

Whosoever punishes one chastises a hundred.

JANUARY 25

On this day in the year 1880, Gustave Flaubert remarked that he had already poured over some 1500 books in preparing for his *Bouvard de Pécuchet*.

The French novelist had frequently complained about the length of time devoted to such preliminary research. Once he mused how he would gladly exchange all the notes he had taken and the 99 volumes he had read for just 3 contemplative seconds to savor the passions of his characters. On another occasion he longed for the life of pure art, where he would not feel forced to absorb all the information written on a given subject.

As the Fulani proverb puts it:

Running and scratching do not go together.

JANUARY 26

On this day in the year 1748, Chesterfield wrote Solomon Dayrolles about wanting to resign from the position of Secretary of State for the Northern Department of the British government.

"I can no longer take my share of either the public indignation or contempt on account of measures in which I have no share. I can no longer continue in a post in which it is well known that I am but a Commis; and in which I have not been able to do any one service to any one man though ever so meritorious, lest I should be supposed to have any power and my colleagues not the whole," he bemoaned to his young friend about being treated as an upper clerk instead of a respected official. "And lately, I tell you truly, I long for rest and quiet, equally necessary to my present state, both of body and mind. Could I do any good, I would sacrifice some more quiet to it; but, convinced as I am that I can do none, I will indulge my ease, and preserve my character."

As the German proverb puts it:

Asses sing badly because they pitch their voices too high.

JANUARY 27

On this day in the year 1822, Robert Owen distributed the first issue of his weekly, the *Economist*.

The Scot manufacturer had advocated the setting aside of necessary capital by the government for the establishment of "villages," based on "cooperation" and "united labor" and organized around scientific agriculture. The journal was dedicated to spreading the "development of principles calculated assuredly to banish poverty from society." But it folded in about 12 months. Two years later Owen put the concept into practice by setting up a self-sufficient community of producers in Indiana. By 1829, the Village of New Harmony also had to be terminated, because of the many failures. He returned to England, dejected in his conclusion that purely voluntary social mechanisms are not viable without prior moral training to overcome the powerful "habits of the individual system."

As the Chinese proverb puts it:

If two men keep a horse, it is thin; if two men keep a boat, it leaks.

JANUARY 28

On this day in the year 1765, Tobias Smollett recorded his puzzlement over the values of the noblemen of Florence, which he was visiting.

"With all their pride, however, the nobles of Florence are humble enough to enter into partnership with shopkeepers, and even to sell wine by retail," the famous traveler noted in his journal. "It is an undoubted fact, that in every palace or great house in this city; there is a little window fronting the street, provided with an iron knocker, and over it hangs an empty flask, by way of sign-post. Thither you send your servant to buy a bottle of wine. He knocks at the little wicket, which is opened immediately by a domestic, who supplies him with what he wants, and receives the money like the waiter of any other cabaret. It is pretty extraordinary that it should not be deemed a disparagement in a nobleman to sell half a pound of figs, or a palm of ribbon or tape, or to take money for a flask of sour wine; and yet be counted infamous to match his daughter in the family of a person who has distinguished himself in any one of the learned professions."

As the Bulgarian proverb puts it:

Only the nightingale can appreciate the rose.

JANUARY 29

On this day in the year 1768, the Massachusetts House sent to Lord Camden in London one of the earliest formulations of the fundamental law in the British Constitution in a letter drafted by Samuel Adams.

"If in all free states, the constitution is fixed, and the supreme legislative power of the nation, from thence derives its authority; can that power overlap the bounds of the constitution, without subverting its own foundation? If the remotest subjects are bound by the ties of allegiance, which this people and their forefathers have ever acknowledged; are they not by the rules of equity, intitled to all rights of that constitution, which ascertains and limits both sovereignty and allegiance? If it is an essential unalterable right in nature, ingrafted into the British constitution as a fundamental law, and ever held sacred and irrevocable by the subjects within the realm, and that what is a man's own is absolutely his own; and that no man has a right to take it from him without his consent; may not the subjects of this province, with a decent firmness, which has always distinguished the happy subjects of Britain, plead and maintain this natural constitutional right?"

As the Catalonian proverb puts it:

The privilege of the few does not make the law for the many.

JANUARY 30

On this day in the year 1860, Louis Pasteur was awarded the Prize for Experimental Physiology by the French Academy of Sciences.

Never hesitant about blazing new trails, the French microbiologist continually found himself in opposition to established authorities. He disagreed with Justus Liebig on the germ theory of fermentation, with Henry Bastian and Félix Pouchet on spontaneous generation, with Claude Bernard and Marcellin Berthelot on the mechanism of biological alcohol formation, with G. Colin on chicken anthrax, with Robert Koch on anthrax vaccination, and with Michel Peter on the treatment of rabies.

As the Japanese proverb puts it:

The lantern carrier should go ahead.

JANUARY 31

On this day in the year 1838, Eugenie de Guerin spoke about an old affection she discovered in herself.

The gentle sister of the poet Maurice de Guerin confided in her journal about her fondness for the three leeches in a vial on the mantelpiece. She loved to care for them. As she changed their water daily, she would look at them with fond memories "because these leeches were brought here for Charles—that Charles came with Caroline—and that Caroline came for thee! Droll sequence this, which makes me laugh at what the heart can string together. What a variety of things!" She would reflect on how the creatures seem able to predict the weather and how she had been consulting them continuously since Maurice had left. "Fortunately the phial always stood at fair. We say over and over again, 'Maurice will have arrived without catching cold, without severe weather, without rain.' Thus it is, my friend, that we keep thinking of thee—that everything makes us so think."

As the Sanskrit proverb puts it:

On seeing a thing be reminded of others connected with it.

FEBRUARY 1

On this day in the year 1958, Shuki el-Quwatli of Syria and Gamal Abdul Nasser of Egypt proclaimed the union of their countries into the United Arab Republic.

Not long after this joint communique by the 2 presidents, the Syrians became disenchanted. Traditional political freedoms in Syria were being compromised. Academic liberties were being curtailed. Local autonomy was being eroded. Power was being centralized in Cairo. Egyptian officials were being given higher pay and privileges. Egyptian military personnel were being assigned major commands in Syria. Native leaders were being eased out of their positions. Finally, the Syrians could stand the drift no longer. A coup was staged in Damascus on September 28, 1961, and Syria again became independent.

As the Bulgarian proverb puts it:

He who calls a wolf invites the pack.

FEBRUARY 2

On this day in the year 1956, Z. Dolecki called for the right to speak out in Poland.

In his poem, "Little Poets May Grow Up," the poet recalled how his fellow Poles had hoped to have been lifted out of Medieval darkness by the October Revolution. But the strictures on thought continue. The youths are weighed down with boredom, benumbed with slogans, and forced to exult of joys that were nonexistent. They cannot live with them any longer. The poem ended with their universal appeal: "We want air!"

As the English proverb puts it:

The stream stopped, swells the higher.

FEBRUARY 3

On this day in the year 1936, John Maynard Keynes opened The Arts Theater in Cambridge.

The British economist was busy rewriting sections of his classic text, *The General Theory of Employment, Interest and Money,* which was to exert a dominating influence on national planning in Western countries for decades to come. Keynes' schedule was also jammed with other duties, such as First Bursar of King's College. But he had chosen to siphon off much needed time toward the establishment of a first-class theater for Cambridge, because he felt the city should not be without one. He contributed substantially to its endowment and guided the enterprise through the financial crises that inevitably plague artistic endeavors during the initial years.

As the Chinese proverb puts it:

If you have two loaves of bread, sell one and buy a flower.

FEBRUARY 4

On this day in the year 1942, Farouk was given the choice of either signing the appointment of the British nominee for Egyptian premier or be deposed.

The British authorities had been anxious over the advances of General Erwin Rommel's Afrika Korps toward Egypt. It was militarily essential that the British forces in Cairo not be distracted by local demonstrations or riots. One of the potential troublemakers was Nahas Pasha, leader of the Wafd, which was the most powerful single element of Egyptian politics. The members had been kept out of office for some time for noncooperation. They were getting edgy and angry. Therefore, to prevent civil disturbances, it was necessary to reinstate Pasha at the earliest moment. But this needed persuading the Egyptian King to whom Pasha was a personal enemy. Farouk adamantly refused. The British then surrounded his Royal Abdin Palace with armored units and presented the ultimatum. The King complied.

As the Arabic proverb puts it:

Kiss the hand you cannot bite.

FEBRUARY 5

On this day in the year 1915, Andrew Carnegie appeared before the Congressional Committee on Industrial Relations to defend his philanthropic foundation against charges of threatening democracy.

When requested to identify his occupation the steel magnate answered: "To do as much good in the world as I can." When Chairman Frank P. Walsh began one of his questions with "Do you not believe, Mr. Carnegie . . . ," Carnegie admonished him with "Now, Mr. Chairman, you say, 'do you not believe?' That implies that *you* believe and you want me to agree. I don't like that. Please be kind enough to say, 'Do you believe?' " As the audience burst into laughter, he tossed a humorous aside to the press corps sitting nearby: "Loud laughter!" The dignity of legislative inquiry broke down completely, as the Chairman ruefully remarked: "We had no trouble in keeping order until you came, Mr. Carnegie." "I am glad of that" came the rejoinder. More laughter from the gallery. He turned with outstretched arms to the crowd and exclaimed: "What an audience! See how the ladies are here! That's one of the triumphs of my life." As he left the room, he commented with considerable satisfaction that he had not "spent a more agreeable afternoon in I don't know when."

As the American proverb puts it:

He is a brave man indeed who plays leap frog with a unicorn.

FEBRUARY 6

On this day in the year 1651, Jules Mazarin fled Paris.

The controller of France's power suddenly became the enemy of the people. Parlement passed a resolution calling for the release of the princes imprisoned by the Cardinal for political purposes. The nobility united against him. The crowd in the streets yelled, "Death to Mazarin!" His Patron the Queen was terrified. Came nightfall, 6 similarly bearded men in identical red jackets and plumed hats sped through several gates in different directions. One of them was Mazarin.

As the Chinese proverb puts it:

The old fox has three holes.

FEBRUARY 7

On this day in the year 1469, Lorenzo di Medici participated in a tournament in Florence in celebration of his forthcoming wedding.

It was a magnificent occasion. The festivities opened with a procession of 9 trumpeters marching into the stadium, followed by 3 pages, 2 squires in full armor, 12 noblemen on horses, Lorenzo's brother Guilliano bedecked in brocade embroidered in pearls and silver, 5 more pages, drummers, fifers, then young Lorenzo himself. He jousted with 4 separate challengers and defeated them all. He was awarded the tournament's first prize and was glorified by the Poet Luigi Pulci as another Achilles. But Lorenzo himself was more realistic and stated that "although I was not a very vigorous warrior, nor a hard hitter, the first award was given to me, a helmet inlaid with silver and a figure of Mars on the crest." He understood well that the recognition had something to do with his being the heir apparent of his powerful grandfather Cosimo and father Piero, to whom ambassadors from Venice and France, cardinals from Rome, and notables from afar have been coming for decades to pay tributes and seek favors.

As the Chuana proverb puts it:

Only the hawk carrying something is looked up to.

FEBRUARY 8

On this day in the year 1802, Pierre Dominique Toussaint of Haiti ordered his military defenders to drive out the 25,000 French troops under Charles Leclerc sent to restore the colony.

Toussaint advised, outlining the strategy of long-term debilitation of the French army, "Do not forget while waiting for the rainy season which will rid us of our foes, that we have no other resource than destruction and flames." Whenever the expeditionary force would leave its base at Port Republican for a sweep into the plains, the guerrillas would harass the rear and attack the less-protected garrison. "Bear in mind that the soil bathed with our sweat must not furnish our enemies with the smallest aliment. Tear up the roads with shot; throw corpses and horses into all the fountains; burn and annihilate everything in order that those who have come to reduce us to slavery may have before their eyes the image of that hell which they deserve."

As the Chinese proverb puts it:

Let your act give your friends no cause for regret and your enemies no cause for joy.

FEBRUARY 9

On this day in the year 1824, 12-year-old Charles Dickens reported for work at Warren's Blacking in London.

For 12 hours a day he labored away in a dirty ramshackle building in the slums with rotting floors and scuffling rats. He covered pots of blacking with oil paper, overwrapped them with blue paper, tied the packages with string, and stuck on the labels—for 6 shillings a week and some lessons from the boss during the dinner break. He wept as he visited his father, who had been thrown into a detention house for indebtedness. He wept as he scurried about in vain trying to raise the 40 pounds for his father's release. He wept as he saw his father transferred to the squalid Marshalsea Prison. The boy was overcome by the "depression of spirit and sinking of heart" as he mingled with the men who have "lost friends, fortunes, home and happiness." But Dickens not only lived through all this grime and sadness, but also acquired an empathy for the downtrodden that was to make his *David Copperfield*, *Pickwick Papers*, and other writings the human-hearted masterpieces they turned out to be.

As the Ukranian proverb puts it:

Do not ask old people for advice, but those who have suffered.

FEBRUARY 10

On this day in the year 1966, Trevor Huddleston stood as usual at the low altar step in St. Mary Magdalene's Chapel in the Church of Christ the King in Sophiatown of South Africa.

Again, the minister began the Preparation: "I will go unto the altar of God . . . even unto the God of my joy and gladness . . . Our hope standeth in the name of the Lord . . . Who hath made heaven and earth." But even as the celebrant and congregation in that early mass were intoning these very words to the white man's God, Huddleston was sad and disheartened over what was in store for the black men in that town before sundown. Joy and gladness was not theirs to be. The law of the church-going white men that there be no intermingling between the races is about to be reaffirmed in action. Now that the white section of Johannesburg is becoming contiguous with the black, something had to be done. A fleet of army lories was enroute, protected by thousands of armed police and Sten guns at strategic points. The black men were to be moved—lock, stock, and barrel. Sophiatown was to be no more.

As the Chinese proverb puts it:

If you give no help to others, you are wasting those prayers to Buddha.

FEBRUARY 11

On this day in the year 1888, Lobengula signed what he thought was a concession of mineral rights to Cecil Rhodes.

The British empire builder parlayed the Amandebelee chief's grant into a British charter approved by Her Majesty a year and a half later. The charter guaranteed broad claims over a vast and vaguely defined region, without stipulated northern boundaries. Rhodes' British South Africa Company could "make treaties, promulgate laws, preserve the peace, maintain a police force, and acquire new concessions. It could make roads, railways, harbours, or undertake other public works, own or charter ships, engage in mining or any other industry, establish banks, make land grants, and carry on any lawful commerce, trade, pursuit or business." Before long, the power vacuum in Central Africa and the bordering southern territories turned into a cauldron of strife and intrigue among the native tribal chiefs and Boer, German, Portuguese, and British representatives. Lobengula himself was inveigled into giving conflicting concessions to various bidders. When Rhodes protested, the Chief insisted that his treaty only granted him the right to dig a single hole. Thus began an endless chain of contentions and battles that continued long after both of them had passed from the scene.

As the Ethiopian proverb puts it:

A man has come; quarrel will come.

FEBRUARY 12

On this day in the year 1912, Yuan Shih-k'ai negotiated the Abdication Edicts of the Empress Dowager and the 6-year-old Emperor Pu Yi.

The emissary from the revolutionary government immediately notified its Provisional President Sun Yat-sen of the successful outcome. The message was profuse with praises for the contemplated republic. "A republic is the best form of government. . . . The whole world admits this. . . . Never shall we allow monarchical government in our China." Having achieved his objective of overthrowing the Manchurian dynasty, Sun resigned his post. Yuan was elected President on February 15. Soon after consolidating his military control and accumulating sufficient financial reserves, Yuan outlawed Sun's revolutionary Kuomintang party, dissolved parliament, and ruled by fiat. In December 1915, he organized a nominally representative Council of State. The Council then implored Yuan to accept the Mandate from Heaven and become the first Emperor of a new dynasty. He ceremonially declined twice and finally acceded on the third petition. Coronation was set for early 1916. When the news broke, widespread rebellion spontaneously erupted throughout the country. Yuan was forced to abandon his still-born dynasty and retire with a great loss of face.

As the Bulgarian proverb puts it:

If you wish to know a man, give him authority.

FEBRUARY 13

On this day in the year 1692, Campbell of Glenylon massacred the leaders of the MacDonald clan of Glencoe in northern Argyllshire.

William III of England had issued an offer of indemnity and full pardon to all Scottish Highland clans who would swear allegiance to him by January 1, 1692. Every clan except the MacDonalds had met the deadline. Their chief MacIan tried to do so before the local magistrates but was told that they were not empowered to give the oath. The same thing happened when he appeared before a military officer at Fort William. Bad weather delayed his trip to the appropriate sherrif's office in Inverary. It was not until January 6 that he was finally able to complete the necessary act. At that time the advisor to the King was Sir John Dalrymple, master of the Stair and Scottish clans, such as the Campbells, who were hereditary foes of the MacDonalds. Sir John seized on the technical violation for his own vengeful purposes. He convinced the King to make an example of the MacDonalds and sent a military mission headed by Campbell against them. It arrived, voicing peaceful intentions, and was received hospitably on February 1. After reconnoitering the situation and refining his plans for 12 days, the party suddenly burst into the homes of the clan's leaders at five that fateful morning. Thirty-eight were shot and killed, as the remaining 300 clansmen fled in a raging snow storm.

As the Indian proverb puts it:

I would rather serve under a vulture as king surrounded by swans, than under a swan surrounded by vultures.

FEBRUARY 14

On this day in the year 1793, Kamehameha was presented with a bull and a cow, the first ever seen in the Hawaiian Islands, by George Vancouver.

The Captain of the British navy returned the following year to Hilo, where the Hawaiian King lived. The Captain's *Discovery* unloaded more livestock. His carpenters constructed the 36 foot *Brittania* as an addition to the King's fleet. His navigator described the greatness of the Christian God. He himself explained the principles of management in government, discipline in military maneuvers, and intercourse with foreigners. Kamehameha was impressed. On February 21, 1794, he offered to place Hawaii under Great Britain's protection. Four days later, Vancouver's aide unfurled the British flag and took possession of the island in the name of the King of Great Britain. A gun salute was fired and the Hawaiians shouted: "We are men of Britain!"

As the Latin proverb puts it:

He sends his presents with a hook.

FEBRUARY 15

On this day in the year 1898, William Randolph Hearst was told over the telephone that the Associated Press correspondent at Havana had just reported that the American battleship *Maine* was blown up.

"Spread the story all over the front page," the newspaper tycoon ordered his editor. "This means war!" For some time he had been exacerbating Spanish-American relations. Hearst had a 17-year-old Cuban Evangelina Cisneros "rescued" from a Spanish dungeon, brought to a rally in Madison Square Garden in New York City, and proclaimed as the Cuban Joan of Arc. He got hold of a personal letter to a friend from the Spanish Minister to Washington, containing some critical comments about the President, and splashed it across his *Journal* with the headline: "The Worst Insult to the United States in Its History." The minister had to resign. When the President vacillated in declaring war, the Hearst papers speared him as "that white-livered cur up there." Eventually, Hearst had his way. On April 19 the Senate voted for war: 42 to 35; the House: 310 to 6.

As the English proverb puts it:

A goose's quill can be more dangerous than a lion's paw.

FEBRUARY 16

On this day in the year 1563, John Dee informed William Cecil of his excitement in finding a copy of *Stenographia* by Trithemius.

While traveling on the European continent on official

business for Sir William, the English scientist, astrologer, and secret agent chanced across the book by the former Abbot of Spanheim. Dee suggested that the "boke would be of vaste use to a Statesmen in your Position." Besides, its "use is greater than the fame thereof is spread." There had been many allegations to the effect that it was a manual of demoniac magic. It contained many names and references to angels and spirits, as well as appropriate invocations to gain their attention, which led to a condemnation of heresy. What Dee discerned beneath the surface, however, were descriptions of the ways of cipher-making and transmission of secret messages. Out of it came his coded technique of communication with ministers at the English Court and with the Queen herself.

As the Chinese proverb puts it:

Let your mind be busy to accomplish; let it be open to understand.

FEBRUARY 17

On this day in the year 1926, Lu Hsun published an essay on emperors.

"The Chinese method of dealing with deities is to try flattering the dangerous ones like the gods of plague and fire, but cheating the benign ones like the guardian and kitchen gods," wrote the Chinese Communist author in his series of articles attacking the hypocrisies of feudal conventions. "The treatment of emperors is no different. Rulers and ruled belong to the same country. In times of strife, 'the winners become emperors, while the losers become criminals.' Usually one becomes emperor and the others become his subjects, and there is not much difference in their attitudes toward each other. Thus, the emperor and his ministers have their ways of hoodwinking the people, while the people have their way of hoodwinking the emperor."

As the English proverb puts it:

What force cannot effect, fraud shall devise.

FEBRUARY 18

On this day in the year 1946, Drew Pearson broke the news story of a Russian atomic espionage network fanning out of Canada.

"The Canadians have taken over a Russian agent, who has given the names of about 1700 Russian agents; also has put the finger on certain officials inside the American and Canadian governments operating with the Soviets," the syndicated columnist announced. The code clerk of the Russian embassy Igor Gouzenko had been caught by the charwoman and security officers in an infraction of security rules by leaving a penciled note lying around the room, instead of keeping it locked within the safe. For this violation, he was ordered back to Russia. But Gouzenko defected, taking with him top-secret directives, dossiers, and papers, describing the large spy ring headed by the Russian military attaché, a Colonel Zabotin, under the NKVD control of the Second Secretary of the embassy, Vitali Pavlov. English and Canadian co-conspirators had been active in the Office of the High Commissioner of the United Kingdom, the Canadian Department of External Affairs, and the National Research Council. By this time, Zabotin had already completed much of his first-priority assignment, including atomic bomb plans, construction of nuclear reactors, and samples of uranium-213 and other materials.

As the Russian proverb puts it:

Confide a secret to a dumb man and he will speak.

FEBRUARY 19

On this day in the year 1902, Harry Houdini sued Werner Graff in the Schöffengericht Köln for slander.

The Schutzmann had accused the American escape artist of being a fraud in an article in the popular *Rheinische Zeitung* of July 25, 1901. Graff defended himself at the trial by saying that Houdini made misrepresentations in his advertising by insinuating that he was able to get out of *anything*. He asserted to the judge and jury that Houdini actually furnished his own handcuffs and chains. Houdini's lawyer maneuvered Graff into consenting to an actual test before the court with a lock of Graff's choice. Graff called on his own policeman to bind Houdini in the German regulation wrist chain and padlock. Without any strain Houdini dropped the loosened restraints from his wrists on the courtroom floor. The judge found for the plaintiff and ordered Graff to extend a public apology. Unknown to the judge and Graff, however, was the fact that Houdini had developed a dozen ways of escaping from that particular device. It was the one with which he had begun his professional career.

As the Japanese proverb puts it:

The wise hawk conceals his talons.

FEBRUARY 20

On this day in the year 1785, Abigail Smith Adams wrote from France to her sister in Massachusetts about reconciling herself to disgusting fashions through force of repeated exposures.

"The first dance which I saw upon the stage shocked me," confessed Mrs. John Adams. "The dresses and beauty of the performers were enchanting; but no sooner did the dance commence, than I felt my delicacy wounded, and I was ashamed to be seen to look at them. Girls, clothed in the thinnest silk and gauze, with their petticoats short, springing two feet from the floor, poising themselves in the air, with their feet flying, and as perfectly showing their garters and drawers as though no petticoat had been worn, was a sight altogether new to me. Their motions are as light as air, and as quick as lightning; they balance themselves to astonishment. No description can equal the reality . . . Shall I speak a truth, and say that repeatedly seeing these dances has worn off that disgust, which at first I felt, and that I see them now with pleasure. Yet, when I consider the tendency of these things, the passions they must excite, and the known character, even to a proverb, which is attached to an opera girl, my abhorence is not lessened, and neither my reason nor judgment has accompanied my sensibility in acquiring any degree of callousness."

As the Latin proverb puts it:

Resist the beginning.

FEBRUARY 21

On this day in the year 1922, Peter Vandermeer was again playing a violin for alms from the passing throng on the streets of Savannah, Georgia.

The music was so beautiful that it attracted the attention of a professional musician, who stopped and inquired about his identity. The violin player turned out to be the once-famous violinist of the Boston Symphony Orchestra. He said he had been blind for 8 years and was destitute. Playing on the streets with a tin cup in various cities was the only way he could eke out a few cents to support his wife and himself on a marginal level for some time.

As the Sumerian proverb puts it:

Fate is a beast well able to bite.

FEBRUARY 22

On this day in the year 1920, 8-year-old Mike McNamara stood in the Bureau of Missing Persons in Brooklyn and explained why he had been away from home for 2 days.

When asked for his name, the boy replied: "They call me Mickey and some call me the Kaiser, but they won't call me the Kaiser any more because I gave Barry Casey a bloody nose." His mother had been busily working as a waitress to support Mike and two other children. Mike recounted how he had hopped a crosstown subway after the bloody-nose affair and transferred to another for Coney Island. On the way he collected newspapers on the train, sorted and refolded them, and sold them to passengers. After two days and nights, he made $1.10, which he showed the police inspector. When asked why he did it, he said simply: "I wanted to make money and help mother."

As the Chinese proverb puts it:

When the parent is affectionate, the child is filial.

FEBRUARY 23

On this day in the year 1534, Jan of Leyden witnessed the decisive victory of the once-persecuted Anabaptists in the election of the town council of Münster.

Lutherans and Catholics refusing baptism into the faith of communal love were driven from the walled city during the freezing winter. Many were penniless and naked. By March no "disciples of the devil" were left within the moat. The town was soon cordoned off by the avenging forces of the old Holy Roman Empire, led by Prince-Bishop Franz von Waldeck. Jan took over the defense when the Anabaptist Prophet Matthys was butchered in a sortie. While running nude through the streets in a trance one day, he received a vision from God: Münster was to become the seat of God's new Israel and Jan of Leyden, the King, assisted by 12 Elders. When the next assault by Waldeck failed, Jan proclaimed himself King of the World. As the siege went on, debauchery piled on food scarcity, in turn piled on cruelty. Led by one of the starving expellees, the besiegers finally gained entry into the city through a secret passage. The defenders capitulated. Jan was captured, chained, and exhibited. In January 1536 he was branded, clawed by pincers, and killed on a blazing iron throne. For several centuries thereafter, his bones hung in a cage from the tower of the Church of St. Lambert's as a public reminder of the fate of heretics.

As the Polish proverb puts it:

The worst Devil is the one who prays.

FEBRUARY 24

On this day in the year 1803, John Marshall promulgated the decision that the Supreme Court shall have the power to declare invalid any act of Congress, which, in the opinion of the court, is unconstitutional.

Two years before, William Marbury had been appointed justice of the peace in the District of Columbia by the President. The document had been duly signed by the Secretary of State but had not been delivered when the incoming President was inaugurated on March 4. The new Secretary withheld the appointment in order to keep the job for one of his own political colleagues. Marbury filed suit directly in the Supreme Court in December. The Constitution itself had defined the original jurisdiction of the Supreme Court in a narrowly delineated class of cases, with power of review over those decided on by the lower courts. This meant that the

Marbury case could not be directly heard by the Supreme Court. However, the Judiciary Act of 1789, in prescribing procedural details of the federal courts, did clearly give the Supreme Court the right to hear such a case. Instead of taking the easier way out, the Supreme Court ruled that it would not hear the Marbury case because the Judiciary Act was unconstitutional. In so doing the Court claimed the power to declare the acts of Congress unconstitutional. The obscure appointment of a justice of the peace thus led to a landmark declaration of power by the Supreme Court. Attempts to impeach Chief Justice Marshall fizzled. The decree stuck.

As the Japanese proverb puts it:

An anthole may collapse an embankment.

FEBRUARY 25

On this day in the year 1850, Jim Watson unearthed a black human skull in a gravel bed at the bottom of a mine shaft in California.

The skull passed from the miner through the hands of the local grocer to the family physician, who believed it predated the Piltdown man. "This knocks the hell out of Moses," said the doctor, as he handed the skull over to the state geologist, Dr. J. D. Whitney. Whitney was terribly excited over what appeared to be the greatest discovery of the decade and became its professional prophet. It was designated the Calaveras Skull. The worldwide scientific community began conjecturing about the character of the Calaveras man. The *American Journal of Science* surmised that the Calaveras man's geological position "is apparently still lower than that of the mastodon." In the meantime the fun-loving fraternal Clampers had been building up the find as "bona fide remains of an aboriginal *Homo Californicus.*" Years later, the facts came out: the Calaveras Skull was nothing more than an exhibit piece stolen from the office of the local dentist by a disgruntled patient, who had tossed it into the mine shaft.

As the Polish proverb puts it:

To believe with certainty, we must begin by doubting.

FEBRUARY 26

On this day in the year 1756, Henri Masers de Latude and a fellow prisoner Allègre engineered the most famous escape from the Bastille.

At that time the prisoners in the stronghold were accorded special privileges in accordance with their rank and with the necessity of keeping their imprisonment a secrecy. Latude's penchant was for fine shirts, the denial of which would send him bursting into paroxyms of rage. At one point he owned 162 shirts, 24 pairs of silk stockings, and 36 napkins. Working steadily for 2 years, Latude and Allègre made a rope ladder 180 feet long with 188 wooden rungs, carefully muffled with rags and another rope of cloth 360 feet long. These were concealed under the floorboards when anyone approached. It appeared to the wardens that Allègre, a former schoolteacher, spent all of his time instructing a diligent Latude in mathematics and engineering. All during the night they removed the loosened flue of their fireplace, climbed through the chimney, pulled up their fabricated ladder and ropes, and slid down to freedom.

As the Welsh proverb puts it:

If thou be not strong, be cunning.

FEBRUARY 27

On this day in the year 1893, Oscar Wilde mailed a letter of disappointment to Pierre Louÿs.

The Irish author had dedicated the original French edition of *Salome* to Louÿs and had been expecting an expression of profuse praise and gratitude from him, "whose name I have written in gold on purple." He complained that even those to whom he had only given copies of the book had sent "charming letters coloured with delicate appreciation." Instead, all he received from the French writer was a telegram of what seemed to Wilde as meaningless drivel. He was completely dejected.

As the German proverb puts it:

He who requires thanks cheapens his gift.

FEBRUARY 28

On this day in the year 1842, Ellenborough arrived in Calcutta as the new Governor-General of India.

After surveying the series of British reverses in Afghanistan, the English lord outlined his first strategic objective on March 15. "To recover Afghanistan if it were possible would constitute a source of weakness rather than strength. The situation, nevertheless, calls for the reestablishment of our military reputation by the infliction of some signal and decisive blow upon the Afghans." Accordingly, one British army sacked Kabul, destroying the finest bazaar in Central Asia, burning the mosque of Ali Mardane, and leveling the rest. Another stormed into the town of Istalif, crowded with refugees from Kabul huddling with fear in the groves of mulberry trees. Every male past puberty was killed; many women were raped. "Tears, supplications were of no avail; fierce oaths were the only answer; the musket was deliberately raised, the trigger pulled and happy was he who fell dead," reported an English participant. "In fact we are nothing but hired assassins." Thus was British prestige restored.

As the Russian proverb puts it:

The tears of other people are just water.

FEBRUARY 29

On this day in the year 1908, Patrick F. Garrett was shot and killed by Wayne Brazle near Las Cruces, New Mexico.

Garrett became famous for his killing of the outlaw Billy the Kid in 1880. when Garrett had been serving as an officer of the law. As sheriff, he became a legend as the scourge of cattle rustlers and the dashing and shooting hero of spectacular arrests. He often said that he would die with his boots on. And so it did happen. He had leased some land to the son of an old settler, who then pastured a herd of goats on it. Garrett remonstrated that this was a violation of the contract. A quarrel ensued and mounted in intensity until that fatal day. Brazle surrendered himself to the local officials after the shooting, asserting that he shot in self-defense after Garrett had reached for his shotgun.

As the Assamese proverb puts it:

A gamecock dies in battle.

MARCH 1

On this day in the year 1906, T. H. Baker of Louisville, Kentucky received a letter from a man in Rutland, Vermont, with the request: "Send me a list of the unsaved men and women of Louisville."

The letter went on to explain that the writer had desired to do some missionary work there and wanted to know on whom he should shower his attention. After thinking it over the Louisville Postmaster sent back a city directory. It was accompanied with a note saying that there were 250,000 names therein and that he felt such an approach would assure everyone in Louisville a square deal.

As the English proverb puts it:

Scald not thy lips on another person's porridge.

MARCH 2

On this day in the year 1901, Rosie Weise confronted her 2-week bridegroom at the Cunard Piers in New York City and started a fight that led to no end of excitement.

It seemed that Rosie had married Isaac on February 20. On the day after the wedding, Isaac had asked her to give him the $800 she had to start a saloon business. When she refused he forcibly grabbed the money and disappeared. Somehow, she managed to find out that he was planning to sail for Liverpool on the Cunarder *Etruria* that day. Rosie and 2 detectives laid in wait. She stood at the entrance to the cabin gangway. Soon she saw Isaac coming down the pier with another woman. In the words of the news dispatch, "Then she started for him with outstretched hands and in an instant all three were engaged in a fierce hair-pulling, scratching, and slapping encounter to the accompaniment of screams of rage and yells of pain and fear. When the detectives, after much difficulty, had succeeded in separating the trio and arresting the man, the latter represented a dilapidated and otherwise sorry spectacle, and his companion had fared little better."

As the Burmese proverb puts it:

You bite my cheek, I bite your ear.

MARCH 3

On this day in the year 1776, Silas Deanne received his instructions from the Committee of Secret Correspondence of the American Continental Congress.

"On your arrival in France you will, for some time, be engaged in the business of providing goods for the Indian trade," the American agent was directed. "This will give good countenance to your appearing in the character of a merchant, which we wish you continually to retain among the French in general, it being probable that the court of France may not like it should [it] be generally known publicly that any agent from the Colonies is in that country." Deanne was to contact certain individuals, who would eventually arrange for a meeting with the French Minister of Foreign Affairs, Count de Vergennes. After establishing his credentials, Deanne was to relay the desire of the American Congress for clothing, arms, and ammunition for 25,000 men, and 100 field pieces for America's defense, for which it promised a great increase in commerce with France. In his correspondence with John Jay, he was the first to use invisible ink in diplomatic circles. He interlined his visible words with invisible ones written with a solution of colorless tannic acid. On receipt in America, the letter was sponged with a solution of iron salts, which combined with the tannic acid to develop a visible dark script. Among other things, Deanne gave the first confirmed report that England was determined to militarily crush the American colonies into an unconditional surrender.

As the Thai proverb puts it:

Birds leave no trace of their flight.

MARCH 4

On this day in the year 1874, Victoria Woodhull sat in court awaiting the opening of the trial on a libel suit brought by Luther B. Challis against her and her associates on the *Woodhull & Claflin's Weekly*.

The paper had printed a story about his alleged seduction of a young girl. This was but one of a long succession of legal and social violences that had studded the lives of Victoria and her sister, Tennessee Claflin. They believed in the expression of principles through direct action. "I despise what squeamy, crying girls and powdered, counter-jumping dandies say of me," Tennie sneered at her genteel generation. They were out to fully exercise their women's rights. They were the first female brokers on Wall Street. They published the most controversial magazine. They were spell-binding suffragettes. They were unabashed free lovers, as Victoria once pointed out before an audience of 3000 in New York's Steinway Hall: "I have an inalienable, constitutional and natural right to love when I may, to love as long or as short a period as I can, to change that love every day if I please." Above all, they were scandal revealers, no matter how much or whom it hurts. This led eventually to the further allegations of illicit relations involving the beloved preacher, the Reverend Henry Ward Beecher. That proved too much for the American people. They finally ignored Victoria and Tennie—even for diversion.

As the Burmese proverb puts it:

He starts chiseling the moment he appears.

MARCH 5

On this day in the year 1934, Carl Sandburg disagreed with John Lewis Hershey regarding the personality of Charles Sumner.

The admirer of the American statesman had sent complimentary copyings from Henry Longfellow on Sumner. In his return letter, Lincoln's biographer pictured Sumner as "spinach, haywire and skunk-cabbage" with "a basic lack of integrity." In his opinion, Sumner "was made for martyrdom, for some scene as big and tragic as the one that John Brown faded out in. Yet what he had was a peculiar sort of respectable mcguffeys-reader success and acclaim." In sum, Sandburg harbored "only aversion for Sumner as a false alarm and stuffed shirt. He wanted to be a dangerous agitator and a perfect gentleman both at once and his critics were correct that you may be either a skunk or a white swan but not both." Sumner's plan would have led to the border states tipping the scales in favor of the Confederacy. This would have resulted in "a weird and aborted area for slavery to flourish as the banyan tree, to languish here and effloresce there, a sort of western-world Balkans to raise hell for an interminable period."

As the English proverb puts it:

You cannot run with the hare and hunt with the hounds.

MARCH 6

On this day in the year 1813, Edward Morgan Forster listened to the Maharajah of Dewas Senior discuss his views about how all of us, including men, birds, and everything, are part of God.

The young secretary then wondered how it was that we became separated from Him. As presented in Forster's account, "He explained it by God becoming unconscious that we were parts of him, owing to his energy at some time being concentrated elsewhere. . . . Salvation, then, is the thrill which we feel when God again becomes conscious in us, and all our life we must train our perceptions so that we may be capable of feeling when that time comes." The significance of his thesis gradually dawned on Forster, as the Rajah described the difficulties intrinsic in the belief that God had consciously created the universe. It would mean that He had consciously created suffering and sin. This the Indian refused to accept. "We were either put here intentionally or unintentionally," said the Rajah. "And it raises fewer difficulties if we suppose it was unintentionally."

As the Yiddish proverb puts it:

Man thinks and God laughs.

MARCH 7

On this day in the year 1931, Oliver Wendell Holmes, Jr., was honored in Washington, D.C., by a symposium of leaders in politics, arts, and the sciences.

When asked for a few comments at the conclusion, the 90-year-old Justice of the Supreme Court expressed the following intimate thought about his end drawing close: "The riders in a race do not stop short when they reach the goal. There is a finishing canter before coming to a standstill. There is time to hear the kind voices of friends and to say to oneself: 'The work is done.' But just as one says that, the answer comes: 'The race is over, but the work never is done while the power to work remains. The canter that brings you to a standstill need not be only coming to rest. It cannot be, while you still live. For to live is to function. That is all there is to living.' And so I end with a line from a Latin poet who uttered the message more than fifteen-hundred years ago. 'Death plucks my ear and says: Live—I am coming.' "

As the Russian proverb puts it:

The falling of a leaf is a whisper to the living.

MARCH 8

On this day in the year 1702, Anne became Queen of Great Britain.

Anne's life had been a concatenation of strife and sadness. She had been separated early from parents and sister. Quarrels with the King and Queen marred her younger days. Four miscarriages and 2 children who died in infancy constituted her lot between 1684 and 1688. Ill health plagued her throughout. Religious militants caught her in their crossfires. Intrigues and jealousies clouded her every action, reaching a climax on her deathbed. On top of it all, her meager abilities, dullness of intellect, and lapses of obstinacy piled obstacles upon obstacles upon the already difficult proceedings.

As the Spanish proverb puts it:

For one who does not know how to suffer, any life is death.

MARCH 9

On this day in the year 1832, Abraham Lincoln announced his first candidacy for political office.

The citizen of New Salem ran for state legislature in Illinois and placed a column in the *Sangamo Journal*. It set forth his position honestly and modestly: "I have no wealth or popular relations to recommend me. My case is thrown exclusively upon the independent voters of this country, and if elected they will have conferred a favor upon me, for which I shall be unremitting in my labors to compensate. But if the good people in their wisdom shall see fit to keep me in the background, I have been too familiar with disappointments to be very much chagrined." He lost.

As the Hungarian proverb puts it:

A bashful beggar has an empty purse.

MARCH 10

On this day in the year 1925, Edgar Wallace voiced opposition to the establishment of compulsory night schools proposed by the Washington Board of Education for children with old work permits.

Representing the American Federation of Labor, Wallace insisted that children should not be forced by economic deprivation to work during the day, and then be forced by the state to attend the "continuation schools" at night. Instead, the children should not be permitted to work at all but go to school during the day under a rigidly enforced school attendance law. The meeting on the welfare of children and workers ended with the forwarding of a strong resolution to that effect to the Board of Education.

As the Arabic proverb puts it:

Teach not the orphan how to weep.

MARCH 11

On this day in the year 1845, Lola Montez received the farewell note from her lover Alexandre Henri Dujarier, who had just been shot in a duel.

This was but one of the many romances and intrigues of the Irish-born Marie Dolores Gilbert, who preferred the identity of a Spanish dancer. The amoureuse had been the mistress of Alexandre Dumas and a string of intellectual and artistic giants. Her greatest conquest was King Ludwig I of Bavaria, who built her a castle and named her the Countess of Landsberg. Lola moved from mistress to political advisor. She engineered a reshuffling of the cabinet when the ministers refused to sign her naturalization papers. She dabbled in university affairs and precipitated internal dissensions among the faculty. Student clubs under her patronage fought the others. When some of the students shook their fists at her one day, she lost her temper and shouted. "I will have the university closed." The mob chased her until she took refuge in a church, to be rescued later by the King's military guard. On February 19, 1848, Ludwig finally yielded to Lola's pressure and closed the university, which he loved dearly. Riots erupted: "Down with the concubine! Set fire to the house on Barestrasse!" Lola was tossed out of Bavaria and Ludwig forced to abdicate.

As the Irish proverb puts it:

A dimple on the chin, the Devil within.

MARCH 12

On this day in the year 1979, James Rosenfield discussed the repeated revampings of the recent television programs of the Columbia Broadcasting System (CBS) with executives of its affiliates in Las Vegas, Nevada.

The president of CBS-TV acknowledged that the affiliates, as well as the public, were confused by the constant shuffling of programs and the insertion of new short-run series. But he pointed out that the competition for audience ratings was getting stiffer. Ranking only second among the Big Three, CBS must respond creatively and vigorously. "We're in a competitive battle and have to play the game as aggressively as we can," he emphasized. "We have to do it this way. We have to experiment with short-flight series because we need a backlog for next fall."

As the Romany proverb puts it:

The dog that trots about finds a bone.

MARCH 13

On this day in the year 1948, Theodore Roethke told Edward Nichols about his being asked by a member of the faculty of Pennsylvania State College as to the honorarium he would want for lecturing there on his way East.

Trying to be accommodating, the poet and former faculty member named a figure of $40 or $50, intending to turn back half for an anonymous prize. To his great shock, the return letter apologized, saying that no money could be obtained for the purpose, tried as his sponsor did with all sources. "Well, hell, the whole thing made me feel like a horse's ass, a fallen angel, a shit merchant all at once," confessed Roethke to his friend. "I reflect somewhat bitterly on the energy I spent & the dough of my own I've spent getting people to come there. You'd think that the damned place would be glad when one of its own boys breaks out with a book that, according to many smart characters, is the best book of verse of this year or last by a country mile; a book, much of which was written there etc. etc. Well, O.K. that's that. I'm getting old, but still remain naive, I guess."

As the Chinese proverb puts it:

Forget favors rendered; remember favors received.

MARCH 14

On this day in the year 1861, Mary Boykin Chestnut expressed her deep distress about slavery.

"God forgive us, but ours is a monstrous system, a wrong and an iniquity!" the daughter of the Governor of South Carolina recorded her sadness in her journal. "Like the patriarchs of old, our men live all in one house with their wives and their concubines; and the mulattoes one sees in every family partly resemble the white children. Any lady is ready to tell you who is the father of all the mulatto children in everybody's household but her own. Those, she seems to think, drop from the clouds."

As the Latin proverb puts it:

What is known is often useful to forget.

MARCH 15

On this day in the year 1884, Otto Leopold von Bismarck presented the first accident insurance bill to the Prussian Reichstag.

The comprehensive system of state insurance for workers providing accident, sickness, and old-age benefits was only one of the Chancellor's many domestic accomplishments. He built canals, nationalized the railroads, assisted the agricultural and industrial interests, and implemented universal suffrage. He also unified the country's currency with a central bank, as well as enacted a uniform code of civil law. All this he had been able to achieve because, to a large degree, he was creatively adaptive to the forces prevailing at the moment. When he controlled a parliamentary majority, he would push across major programs. When the Conservatives were cooperative, he worked with them. When they were refractive, he joined with the National Liberals. Then back again with the Conservatives, and so on.

As the German proverb puts it:

The wise man makes greater use of his enemies than the fool does of his friends.

MARCH 16

On this day in the year 1888, William Booth telegraphed encouragement and praise to his Salvation Army evangelists who had been thrown into jail for marching with music on a Sunday in the English town of Torquay.

The General then notified the Local Board on March 26 that he was not about to tell his followers "that they should, for fear of this ill wind or ill-treatment which may be meted out to them, cease to do that good work which is permitted to go on unhindered in every other portion of Her Majesty's Empire. The experiment of marches without music has been fully tried in Torquay, and has resulted in the conviction that the music is essential to the gathering into our barracks of those whom it is especially our duty to care for." Salvationist reinforcements poured in from the rest of Devonshire; Torquay police organized surveillance and enforcement networks. "We are all determined to go on, again and again, yes, again and again!" Booth hurled defiance in St. James Hall at Piccadilly. "Bandsmen are volunteering from all parts of the west country and when they have all done their best, if the opposition still goes on, we will send down officers and men from London." Eventually, Parliament passed the Fowler Bill that ended the local prohibition. The Salvation Army marched over another roadblock in its golden era of rapid expansion.

As the Chinese proverb puts it:

If the water buffalo refuses to drink, do not try to bend its neck.

MARCH 17

On this day in the year 1929, Pierre Teilhard de Chardin became overcome with "an odd mixture of pleasure and pain" in Tientsin.

The Jesuit paleontologist had been involved with the discovery of the Sinanthropus fossil in the Chou-Kou-Tien fissure about 30 miles from Peking the previous December. He had just returned again to the same Jesuit house. But on this occasion, he was seized with the feeling of exile. Teilhard found himself with "old, happy memories of this place, mingled with a certain nostalgia for Europe, and saddened a little, too, by an awareness in mind and body of departing youth." He no longer felt the way he did as when he first arrived 6 years earlier. Instead, he was recalling how "my own 'soul' then was practically brand new. But now I give myself the impression of a veteran fighter, not exactly skeptical, but pretty tough, a man who has no use any more for anything but the activity—and the friendship—that science brings, in so far, of course, that it allows me scope for action."

As the French proverb puts it:

Few persons know how to grow old.

MARCH 18

On this day in the year 1970, Lon Nol deposed Norodom Sihanouk, who was on a trip to Moscow.

Up to that time, the peace-loving Cambodians went about

their evenly paced living, carefree of the war in neighboring South Vietnam. True, the North Vietnamese troops had used the eastern regions for staging purposes. But the Cambodian Head of State Prince Sihanouk had succeeded in walking a political tight rope and prevented Cambodia herself from becoming an active battlefield. The General, however, cast his lot with the Americans and demanded that the Communists leave the country. Within 6 weeks American and South Vietnamese ground and sea forces invaded Cambodia. Battles spread through the land. Fighting reached the outskirts of the capital Phnom Penh within 3 years. Communist troops roamed over two-thirds of the country. American planes dropped over 50,000 tons of bombs a month around the city. Industry was crippled; plantations, harbors, and facilities destroyed; airports shelled; towns leveled. A million refugees took to the roads. A dispatch from Phnom Penh in May, 1973 described a waiter beside the pool of the once-elegant Hotel Le Phnom responding to a guest asking for lemons. "I am sorry, sir. After three years of war, there are no lemons," he shook his head. "And after three more years," he made a swooping gesture of dive-bombing planes with his hands, "there will be no more Cambodia."

As the Swahili proverb puts it:

When elephants fight, only the grass gets hurt.

MARCH 19

On this day in the year 1314, Jacques de Molay was burnt at the stake on a tiny island in the Seine.

Molay was the leader of the Templars—descendants of the Poor Knights of Christ, founded 2 centuries before by the pious Hugues de Payns to protect Christian pilgrims to the Holy Land. In time their strongholds became the security vaults of the wealthy. The city of Gaza, the island of Cyprus, and other massive gifts were bestowed on them. The accumulated resources were most remunerative as high-interest loans to stranded pilgrims, merchants, and princes. By the latter part of the thirteenth century, they were rich and powerful. King Philip the Fair plotted to take them over and Pope Clement V served as a partly unwitting instrument. Agents of the King's ambassador to Italy Guillaume de Nogaret infiltrated the Order. Rumors were spread about homosexuality, devil worship, spitting at the crucifix, and other evil doings among the knights. While Molay was in Paris responding to the Pope's appeal for a new crusade, the King's men arrested him on Black Friday, October 13, 1307. He was tried before the commission of cardinals on the basis of false testimony obtained from others under torture and executed at the hands of the Paris Inquisition. Within a year, Pope Clement died— they said of cancer; King Philip died of a heart attack while hunting; Ambassador Nogaret and the 3 principal accusers also died from various causes.

As the Turkish proverb puts it:

Allah postpones but does not overlook.

MARCH 20

On this day in the year 1948, Tito announced Yugoslavia's independence from the Soviet monolith in a letter to Vyacheslav Mikhailovich Molotov.

The deepening schism became gradually visible to the public through a series of signs. On May 25 the year before the Soviet leaders did not send any note of birthday congratulations to the Marshal, which they had been doing for years. Rumors spread that the scheduled June meeting of the Cominform was to be held in Prague instead of Belgrade as originally planned. On June 26 the Manchester *Guardian* published an article about the impending crisis between Yugoslavia and the Soviet Union. Then on June 28 Cominform passed a resolution to oust Yugoslavia. The Yugoslavians reasserted their determination over Radio Belgrade on June 30. The world feared for little Yugoslavia. But no cause for alarm. Tito stuck to his guns and emerged stronger than ever internally and externally vis-à-vis both the United States and the Soviet Union.

As the Scottish proverb puts it:

There is a time to squint and a time to look straight.

MARCH 21

On this day in the year 1562, Thomas Gresham wrote Elizabeth I about the necessity of modernizing the British naval armaments and offered to undertake the task himself.

The Greshams had been the dominant influence on the commercial policies of England for over 4 reigns. They did not have to go through any intermediaries to see their royal patrons. Thomas' father had served as Lord Mayor of London and had profited the greatest from the confiscation of Church lands during the Reformation. Like his father, Thomas was Royal Agent, a liaison between royal and mercantile interests. He himself was a purveyor of munitions, among other things. He negotiated with foreign courts. He maintained an information-gathering and mail network. He raised money for the crown. He was a stout Protestant. It was not surprising, therefore, that the Queen immediately ordered large quantities of muskets, pistols, cuirasses, and powder from him on receipt of his brief note.

As the Japanese proverb puts it:

Stand in the shade of a large tree.

MARCH 22

On this day in the year 1967, Chou En-lai again yielded precedence to his junior in the Chinese Communist party.

Relinquishing seniority for the sake of harmony was not unusual for the Premier. When Liu Shao-ch'i had become popular in 1945, he stepped down from the second-ranking political position to make room for Liu. When Liu was deposed by the Party for political heresy after a few years, Chou resumed his former status. Again, on this occasion, Chou welcomed another lower-ranking member, Lin Piao, as "the comrade in arms closest to the Party Chairman." When Lin too was later disgraced in an aborted coup against the Chairman, Chou resumed his former rank, as he continued to keep China's administrative organization going as the Chairman's deputy for operations. Despite repeated self-effacement, he had somehow always managed to retain key positions within the Party, enjoy the confidence of every chairman through six changes of leadership, and remain in the small inner circle.

As the Italian proverb puts it:

Shift your sails with the wind.

MARCH 23

On this day in the year 1839, Lin Tse-hsu cordoned off the Chinese factories in Canton.

The Imperial Envoy had been sent by the Emperor for the purpose of putting an end to the opium traffic. Lin had summoned the collaborating Hong merchants and threatened to strangle them if they did not cease and desist. With 20,000 chests of opium aboard 20 or more ships at anchor in the harbor, the foreign and Chinese merchants offered to surrender only 1000 as a compromise. Lin took the hard line and ordered the workers to leave their jobs under penalty of decapitation. All the opium from foreign ships were seized and confiscated. In July a fracas involving a group of American and British sailors and Chinese farmers ended in the death of one of the farmers. The question of extraterritorial rights raised the heat of friction with neither side willing to give in. One thing led to another. Lord Palmerston finally took the position that the opium trade, which had accounted for half of the British exports to China, was essential for maintaining Britain's balance of payments and its discontinuation would be disastrous for the economy of India. China was roundly condemned by Britain for her "provocations" and "arrogance" and the Opium War was declared.

As the Serbian proverb puts it:

When they want to kill a dog, they first say it is mad.

MARCH 24

On this day in the year 1875, Sidney Lanier denounced commercialism as an evil in disrupting the harmony in national life, as he wrote about his latest poem to Gibson Peacock.

In an earlier letter to Paul Hamilton, the American poet had set forth the same theme, "Trade, Trade, Trade; pah, are we not all sick? A man cannot walk down a green alley of woods, in these days, without unawares getting his mouth and nose and eyes covered with some web or other that Trade has stretched across, to catch some gain or other. 'Tis an old spider that has crawled all over our modern life, and covered it with a flimsy web that conceals the Realities. Our religion, our politics, our social life, our charities, our literature, nay, by Heavens! our music and our loves almost, are all meshed in unsubstantial concealments and filthy garnitures by it." When his poem was published in June 1875, it started with the lines:

O Trade! O Trade! would thou wert dead!
The Time needs heart—'tis tired of head . . .

As the Chinese proverb puts it:

To enjoy life in the mountains, let there be no aligning of the trees, no arranging of the rocks, and no contriving of the heart.

MARCH 25

On this date in the year 1978, Ian Viner received support from Aborigine groups for his move toward placing control of Aborigine affairs in Queensland in the hands of the Australian Parliament.

The dispute began in 1976 when a rich bauxite deposit was discovered in a little Aborigine reserve in Aurukun and Mornington Island. Premier Johannes Bjelke-Peterson of Queensland wanted to move the tribe and open the mine. Three foreign companies were to operate the enterprise and the Aborigines were to receive 3% of the profits. The latter did not want to leave their ancestral homes and hunting grounds. But the Australian Minister of Aborigine Affairs intervened and announced on March 22 that the federal government would pass laws to supersede the state's rights over the Aborigines. The State Premier vowed a fight against the interference of the central government in the internal matters of the state of Queensland. In either case, the fate of the Aborigines will still rest in the hands of others.

As the Spanish proverb puts it:

A peasant between two lawyers is a fish between two cats.

MARCH 26

On this day in the year 1913, Albert Schweitzer sailed from Bordeaux for Africa.

The Alsatian music scholar and theologian began his new life as medical missionary as he arrived with 70 packing cases of supplies at Lambaréné on the Ogowe River 50 miles south of the equator in Gabon. He worked indefatigably and maintained strict discipline for maximum efficiency. There were so many sick people to take care of. No sooner was a rudimentary hospital built out of the bushes, when the facilities were overloaded and successive extensions had to be built. When the writer John Gunther showed interest some 40 years later in what the native workmen were getting to eat, the doctor mentioned, "Seven bananas a day." "Would they work better if they get 8 bananas?" "No," Schweitzer's eyes flashed. "That would disturb discipline and morale. If somebody does particularly good work, I may give him extra fare, but I do so secretly, so that the others will not know."

As the Bihari proverb puts it:

He who holds the ladle controls everybody.

MARCH 27

On this day in the year 1954, Lewis Mumford called for the cessation of further experiments on and explosions of hydrogen bombs.

"If as a nation we have become mad, it is time for the world to take note of the madness," decried the American author and social critic in a letter to the *New York Times.* "If we are still humane and sane, then it is time for the powerful voice of sanity to be heard once more in our land." But no one heard and no one took note within the governments of power. The routine announcement by the governments of power after each test explosion that "we will not be the first to use the hydrogen bomb" always seems sufficient to satisfy peace-loving citizens. And the process goes on.

As the Congolese proverb puts it:

If you don't want the gun to go off, don't cock the trigger.

MARCH 28

On this day in the year 1750, Benjamin Avery presented a full account of the efforts being made for "introducing Spiritual Power into America" to the General Meeting of the Dissenting Deputies.

The American colonial warned his compatriots of the dangers of the very religious domination from which they had escaped. He spoke of how Thomas Sherlock, after becoming Bishop of London in 1748, outlined his objective of sending bishops to the colonies and establishing the Church of England there on a firm footing, beginning with one in Barbados and another in Virginia. The colonials themselves had not intimated a need for higher clergy, but Sherlock was determined, as he had alluded to a friend on September 9: "The business of the diocese and of the plantations . . . sits heavy on me." Word of the plan reached the Connecticut representative in London, Eliakim Palmer, who immediately passed on his concern to Governor Jonathan Law to bear "the strongest testimony (as your agent) against it" as a program having "so Direct a Tendency to Introduce Ecclesiastical Tyranny amongst a people whose ancestors have so severely felt the bad effects of it as ours have done—I have given the Alarm to our Brethren on this side of the Water who as a Body have deputed Dr. Avery and myself to attend four Great Men upon the Affair."

As the Ruandan proverb puts it:

The fire goes where there is still grass.

MARCH 29

On this day in the year 1904, Anton Pavlovich Chekhov again objected to the stage interpretation being given to his *Cherry Orchard*.

"Stanislavski has butchered my play," the Russian playwright stated in a letter to his wife. The disagreement was evident from the very first rehearsal. Chekhov had conceived his play as a gay comedy, "in places even as a farce." But the director read it as a social drama of the minor rural nobility giving way to the nouveaux riche. The actors and actresses followed Stanislavski's cue and the posters referred to it as a drama. Despite Chekhov's apprehensions, the opening night was a huge success. The ovation was thunderous. The author was applauded with grandiloquent testimonials as he stood on the stage in the midst of bouquets, wreaths, and gifts for over an hour after the final curtain. Even so, Chekhov insisted that Stanislavski had committed an error of interpretation, while Stanislavski insisted that Chekhov had exceeded the limits of his expertise.

As the Livonian proverb puts it:

A fisherman is wise in the morning, a shepherd in the evening.

MARCH 30

On this day in the year 1907, Lamsdorf, who had just died not long before, was being remembered in the St. James Club in London for his comment on dull-wittedness being a diplomatic asset.

"The raw university enthuse is qualified by no more than certain fixed ideas culled from the old world of learning and would paralyze the policy of any other nation in the world but England," the Count had said. "With England, it does not matter." Someone pressed him, "But why not, Count?" He got the reply: "The young English diplomat is so stupid and looks so dull that all the world thinks he must have something deep, some profundity, behind it all. An English ambassador does a thing so insane that it appears a ruse."

As the Yiddish proverb puts it:

What is the use of cleverness if foolishness serves?

MARCH 31

On this day in the year 1950, Fred Allen comforted Groucho Marx about the declining popularity of his radio show.

"I am beginning to regard myself as the kiss of death to any branch of the amusement industry" with which he was connected—so wrote Marx to his fellow comedian on March 20. "When I reached big-time vaudeville it immediately began to rot at the seams. During the days when I was a movie actor, no theater could survive unless it gave away dishes, cheese and crackers, and, during Lent, costume jewelry." Now he was wondering whether he was doing the same thing to radio noting that his own Hooper rating had dropped to fifth place. Allen replied, "Vaudeville committed suicide, the picture business ran out of adjectives and radio was thrown to the cretin. . . . if you want to give television the buss of rigor mortis you had better hurry." Allen assured him that Marx was not a contributor to the decaying state of the entertainment world. "After a few recent shows, dogs in this section have been dragging television sets out into the yards and burying them."

As the Chilean proverb puts it:

If the wise man does not approve, it is bad: but if the fool applauds, it is worse.

APRIL 1

On this day in the year 1879, Paul Cezanne sent a letter to Camille Pisarro, declining to continue exhibiting his works with the impressionists.

By this time the French artist had developed his own concept and style of painting. He freed himself from the deductive reasoning of the classical masters, as well as the subjective viewing of his impressionist predecessors. To him, both approaches led to a dissolution of reality. He wanted to feel the sensation realistically and directly in the presence of Nature herself. There was to be neither logical constraints nor emotional shimmerings. There was to be no sacrificing of her vibrancy. He spoke of realization and modulation—the bringing into being and the adjusting to color. The overall effect of his newly found harmony of form and color on the viewer was a spontaneous appearing before his very eyes of form in the patches of color and its receding back into the canvas, as it were. There was a vital intensity and solidity in the flat planes never before achieved. As recapitulated in his own words at age 70, "Now the idea to be insisted on is—no matter what our temperament or power in the presence of nature—to produce the image of what we see, forgetting everything that has been done before, which I believe, should enable the artist to express his entire personality, great or small."

As the English proverb puts it:

Eagles fly alone.

APRIL 2

On this day in the year 1453, Mohammed II began his long artillery bombardment of Constantinople, which led to its capture on May 29.

The Ottoman Sultan took immediate steps to consolidate his hold over the neighboring regions. One of his first acts was the prohibition of Christian shipping through the Bosporus. On November 10 2 Venetian ships loaded with grain decided to run the blockade, since they had always passed unmolested before to and from the Black Sea. One volley from the watchful cannons sank both of them. The Captain and 30 sailors escaped the explosions and swam ashore. They were captured, chained, and brought to Adrianople, where Mohammed was based. The Sultan ordered the crew beheaded and the captain impaled. He was bound and pulled down on a sharpened spike. The point thrusted through his anus, speared through his guts, and perforated his shoulders. There the captain writhed and moaned until he died 10 hours later. The bodies were then fed to the wild animals at Demotica.

As the Russian proverb puts it:

If the thunder is not loud, the peasant forgets to cross himself.

APRIL 3

On this day in the year 1851, Mongkut ascended the Thai throne in the presence of 150,000 peasants.

After the monk, who had been carrying his cast-iron bowl and begging for food with downcast eyes for 27 years, became King, he was particularly emphatic about preserving the Thai culture as he went about reforming the laws and modernizing the operations of the government. He insisted on Thailand's independence from foreign domination. The

French were overrunning Cambodia over which the Thais had claimed sovereignty. The British warships were shelling a Malayan city, also claimed by Thailand. During the period of strained relations between Thailand and France around 1865, England offered, actually demanded, that she represent Thailand in Paris. Mongkut adamantly refused and sent his own ambassador. "It is for us to decide what we are going to do," the ambassador was instructed, "whether to swim up-river to make friends with the crocodile or to swim out to sea and hang on to the whale."

As the Georgian proverb puts it:

The cock cannot profit from the friendship of a fox.

APRIL 4

On this day in the year 1835, Charles Brown replied to Walter Savage Landor, who begged for a few sentences of exoneration or criticism concerning his family crisis.

"For more than eleven years I have been intimate with you, and, during that ime, frequenting your house, I never once saw you behave towards Mrs. Landor otherwise than with the most gentlemanly demeanor, while your love for your children was unabounded," the longtime friend gave succor to the English man of letters against the hysterical and libelous outbursts of his wife. "I was always aware that you gave the entire control into her hands over the children, the servants, and the management of the house; and when vexed or annoyed at anything I could not help but remark that you were in the habit of requesting the cause to be remedied or removed as a favor to yourself. All this I have more than once repeated to Mrs. Landor in her accusations against you, which I could never well comprehend."

As the Czech proverb puts it:

It is an unhappy house, when the hen crows and the cock is silent.

APRIL 5

On this day in the year 1651, Christopher Jones tacked the *Mayflower* out of Plymouth Harbor, leaving the small group of Pilgrims on their own on the strange continent.

Soon after the Captain's departure, their Governor John Carver died. The mantle passed to 32-year-old William Bradford, whose courage, vigor, and wit pulled the Pilgrims through many a tight situation. Yet had it not been for an unusual combination of happenstance, the small group might well have perished. This was the timely appearance of Squanto. The Indian had been kidnapped with 20 others by an English Captain Thomas Hunt in 1614 and sold as a slave at the Malaga market in Spain. He fell into the hands of some local friars, then slipped away to London, where he lived with John Slamie, treasurer of the Newfoundland Company. Through the good offices of the executive, Squanto returned home with Captain Thomas Dermer, who had set out to explore New England in 1619. When he landed, he learned that the plague had wiped out all his people. He took a liking to the Pilgrims, when they appeared on the scene. The English-speaking Squanto taught them how to plant and cultivate corn, how to space the hillocks, how to fertilize with fish, when to catch the herring, how to build traps, how to keep the wolves away, and so on. He was, according to the Pilgrim records of the day, "a speciall instrument sent by God for their good beyond expectation."

As the Scottish proverb puts it:

He doubles his gift who gives in time.

APRIL 6

On this day in the year 1915, William Hale Thompson was elected Mayor of Chicago.

The Mayor-Elect promptly threatened that "the crooks had better move out of town before I am inaugurated." He was inaugurated. The crooks did not move out of town. Business went on as usual.

As the Colombian proverb puts it:

Old dogs bark sitting down.

APRIL 7

On this day in the year 1839, Louis Joseph Papineau began to doubt that France would come to the aid of Canadian independence, which he had been trying to promote.

"France and England are sitting on a volcano and many kind-minded people fear the instantaneous explosion," the political fugitive concluded after a short stay in Paris. He did not believe that France, being concerned with possible trouble on her eastern borders, would care to aggravate her relations with England. Then, too, many Frenchmen felt the question was actually moot, since it was their expectation that Canada would eventually be swallowed up by the United States anyway. But most discouraging to Papineau was his growing impression that Frenchmen as a whole were not the type that would stick with a cause through a long struggle. To him, "Parisians especially were in a giddy round of pleasures and dissipation which does not let penetrate too deeply in their hearts the desire to prove, through sacrifices, the sincerity of the liberal opinions."

As the Jamaican proverb puts it:

If you must lean, don't lean on vines.

APRIL 8

On this day in the year 1923, Henry Ford was urged by his admirers in Georgia to become a presidential candidate.

After a preliminary survey and a few trial balloons, the auto magnate released the statement: "I don't know where this boom started, but I'm not interested in it." Mrs. Ford explained it this way: "If Henry goes to the White House, he will have to go without me."

As the Scottish proverb puts it:

No man can thrive unless his wife lets him.

APRIL 9

On this day in the year 1939, Marian Anderson gave a concert from the steps of the Lincoln Memorial in Washington to an audience of 75,000.

The American contralto had been denied permission to

perform in Constitution Hall by the Daughters of the American Revolution because she was black. The wife of the President, Eleanor Roosevelt, resigned in protest and offered the more prestigious and symbolic platform for her appearance. Among those in attendance were the Chief Justice of the Supreme Court, Congressmen, and members of the cabinet. Some years later, Anderson was asked in an interview about her reactions to the episode. "Oh, it's been such a long time ago I've forgotten about it," she replied.

As the Arabic proverb puts it:

Forgiveness is perfect when the sin is forgotten.

APRIL 10

On this day in the year 1868, Jay Gould was investigated by the New York Senate with respect to irregularities with the finances of the Erie Railroad Company.

The Committee ascertained that "large sums of money were expended for corrupt purposes by parties interested in legislation concerning railways during the session of 1868." Actually, this had been only one phase of the continuing competition between the financier and Cornelius Vanderbilt. While the latter was avidly acquiring Erie stocks to control the railroad, Gould and his associates were secretly scheming to make more money by manipulating them. Under Vanderbilt's influence, a presiding judge had ordered that no further stocks were to be issued. The price shot up 30 points. But somehow, Gould had gotten hold of 100,000 illegally issued shares. These were sold and checks converted into cash as quickly as they came in. Vanderbilt himself lost $7 million in the process. Gould then tried to consolidate his gains by bribing the state legislators into legalizing the fraudulent stock issues. A bill was cooked up for the purpose. Vanderbilt passed money around to defeat it. Gould passed more. One senator accepted $75,000 from Vanderbilt and $100,000 from Gould. The bill was passed.

As the Hungarian proverb puts it:

The law moves on golden wheels.

APRIL 11

On this day in the year 1904, Georg Gapon formed the Assembly of Russian Factory and Mill Workers in St. Petersburg.

Russia's first large legal trade union grew rapidly. Eleven branches were formed within a year. The membership soon rose to 9000. In his desire to expand even more rapidly, Gapon sought the endorsement of 4 influential labor leaders. But they were suspicious of Gapon's association with government officials. As required for continued legal recognition, the union was subject to certain controls by the chief of police. They therefore requested, as the price for their cooperation, that a list of demands be presented by the Assembly to the Tsar. This placed Gapon in the difficult position of allowing his organization to be dragged into political activities, which would assuredly put him on a collision course with the police. Yet there appeared to be no other alternative if his movement was to gain momentum. After a tiring and fruitless argument, Gapon agreed: "So let it be!" On the cold afternoon of January 22, 1905, union men and women with Red Cross armbands linked arms and marched toward the Winter Palace. The Tsar's troops opened fire, leaving hundreds killed and thousands wounded. "Bloody Sunday" surgically ended the Gaponovshina labor movement.

As the French proverb puts it:

He pays too high a price for honey who licks it off thorns.

APRIL 12

On this day in the year 1709, Richard Steele founded the *Tatler*.

Joseph Addison soon joined Sir Richard and the two journalists made the periodical one of the best of its kind. "The general purpose of the paper." Steele explained in the first collected volume, "is to expose the false arts of life, to pull off the disguises of cunning, vanity, and affectation, and to recommend a general simplicity in our dress, our discourse, and our behavior."

As the English proverb puts it:

The best luxury is simplicity.

APRIL 13

On this day in the year 1279, Kublai Khan's fleet encircled the Chinese flotilla southwest of Canton and crushed the last vestige of military resistance.

The grandson of Genghis Khan had completed the conquest his grandfather had begun. During the interim period of 74 years, however, the Mongols had come to adopt the ways of the Chinese to such an extent that Kublai himself became a Son of Heaven, Emperor Yuan Shih-tsu of the Yuan dynasty. Before 2 centuries had passed, there were no more Mongols in China—not slain but assimilated.

As the Chinese proverb puts it:

With patience the mulberry leaf becomes a silk gown.

APRIL 14

On this day in the year 1949, Roy J. Harris uncovered a widespread scandal within the Illinois press.

The newspapers had been vigorous and vociferous in exposing corruption in government, business, and labor unions for decades. But for the first time, a major disgrace involving not one or a few isolated newsmen, but organized dozens under the control of the office of Governor Dwight H. Green, was uncovered for the public to see. The reporter from the *St. Louis Post-Dispatch* described how "editors and publishers of at least thirty-two downstate newspapers were on the state payroll." The main assignment to many of them "was to print canned editorials and news stories lauding accomplishments of the Republican state administration."

As the Bantu proverb puts it:

He who takes a light to find the whereabouts of a snake should commence at his feet.

APRIL 15

On this day in the year 1846, Tabitha Brown joined one of the wagon trains in the Great Migration westward.

Grandma Brown was 62 years old, 5 feet tall, and 108 pounds when well fed. She was partly paralyzed and walked with a cane. She fought no savages, trapped no beavers, converted no heathens. But she had courage and stamina. As she crossed the plains and the Rockies, she nursed the sick along the way and endured the near-starvation when the cattle were rustled off by the Rogue River Indians. After arriving in Oregon, she started one of the first schools in that part of the country. It was for both the rich and the poor. Those who could afford paid a dollar a week for board and tuition. Hobbling about with a lame leg, she worked feverishly to keep the institution going, mixing 10 pounds of flour daily for the needed bread. Today it is known as the Pacific University.

As the Japanese proverb puts it:

Mountains are esteemed not because they are high, but because they have trees.

APRIL 16

On this day in the year 49 B.C., Marcus Tulius Cicero was advised by Julius Caesar to remain aloof from the struggle between him and Pompey.

The letter from the Roman commander was friendly. He guaranteed Cicero's safety. Sentimentally, the statesman had leaned toward Pompey, who he felt would better preserve the republic. But he straddled the fence for several more months, waiting to see how the tide of battle would flow. When news came that Pompey's lieutenants had maneuvered Caesar's forces into a dangerous box in Spain, Cicero decided to jump on Pompey's bandwagon and went straightway to join him in Greece. By this time, however, Pompey had grown lukewarm toward him because of his vacillation. Even more unfortunately for the orator, Caesar recouped his fortunes and defeated Pompey decisively at the battle of Pharsalus in 48 B.C. Nevertheless, Cicero was allowed to depart for semiexile in southern Italy. When Caesar finally visited Tarentum, Cicero greeted him with great trepidation. But Caesar was magnanimous and embraced him. After chatting affectionately for a long time he invited Cicero to live as though nothing untoward had ever happened.

As the Arabic proverb puts it:

Pardon is the choicest flower of victory.

APRIL 17

On this day in the year 1895, Li Hung-chang signed the Treaty of Shimonoseki, accepting defeat and most of the terms imposed by Japan.

The Japanese navy had broken the back of the Chinese fleet at the mouth of the Yalu River. The Japanese army had crushed the Chinese force in Korea and Manchuria. It was no contest. After 6 months China sued for peace. Korea was to be independent. China was to pay indemnity, cede Formosa, the Pescadores, and the Liaotung Peninsula on the mainland, and open up several ports to Japan on a most-favored nation basis. Afraid of the rising Japanese power, Germany, France, and Russia intervened and demanded that Japan restore the Liaotung Peninsula to China on grounds that "Japan would be a constant menace to the capital of China, render illusory Korean independence, and be a perpetual obstacle to the peace of the Far East." Being close to financial and military exhaustion and aware of the presence of 30 Russian warships in Asian waters, Japan backed down on this item. The Sino-Japanese War and the triple intervention dramatically exposed the weakness of China, which continued under foreign domination and exploitation for yet another half century.

As the Indian proverb puts it:

Whosoever carries the bludgeon owns the buffalo.

APRIL 18

On this day in the year 1951, Douglas MacArthur returned to San Francisco after an absence of 14 years.

The General of the Army's all-absorbing theme of life had been: "There is no substitute for victory." He had been first in his class at West Point. He had conquered the Japanese decisively in the Pacific in World War II. He had subjugated their Emperor, ruled their country, and changed their customs in the post-war period. When his Commander-in-Chief Harry Truman ordered him to adjust his strategy in the subsequent Korean War to that of a stalemate, MacArthur imperiously balked. The President stripped him of his command. And MacArthur ended his otherwise glorious military career by being fired.

As the Sudanese proverb puts it:

Do not insult the crocodile until you have crossed the river.

APRIL 19

On this day in the year 1562, Don Carlos pitched headlong down a staircase after missing a step, knocked his head against a closed door, and fell unconscious.

The heir to Felipe II of Spain recovered but suffered alarming symptoms on the tenth day. Nine specialists and 50 consultations were called. Three options were finally proposed. The first was trepanations by Dr. Andreas Vesalius to let out the diseased blood pressing on the brain. The second was the alternating application of a black "repercussive" ointment and a white "attenuative" ointment by a Moor from Valencia. The third was placing the century-old miracle-working cadaver of the Franciscan Fray Diego beside the patient in bed. All 3 were tried. It was said that the miracle finally saved the prince's life, although he turned out crippled, hunchbacked, and mentally not-all-there.

As the Persian proverb puts it:

Drowning people snatch at foams.

APRIL 20

On this day in the year 1967, Janet Flanner reported from Paris on the widespread damage to 25 coastal villages in Brittany brought about by floating sheets of oil from the wreckage of the commercial tanker, *Torrey Canyon.*

"The real lost ones up there are the seabirds, of value only to the balance of nature," the *New Yorker* feature writer concluded her dispatch. "An estimated twenty-five-thousand of them perished last week—rendered flightless by the oil on their feathers and waterlogged, drowned, starved, poisoned, or chilled to death. They were almost the entire population of the largest bird sanctuary in this part of Europe—on the Ile Rouzic, offshore from Perrosquires, near Lannion. The present loss also stretches into the future, since this is the sanctuary nesting season for the cormorants, guillemots, and penguins, and for the only colony in France of the rare puffins, now feared completely wiped off."

As the American proverb puts it:

The avaricious man will sell his share of the sun.

APRIL 21

On this day in the year 1883, John D. Rockefeller, Sr., instructed a subordinate to "see how much we could afford to decline the market if we could get the entire business in refining, taking into account the profit and the extra crude we would thereby pump."

The Standard Oil official recommended caution. It became apparent from past experience that price-slashing would not drive all the small independents out of business as readily as large competitors. The faster shut-down and start-up times of the smaller firms favored them in such a contest. If Standard were to cut price to cost, the smaller companies would merely keep producing the oil and hold on to them until prices go up again. If the price war were to be intensified below cost, they would simply stop altogether and wait. In the meantime the Standard giant would lose at an enormous rate, which could not be sustained for any length of time. Then when Standard could take the massive losses no longer and raise the price at last, the independent simply would start up again with ease. When confronted with such an analysis, Rockefeller decided to give up this line of attack and resort to a much more complex envelopment.

As the Spanish proverb puts it:

The best art of the swimmer is knowing how to secure his clothes.

APRIL 22

On this day in the year 1953, Clare Booth Luce stepped off the gangplank in Naples as the new Ambassador from the United States.

She arrived, however, without the money bags of her predecessors. While they were able to hand over $2.8 billion in direct economic aid to the Italians, she could arrange for only

$105 million in fiscal year 1954. Mutual defense assistance in the form of American offshore procurement contracts in Italy decreased over 75% during her first year. But the Ambassador worked diligently at her job. She was especially sensitive in her public relations. When an Italian LAI plane crashed at Idlewilde in New York, she switched her booking from an American airline to LAI. When Prime Minister Alcide De Gasperi died, she rushed back from leave to attend the funeral. When a flash flood damaged the Amalfi coast, she hurried to the scene of the disaster and made a round of the hospitals.

As the Indian proverb puts it:

If you can't give sugar, then talk sugar.

APRIL 23

On this day in the year 1843, William Miller and his disciples in the United States awaited for the end of the world, which he had prophesized would occur that day.

But the world went on.

As the American proverb puts it:

Let any guy talk long enough, he will have believers.

APRIL 24

On this day in the year 1916, Padraic Pearse set the revolution in action in Dublin, which he had hoped would give birth to the Irish Republic.

The 1500 insurgents received scant help on that Easter Sunday. The poet's sister hysterically called out to him as he was marching off, "Come home, Pat, and leave all that foolishness!" Irish men and women stood on the street corners muttering, "I hope every one of them gets shot." The rebels succeeded in burning the General Post Office and occupying the College of Surgeons. Equipped only with crowbars, pikes, shotguns, and 1870-vintage German mausers, they were no match for the British regulars with machine guns and artillery. The uprising ended as a fiasco. But the rebels had been inspired by the statement of the patriot Fintan Lalor: "Somewhere and somehow and by someone, a beginning must be made, and the first of armed resistance is always premature, imprudent, and foolish."

As the Chinese proverb puts it:

To be a person of principle, first be a person of courage.

APRIL 25

On this day in the year 1227, Ulrich von Lichtenstein began his 5-week tilting trip from Venice to Vienna.

He was preceded the day before by a herald with an open letter to the knights of Lombardy, Austria, and Bohemia. One and all were notified that the goddess of Venus will rise from the ocean near Venice and ride northeastward, with a challenge to every warrior enroute. He who dares to meet her will gain favor with the ladies. He who unhorses her will be given all the horses in her retinue. He who refuses to tilt with her will be forever disgraced. Everyone recognized, of course, that under the ornate white dress and pearl-bedecked braids was von Lichtenstein himself. He had been knighted 5 years earlier at the wedding feast of the Duke of Saxony. There he fell in love at first sight with one of the beautiful guests and made a sacred vow to devote his newly earned knighthood in her service. Now he had the confidence for a public demonstration of his worthiness. In the series, he broke 311 lances, unhorsed 4 opponents, and was never unhorsed himself. But when his niece presented his message of chivalry to the fair lady, the reply was quick: von Lichtenstein was too presumptious and ugly to be deserving of her, even as a distant admirer.

As the English proverb puts it:

One cannot love and be wise.

APRIL 26

On this day in the year 1336, Francesco Petrarca gained sudden enlightenment on the meaning of life.

The early Renaissance Italian humanist had been wanting to climb Mont Ventoux for years. He finally undertook to do so with his brother. They reached the summit after an exhausting struggle up the steep slope. Inspired by the scene from the peak with the mountains of Lyons to the right, the sea near Marseilles breaking against Aigues Mortes to the left, the Rhone directly ahead, and the snow-covered Italian Alps in the distance, his mind turned to loftier meditations. Will he always be ready to meet death with equanimity as the remainder of life after 40 flows into old age? At this point he took out Augustine's *Confessions*, which he had brought along, opened it at random, and casually looked into the page. His eyes fixed on the passage: "And men go to admire the high mountains, the vast floods of the ocean, and the revolution of the stars—and desert themselves." Struck by the thought that the passage had been written just for him, Petrarca slowly closed the book—a changed man.

As the French proverb puts it:

If a person cannot find peace within himself, it is useless to look elsewhere.

APRIL 27

On this day in the year 1915, Franz Kafka again felt depressed over his lonely state of existence.

"Incapable of living with people, of speaking," the Austrian novelist saw himself in his diary. "Complete immersion in myself, thinking of myself. Apathetic, witless, fearful. I have nothing to say to anyone—never."

As the Egyptian proverb puts it:

The person who eats alone chokes alone.

APRIL 28

On this day in the year 1503, Gonzalo de Cordoba marched out of his stronghold at Barletta.

Instead of engaging the French Duke of Nemours with an equal force of 6500 arrayed before him at Canossa, the Spanish commander sped to Cerignola, 16 miles across the Ofanto River. There he stationed his men behind a ditch, with this 13-gun artillery protected by a hastily built rampart. The Duke soon caught up with them, eager to show off the finest cavalry in Italy. Just then an explosion blew up Gonzalo's artillery magazine. The French could not hold back any longer at this stroke of good luck and charged—only to find that the innocently looking ditch turned out to be an excavated obstacle with sharpened stakes. Seeing his forward ranks impaled, the Duke wheeled his cavalry along the ditch trying to cross the barrier at another point. The Spanish harquebusiers at the flanks had a field day. Nemours himself was blasted off the saddle. Finally Gonzalo unleased his own cavalry. Three thousand Frenchmen were killed as compared to 100 Spaniards.

As the Scottish proverb puts it:

If you don't see the bottom, don't wade.

APRIL 29

On this day in the year 1739, John Wesley delivered his great sermon on "Free Grace" at Bristol.

The founder of Methodism waxed eloquently over God's love. "The grace of love of God, whence cometh our salvation, is *free in all* and *free for all.*" He preached on with fiery emotion. "To say, then, He did not intend to save all sinners is to represent Him as a gross deceiver of the people. You cannot deny that He says, 'Come unto me, all ye that are weary and heavy laden.' If, then, you say He calls those that cannot come; those whom He knows to be unable to come; those whom He can make able to come, but will not; how is it possible to describe greater insincerity?. . . This is blasphemy clearly contained in the *horrible decree* of predestination. And here I fix my feet. On this I join issue with every assertion of it. You represent God as worse than the devil; more false, more cruel, more unjust . . ." And so went his denunciation of those who proclaimed the doctrine of predestination.

As the Turkish proverb puts it:

If Allah closes one door, he opens a thousand others.

APRIL 30

On this day in the year 1849, Andrew Gordon began his trek from St. Joseph, Missouri, to seek gold in California.

Within 9 days his party of 15 wagons met 2 others that had turned back. "Two of their men died of cholera; they had three left, and these survivors had hollow eyes and caved in cheeks, and looked as if they were about done for." On the cover of their wagon, the words were still legible: *Going for Gold*. The trail grew rougher as they encountered mounds of things that others had thrown away to lighten their loads. Dead mules and oxen became a common sight. Next came the blazing August heat. "I hardly know whether I am alive or dead." Finally, on September 23, the Gordon train arrived at San Francisco. Ten thousand people were scrambling about in the town built for 800. He checked into a so-called hotel. Four persons were stacked in bunks, one atop another. For this, they had each to pay $10 per night. "Are we crazy?" Gordon rhetorically summarized his estimate of the situation in his diary the following day.

As the Spanish proverb puts it:

Many go out for wool and come home shorn.

MAY 1

On this day in the year 1885, Sidney Webb joined the Fabian Society at the urging of George Bernard Shaw.

The 2 complemented each other most effectively. The Irish author was a brilliant, incisive, and imaginative genius, eloquent in word and speech. The English socialist was an encyclopedic reader and meticulous gatherer of facts, conversant with practical requirements of achieving political reform. What necessary skill was deficient in the one was amply blessed in the other. Shaw talked about this collaboration in his letter of June 17, 1948, to Archibald Henderson. In building up the Society Shaw envisioned himself "as the constructor of the fundamental theory and frames of reference (often deduced from a single observation or personal experience), whilst Webb, with his miraculous memory for facts and power of reading books almost as fast as he could turn over the leaves, was the inductive empiric of the partnership and wasted none of his time in theory and logic." Furthermore, "Webb was intensely English and I ineradicably Irish, so that our views often clashed at first impact and our fierce argu-

ments worked out to a unique conclusion of which we would
have been separately incapable."

As the Swedish proverb puts it:

When the blind person carries the lame, both go forward.

MAY 2

On this day in the year 1927, Edna St. Vincent Millay
thanked Llewelyn Powys for dedicating *The Verdict of
Bridlegoose* to her.

"It is a lovely book," said the American poetess, who had
been ill for some time and could not see well enough to read.
"Nobody can express as you do how precious a thing is life,
and how delicate & how to be cherished. I shall never forget
the old janitress. It is incredible that she could die, who in her
youth had seen wild deer with golden branches on their
heads."

As the Turkish proverb puts it:

One who has been near death knows the value of life.

MAY 3

On this day in the year 1621, Francis Bacon was impeached
by the House of Lords for corruption in office.

"The Lord Viscount St. Alban to pay a fine of 40,000
pounds," the verdict stipulated. "To be imprisoned in the
Tower during the King's pleasure. To be forever incapable of
holding any public office, place or employment in the commonwealth. Never to sit in Parliament nor come within the
verge of the Court." Yet when Parliament had opened for the
session in January, Sir Francis was sitting at the pinnacle of
glory. He was Lord Chancellor, Baron Verulam, and Viscount St. Alban. His new book *Novum Organum* was receiving the plaudits of all Europe. His palatial residences, with
gilded statues of Jupiter and Apollo, were the gathering
places of noblemen, knights, and celebrities. Ben Jonson de-
claimed verses in his honor. He was the King's favorite. Who
dare harm Sir Francis?

As the Greek proverb puts it:

Call no man happy till he dies.

MAY 4

On this day in the year 1961, Richard S. Peters expressed dismay at the state of education as a discipline.

The professor from Birbeck College of the University of London said he was "appalled by the looseness, fogginess, and general lack of rigor that one meets when reading some of the literature on issues such as 'democracy in education,' 'equality of opportunity in education,' and the 'aims of education.' "

As the Hindi proverb puts it:

Knowledge is useless to the person without discernment.

MAY 5

On this day in the year 1837, Horace Mann was agreeably surprised in meeting his friend B. Taft, who reminded him of their association in establishing the Worcester Hospital.

"If ever I performed a disinterested act, it was in my efforts to found that institution; and I have been fully rewarded therefor," the American educator reflected to himself that evening. "Indeed, I have observed that acts emanating from worthy motives have almost always invariably yielded me an ample requital of pleasure; while those which sprung from a selfish motive, however intellectually judicious, have, at least in their connections and remoter results, ended in annoyance or injury. Is this fancy? Or is there some mysterious, indissoluble connection between embryo motive and physical result, just as there is between the invisible, impalpable quality of a germ, and the self-exposing, self-diffusing character of the fruit? Surely it is not above or beyond the wisdom of the Deity to ordain such a connection."

As the German proverb puts it:

God knows who are the best pilgrims.

MAY 6

On this day in the year 1854, Giuseppe Verdi received wild applause for his *La Traviata* in Venice.

Yet it was only 14 months before that the première in the same city had been a disaster. The tenor had lost his voice.

The baritone had performed perfunctorily because he felt the role was beneath his dignity. Whenever the plump soprano coughed during the touching scene of her tuberculosis, the audience would roar with laughter. But Verdi was not discouraged. He knew that in time the greatness of the work would reveal itself. "I am not upset," he wrote to the conductor Ignazio Mariani. "Either I am wrong or they are. For my part I do not believe the last word on *Traviata* was spoken." Indeed it was not. The opera has since become one of the most popular in all repertories.

As the French proverb puts it:

Patience is the art of hoping.

MAY 7

On this day in the year 1824, Ludwig van Beethoven gave the opening performance of his *Ninth Symphony* in Vienna.

"The gigantic creations," in the praises of the critics, were received "with deepest appreciation" and "closest attention." The ovation for the composer was enthusiastic, as he bowed again and again. But the receipts disappointed him. The account after the concert showed less than $600 left for him. When everybody sat down at the celebration dinner which Beethoven had arranged, he accused his biographer Anton Schindler of conniving with the theater management and cheating him out of his rightful due. Beethoven further stated that he had been informed of the fraud by a reliable source and that he had brought Count Karl Brühl along to audit the figures. Beethoven's guests felt insulted and left.

As the Hebrew proverb puts it:

Spread the table and contention will arise.

MAY 8

On this day in the year 1958, Linus Pauling repeated his warning on the long-term menace of the radioisotope carbon-14 liberated in atomic tests.

On the basis of the ongoing rate of testing, his calculations predicted that a year's explosion of 30 megatons would ultimately lead to 230,000 seriously defective children and 420,-

000 embryonic and neonatal deaths. Bomb tests carried up to then would lead to an estimated genetic damage of over a million seriously defective children and over 2 million embryonic and neonatal deaths from all radioisotopes produced. "As other people have pointed out, these numbers will represent a minute fraction of the total number of seriously defective children and of embryonic and neonatal deaths during coming centuries," the Nobel Laureate in chemistry admitted in his letter to a newspaper editor. "But I feel that each human being is important, and that it is worthwhile to calculate the numbers of individual beings who will be caused to suffer or to die because of the bomb tests, rather than talk about 'negligible effects,' 'undetectable increase,' 'extremely small fraction.' "

As the Sanskrit proverb puts it:

Noninjury is the highest duty.

MAY 9

On this day in the year 1746, Voltaire was finally admitted to the French Academy.

The philosopher succeeded only after yet another determined campaign in which he touched all bases and manipulated all levers. He publicized his great regard for the Jesuits. He elaborated on his admiration for the King. He praised the royal mistress to the skies. When the amiable Pope Benedict XIV accepted the dedication of his *Mahomet,* Voltaire ended his letter of appreciation with the sentiment: "With the utmost respect and gratitude I kiss your sacred feet."

As the Chinese proverb puts it:

He who sacrifices his body to fame is a caged pheasant.

MAY 10

On this day in the year 1920, Thomas Mann allowed the first chapter of *The Magic Mountain* to appear in a local newspaper.

The German author had already received warm compliments as he read excerpts from the manuscripts to an audience 2 weeks before. The critic Berthold Brecht was especially commendatory. To him, the novel conveyed the sense of a "refined or naive guerrilla war against death. . . . The general fate of the many who are watching death has created a peculiar culture—a certain *savoir mourir* perhaps—which in its playful charm hides the painful difficulties which have been inwardly overcome." Each description was rich in metaphysical ramifications. "The story of the dying woman who does not want to die, who kicks her legs in opposition when the priest comes to her, is incomparable in its mixture of profound horror and charming grandeur. So also is the story of the dying boy who makes a frivolous little play for the ladies out of his terribly lonely and intense battle with death in its mixture of restraint and love."

As the Pashto proverb puts it:

Do not die before your appointed time.

MAY 11

On this day in the year 1864, Ulysses S. Grant reported his heavy losses after 6 days of hard fighting at the Battle of Spottsylvania to the Union army's Chief of Staff but "propose to fight it out on this line if it takes all summer."

Up to that point 11 general officers and 20,000 men had lost their lives. But the battle was won in another 2 days and the Confederates were forced to retreat from their strategic positions. The Lieutenant General promptly sent off a message to Secretary of War Edwin M. Stanton, recommending promotions for "the gallant and distinguished services in the last eight days' battles." The list included the rank of major general for Brigadier General George C. Meade, Colonel S.S. Carroll, and Colonel E. Upton.

As the Jamaican proverb puts it:

If you want milk, feed the goat.

MAY 12

On this day in the year 1495, Charles VIII celebrated his conquest of Naples.

Feeling that he had successfully consolidated his claim, the King of France left for home on May 20. But the League of

Venice had not been broken. The Italian army of nearly 20,-
000 strong regrouped on the banks of the Taro tributary to
the Po, and the Fourth Marquis of Mantua, Francesco Gonzaga, was determined to destroy the French army of 10,000.
During the engagement, however, Gonzaga had not seen fit
to fortify the foot of the mountain track, which would have
bottled up the enemy. Instead, he allowed it to file out unmolested. As he attacked them across the river, his fragile communication chain broke down, when some of the specially
designated officers were killed. Confusion resulted. Furthermore, he had made no provision for effective control of his
mercenaries, who became sidetracked from fighting into the
more remunerative looting. Many units deserted. As a result,
3500 Italians, including all of Gonzaga's relatives, lost their
lives. Only 200 Frenchmen died, as the rest resumed their
march northward unmolested.

As the English proverb puts it:

He is the best general who makes the fewest mistakes.

MAY 13

On this day in the year 1955, Hu Feng wrote a self-criticism
of his own views on literary excellence in the *Jen Min Jih
Pao.*

For a number of years the Chinese writer had become progressively critical of the orthodox doctrine regarding the
place of authors in a proletarian society. He kept praising the
realism of Balzac, Shakespeare, and other Western authors.
By 1949 he was repeatedly condemning his Chinese confreres
for following the official line. He contended that the insis-
tence on Maoist ideology rather than the facts of life as the
guide to serious literature was an error. The authorities said
nothing in response. Encouraged by some of his supporters,
he grew so bold as to send a long memorandum to the Central Committee in July 1954, challenging the Party's exhortations that writers should steep themselves in Marxism; amend
their bourgeois way of life; mingle with peasants, workers,
and soldiers; join in the advancement of national traditions;
and serve the people. He proclaimed these as "5 daggers
stuck into the heads of the writers." Ten months later, he realized he had gone too far and wrote the retraction in the

Party newspaper in an attempt to salvage his fortunes. But by that time the observing officials had decided that his time was up. He was expelled from the Union of Chinese Writers on May 25 and arrested in July.

As the Samoan proverb puts it:

The grasshopper flies about, but the kingfisher watches him.

MAY 14

On this day in the year 1911, Louis D. Brandeis led the Supreme Court in dissolving the Standard Oil Company of New Jersey into 29 separate corporations.

The Justice felt that the ruthless antilabor practices of trusts were bringing about a revolution of violence. He continued this line of argument for years thereafter, emphasizing the dangers of enlarging trusts being taken over by more powerful socialists. The expropriators of little entities would themselves be expropriated. Vigorous trade unions were seen as a counterforce to this threat to democracy. He reminded his fellow citizens of how a Roman emperor "is said to have remarked in regard to his people that he wished that the Christians had but one neck that he might cut it off by a single blow of his sword." Brandeis suggested the possibility that the socialists may likewise say: "Let these men gather these things together; they will soon have them all under one head, and by a single act we will take over the whole industry."

As the Turkish proverb puts it:

Even the tallest tree has an ax waiting at its foot.

MAY 15

On this day in the year 1532, Thomas More resigned his Great Seal.

The Lord Chancellor was thrown into the Tower soon thereafter and beheaded on July 6 for his refusal to approve King Henry VIII's marriage to Anne Boleyn. Sir Thomas himself had premonitions of such trying times to come when he had accepted the post. "Long having meditated leisure, lo

I am unexpectedly thrown into the stream of affairs," he had prophesied to Desiderius Erasmus. "My friends here exult vehemently and congratulate me . . . You perhaps will pity my fortune."

As the Chinese proverb puts it:

Swim not in the tides of the world and their storms will not lash against your breast.

MAY 16

On this day in the year 1960, Titamaua, Bogugsep, Fafato, and 13 other Miamin warriors stood trial for the murder of Wabuo of the Suwana tribe.

The raiders had surrounded the doomed house at night. At daybreak, they called for Apominga and his wife. As the couple stepped out, Bogugsep hacked Apominga with an ax. Titimaua severed the limbs, opened the chest, and cut out the liver. The other members carefully wrapped the pieces in leaves. Wabuo was next, then a third. The wives were carried off with the packages. On their return the Miamin tribe held a feast of flesh and taro. In his summation of the case, Chief Justice A. H. Mann of the Supreme Court of the Territory of Papua and New Guinea reviewed the mores of the defendants. "Apparently they have to rely upon raids of this kind to obtain wives for their young men, and the killing, cutting up and eating of the women's husbands appear to be accepted by the women as something inevitable and final, so that they simply accept the position and make no attempt to escape. The cannibalism involved was merely ritualistic and was not made the occasion of any very obvious form of celebration. On the other hand, it was evidently not solely a matter of obtaining fresh meat." Under the circumstances he recommended that the death sentence be commuted. It ended as a 3-year imprisonment.

As the French proverb puts it:

To understand everything is to forgive everything.

MAY 17

On this day in the year 1926, Don Marquis lectured to a large Yale audience in Sprague Hall, delighting the students with nuggets of humor, such as King Solomon being the first columnist of note.

The American writer stood at the crest of his popularity. In 1922 he was enjoying the exceptional salary for a newspaperman of $20,000 from the New York *Herald Tribune;* his play on Broadway, *The Old Soak,* was receiving rave reviews: 3 new books were being released; his feature column, *the lives and times of archy and mehitabel,* was being avidly read—life was great. Within a few years, however, the situation changed radically. He had to pay back $5000 out of $14,000 unearned royalties on his books. The endless stream of bills for the maintenance of 2 households with their servants and entertainments was swamping him. He was so weak physically that he had to lie down after several hours of work. He regretted having "scattered his good stuff so widely." In a sad note to his publisher, he wondered whether "it may be too late, now, to do anything with the ability I have—especially as the potboiler problem is always present—but I'm giving myself a last fling before retiring permanently to the ranks of the superannuated hacks." He was a sick man on a treadmill, severely anxious over eluding fame.

As the Swedish proverb puts it:

Luck never gives but only lends.

MAY 18

On this day in the year 1909, Sergei Diaghilev presented the world premier performance of his Ballet Russes in *Prince Igor* at the Théâtre du Chatelet in Paris.

The impresario staged one of the most memorable ballet openings in the history of the dance with Michel Fokine as choreographer, Nicholas Roerich as designer, and Alexander Borodin as composer. A new era of art form was introduced. The elements of dancing, painting, and music were unified in one expression. Other artistic teams of his included Fokine, Marc Chagall, and Igor Stravinsky in *The Firebird* and Leonide Massine, Erik Satié, Jean Cocteau, and Pablo Picasso in *Parade.*

As the Chinese proverb puts it:

Behind the able person are able persons.

MAY 19

On this day in the year 1893, Emilio Aguinaldo landed back in the Philippines on an American ship.

The Filipino leader quickly organized a military contingent with American aid to fight the Spaniards. American troops arrived later to join him. The combined forces captured Manila on August 13. Aguinaldo then set up a government, convened a congress, and promulgated its constitution as an independent Philippines on January 21, 1899. But the United States had ideas of its own, using its expeditionary army to batter the Filipino troops and chase the remnants from one part of the country to the other until Aguinaldo himself was captured in March 1901. All resistance ceased a year later. The United States then picked up all the marbles and annexed the Philippines itself.

As the Egyptian proverb puts it:

The camel has his scheme and the camel driver has his.

MAY 20

On this day in the year 1498, Vasco da Gama anchored off Calecut, one of the main trading ports of southern India.

The Portuguese explorer had been sent a year before by King Dom Manuel to make geographical discoveries and obtain new sources of spices. For some reason, the negotiations made little headway with the natives. Relationships worsened with time. The Portuguese seemed to have little notion of the local customs and practices. Soon after arrival, the Captain of the ship notified the appropriate high government officials of his desire to make a gift to the King. The officials came and asked what the Captain had in mind. He showed the items: 12 strips of cloth, 4 scarlet hoods, 6 hats, 4 strings of pearl, 1 case of sugar, 2 casks of oil, and 2 of honey. As recorded in the explorer's journal, "When they saw the present they laughed at it, saying that it was not a thing to offer to the king, that the poorest merchant from Mecca, or any other part of India, gave more, and that if he wanted to make a present [as an ambassador from the King of Portugal] it should be in gold, as the king would not accept such things. . . . Upon this they declared that they would not forward his presents, nor consent to his forwarding them himself.

When they had gone, there came certain Moorish merchants and they all deprecated the present which the captain desired to be sent to the king."

As the Slovakian proverb puts it:

The person who wishes to possess must give.

MAY 21

On this day in the year 1947, Bernard Berenson was again bewildered by the behavior of Ignazio Silone toward him.

The 82-year-old connoisseur of art had been enjoying Silone's writings. Yet somehow he was unable to get the author to say very much during the 2 or 3 times they had gotten together. Berenson wondered why. "If I intimidate him why does he accept my invitation?" he pondered in his diary. "Yet he must open his mouth with others or Sylvia Sprigge (for instance) would not be so devoted to him. Do I represent the unclimbable, impenetrable Pharisia, so that he thinks it useless to talk? I cannot make it out, but am more baffled than offended." Perhaps he was already getting an inkling of what he was to realize two years later: "I seldom open a book published today . . . without finding something that increases my feeling of having survived my world, of having been left behind, of being a tolerated ghost in a society 'that knew not Joseph.' "

As the Turkish proverb puts it:

The dog barks but the caravan passes.

MAY 22

On this day in the year 1837, Philip Hone decried the loss of life by steamboats in America, especially in the Western waters.

Such accidents seldom occurred in Europe, where the knowledge about steam devices was no better. "But we have become the most careless, reckless, headlong people on the face of the earth," the New Yorker noted in his chronicle. " 'Go ahead!' is our maxim and password; and we do go ahead with a vengeance, regardless of consequences and indifferent about the value of human life. What are a few hundred persons, more or less? There are plenty in this coun-

try, and more coming every day; and a few years in the life
of a man makes very little difference in comparison with the
disgrace of a steamboat being beaten in her voyage by a rival
craft."

As the English proverb puts it:

People take less care of their conscience than their reputation.

MAY 23

On this day in the year 1962, Reubén M. Jaramillo, his preg-
nant wife, and 3 adolescent sons were dragged from their
home in Tlaquiltenango.

The Mexican revolutionary had been threatening rebellion
if agrarian reforms were too slow in coming. Aided by the
peasants of Morelos, he managed to elude the troops and police sent by President Ruiz Corines for several years. When
Lópes Mateos became President, he offered Jaramillo am-
nesty and promised to reinstate the halted reforms. Nothing
significant happened. The latter could wait no longer. In 1961
he led 5000 landless peasants in occupying unused land in
Michapa and El Guarin, including tracts owned by a friend
of the Morelos Governor. Jaramillo was declared an outlaw
for trespassing on private property. When the government decided in early 1962 to dam the Alto Amacuzac and San
Jeronimo rivers for electric power and irrigation, it became
clear that the 40,000 hectares occupied by Jaramillo's
peasants would become the breadbasket of the region. The
peasants were immediately cleared off the land in February.
Jaramillo and his family were arrested not long thereafter,
driven to the Xochicalco ruins, and there riddled with sub-
machine gun slugs.

As the Arabic proverb puts it:

*Never sit in the place of a person who can say to you,
"Rise!"*

MAY 24

On this day in the year 1969, Jack Elam lifted the curfew he
had imposed on Greensboro during two days of violence at

the North Carolina Agricultural and Technical State University.

The trouble started at nearby Dudley High School. A militant student was barred from the campus ballot. The bitterness among his supporters grew and spread. It burst into anger as they disrupted the election. The university students took up the cause. Gangs armed with guns and chains roamed the neighborhood. Rocks were thrown at passing cars and gunshots fired at the police. The disturbances climaxed in a 2-day exchange of fire between snipers and 500 national guardsmen. It was only after at least 5 policemen were injured and 1 university honor student was killed that the unrest quieted down and the mayor was able to lift the state of emergency.

As the French proverb puts it:

A little bit of bile spoils a great deal of honey.

MAY 25

On this day in the year 1912, Boni De Castellane declared in Troy, New York, that his one ambition in life was to establish a hotel in which the guest may commit suicide at whatever time and in whatever way he chooses.

The Count explained that he had gotten tired of living an empty life of leisure and had decided to go into business. "This is my plan," he announced. "I open a hotel. We call it 'Paradise Found,' or some other beautiful name. The man who is tired of life comes there. He has arranged his affairs. He wants to sleep, sleep, sleep. He enters the hotel and registers. The clerk asks: 'A room with or without, sir?' He means with or without cremation. Very well, the guest wants it with. The clerk remarks: 'That will be $175—yes, in advance, please.' You see there's no fuss about it. The guest knows all about the place and knows why he has come there. He goes to his room. Then, pouf!"

As the English proverb puts it:

Business is business.

MAY 26

On this day in the year 1816, George Gordon Byron met Percy Bysshe Shelley on the shores of Lake Geneva.

The 2 English poets became close friends. One day while they were on a rowboat a violent storm blew up. In his later account of the experience to John Murray, Byron mentioned how concerned he became because Shelley could not swim. "I stripped off my coat—made him strip off his and take hold of an oar, telling him that I thought (being myself an expert swimmer) I could save him, if he would not struggle when I took hold of him—unless we got splashed against the rocks, which were high and sharp, with an awkward surf on us at that minute. We were about a hundred yards from shore, and the boat in peril. He answered me with the greatest coolness, that 'he had no notion of being saved, and that I would have enough to do to save myself, and begged not to trouble me.'"

As the Chinese proverb puts it:

The pine tree reveals its sturdiness in winter.

MAY 27

On this day in the year 1905, Heihachiro Togo destroyed the Russian Baltic Fleet off the coast of Tsushima.

The opposing flotillas did not differ much in overall tonnages. But for years the Japanese had been assiduously preparing for a decisive battle on their home grounds. They built ships that surpassed the Russian ones by several knots. The ammunition was far more devastating. The morale of the Japanese sailors was heightened by the conviction that in their hands rested the survival of the country. Admiral Togo's fleet crossed the T a couple of times and blasted the Russian ships in the process. When the smoke cleared, 8 of the 12 ships of the Russian battleline were sunk and 4 captured, together with the commander Admiral Zinovi Rozhdestvensky. Forty-eight hundred Russian sailors were killed or drowned and 6000 taken prisoners. Japanese losses were set at 3 torpedo boats sunk, several ships damaged, and 700 seamen killed or wounded.

As the Hindustani proverb puts it:

Every cock fights best on his own dunghill.

MAY 28

On this day in the year 1953, Edmund Hillary and Tenzing Norgay rested at 27,500 feet on Mount Everest before the final accent to the top.

After belaying and assisting each other in the closest of teamwork, they stood on the top of the 29,028-foot peak on May 29 at eleven-thirty in the morning. While the Australian mountaineer was admiring the great stretch of scenery below them, as recounted in his report, the sherpa "had made a little hole in the snow and in it he placed various small articles of food—a bar of chocolate, a packet of biscuits, and a handful of candies. Small offerings, indeed, but at least a token gift to the gods that all devout Buddhists believe have their home on this lofty summit. While we were together on the south col two days before [expedition leader John] Hunt had given me a small crucifix which he had asked me to take to the top. I, too, made a hole in the snow and placed the crucifix beside Tenzing's gifts."

As the Albanian proverb puts it:

Even the hen looks toward heaven when she drinks water.

MAY 29

On this day in the year 1803, John Wetherall experienced a crisis at sea with the Royal Navy sailing through the Queen's channel to Spithead.

"At 4 P.M. stuck on the Goodwin Sands having caught a fresh air of wind from the ENE. 'What ho, she comes!—Take in the royals topgallant-sails and all of the light-sails. Brace the yards to the wind. Out Boats. Fire signal guns for assistance. Be smart my brave fellows, exert yourselves to get the Ship afloat. Run away the Steam Anchor to the S.E. Well done my brave boys. Now man the barrs and heave away the Cabstern. Drummer beat up and fifer play a merry tune to give the men life to heave the Ship afloat . . .' Such was the language of this terrified tyrant to his men when he thought his honour was in danger," related the seaman's log. "And in one minute after she was afloat, 'Silence, damn you all!' was the first salute of honour the Moment he found the Ship was afloat."

As the Chinese proverb puts it:

The friendship of officials is as thin as their papers.

MAY 30

On this day in the year 1850, Edward Amasa Parks attempted to reconcile intellectualism and pietism in a sermon before the Congregational ministers in Boston.

He spoke of the theology of the intellect, preferring the general to the specific, which "conforms to the laws, subserves the wants and secures the approval of our intuitive and deductive powers" and of the theology of the feelings, preferring the specific to the general, which "is suggested by, and adapted to the wants of the well-trained heart." Confounding the former scientific type with the latter poetic type ruins both. Rather than an intruding domination of one over the other, he hoped for a mutual enriching: "That the intellect will yet be enlarged so as to gather up all the discordant representations of the heart and employ them as the complements, or embellishments, or emphases of the whole truth; that the heart will be so expanded and refined as to sympathize with the most subtle abstractions of the intellect; that many various forms of faith will yet be blended into a consistent knowledge, like the colors in a single ray; and thus will be ushered in the reign of the Prince of Peace . . . when the fancy shall wait upon rather than trifle with the judgment, and the judgment shall not be called as now to restrain the fancy, when the passions shall clarify rather than darken the reasoning powers, and the conscience shall not be summoned as now to curb the passions, when the intellect shall believe, not without the heart, nor against the heart, but *with the heart into salvation . . ."*

As the Croatian proverb puts it:

While scholars philosophize, fools live.

MAY 31

On this day in the year 1900, Frederick Sleigh Roberts captured Johannesburg.

Pretoria fell a week later and formal resistance in the Boer War came to an end when the British forces linked up at

Vlakfontein on July 4. Transvaal was absorbed into the British Empire on September 3. Guerrilla warfare continued, however, causing endless disruptions in communications and exasperating all attempts to bring it to an end. Erection of a line of protective blockhouses was ineffective. Pursuit produced no better results. Field Marshal Horatio Herbert Kitchener, who had taken over the command from Field Marshal Roberts, finally resorted to the Spanish tactics that has been used in Cuba. Flying columns of mounted infantry swept through the country. Farms providing sustenance for the Boer raiders were burnt. Some 120,000 Boer women and children were herded into concentration camps, in which some 20,000 died of disease and neglect. By means of such measures, the guerrilla activities were slowly ground to a halt after 18 months.

As the English proverb puts it:

Destroy the nest and the birds will fly away.

JUNE 1

On this day in the year 1857, Manuel Domínguez was hooked under the chin and then in the eye of Barrabás, the greatest gray bull of Concho y Sierra.

The Spanish matador recovered and was back in the ring within 3 months. For the next 17 years of bullfighting, the 1-eyed Domínguez was hailed as Desperdicios—the Cast-off Scraps, from the way which he had contemptuously cast the gouged-out eyeball aside.

As the Bulgarian proverb puts it:

No hero without wound.

JUNE 2

On this day in the year 1937, Waldo H. Dubberstein told a Chicago audience that the collective bargaining being pressed throughout the country by the labor unions at the time had actually been in use for 5000 years.

The instructor in oriental history at the University of Chicago described the formation of unions by skilled craftsmen around 3063 B.C. "As the guilds were responsible to society for the good behavior of their members, collective bargaining became a part of the day." Among the things discussed by the citizens of Babylon over beakers of beer were old age pensions and governmental interference in industry. "The government attempted to regulate by price fixing and monopoly, having full control over the salt industry and fishing rights," he related. "The government, believing that high prices would bring down prosperity, made unsuccessful attempts to lower them."

As the Danish proverb puts it:

Young pigs grunt as old pigs grunted before them.

JUNE 3

On this day in the year 1162, Thomas Becket was consecrated Archbishop of Canterbury.

The post was procured for him by Henry II. But the King did not realize what he had bargained for. He had always know Becket as a worldly man of affairs. Becket was not even a priest before his election as Archbishop. He had been Chancellor to the King, managing all secretarial functions and revenues, as well as itinerant judge. He had been a lavish spender, taking along rare silks, tapestries, and a personal entourage of 200 when he traveled to Europe to arrange for the marriage of Henry's 3-year-old son to Louis VII's infant daughter in France. He had also been a military man, providing some 5000 soldiers in the war against France in 1159. In all this he had been very responsive to the King's desires. The King had imagined that he would continue to be so in his new post. It seemed, however, that overnight the Archbishop became determined to serve the Church above all and directed his entire being and talent for insistent innovations along this direction. He set out to insure the complete freedom of the Church from secular constraints. This led eventually to the head-on conflict between Becket and his royal patron, ending with Becket's murder in the Cathedral by 4 barons on December 29, 1170.

As the English proverb puts it:

A person is the creature of circumstances.

JUNE 4

On this day in the year 1921, Rabindranāth Tagore asked
C. F. Andrews whether his country's freedom was to come
directly from the King's Messenger or from the British Parliament.

The Indian sage had long warned against the phantasy of
independence, as aggressively embodied in the viciousness of
violence. In an earlier letter to his friend, he had tried to
point out that *Sarawāj* (self-rule) is *maya* (illusion). Like a
vanishing mist, it leaves "no stain on the radiance of the
Eternal. However we may delude ourselves with the phrases
learnt from the West, *Sarawāj* is not our objective. Our fight
is a spiritual fight—it is for Man. We are to emancipate Man
from the meshes that he himself has woven round him—these
organizations of national egoism. The butterfly will have to
be persuaded that the freedom of the sky is of higher value
than the shelter of the cocoon. If we can defy the strong, the
armed, the wealthy—revealing to the world the power of the
immortal spirit—the whole castle of the Giant Flesh will van-
ish in the void. And then Man will find his *Sarawāj*."

As the Chinese proverb puts it:

> *The silkworm, which weaves its cocoon and stays inside, is
> imprisoned; the spider, which weaves its web and stays out-
> side, is free.*

JUNE 5

On this day in the year 1871, Cakobau was given a new all-
white ministry to replace the "native government" at Levuka
in the Fiji.

The decline of self-rule was predestined since the first
tradesmen and missionaries arrived in the Southwest Pacific
islands in the 1790s. On October 10, 1874, the unconditional
Deed of Cession transferring sovereignty to Queen Victoria
was forced on Cakobau and the other chiefs. "The whites
who have come to Fiji are a bad lot . . . if we do not cede
Fiji, the white stalkers of the beach, the cormorants, will
open their maws and swallow us," lamented Cakobau. He
kept hoping that somehow the annexation would at least
unify the natives and the whites so that the stronger could
support the weaker against the marauders. But disillusion-

ment was not slow in coming. Finally, Cakobau presented to the Queen's representative for delivery to Her Majesty "the only thing he possess that may interest her"—his favorite war club.

As the Congolese proverb puts it:

The key that opens is also the key that locks.

JUNE 6

On this day in the year 1942, Frank J. Fletcher and Raymond A. Spruance emerged victorious in the Battle of Midway over Isoroku Yamamoto and Chuichi Nagumo.

The Japanese admirals had thought that there were no American carriers in the Central Pacific and that most of the remaining American ships were cruising north to meet the Aleutian threat. So the commanders sent half of their attack planes against Midway on the early morning of June 4. In the middle of the hour-long preparation for a second strike against the island, in which their reserve planes were being stripped of armor-piercing bombs and torpedoes and rearmed with incendiaries and fragmentation bombs, Nagumo was startled with a report from his search planes that a formation of large American warships was sighted to the northeast. In the meantime, attack planes from the American carriers, *Enterprise* and *Hornet*, and half from the *Yorktown* had already been launched against the 4 Japanese carriers at seven to seven-thirty in the morning. By ten twenty-five the *Akagi*, *Kaga*, and *Soryu* were flaming wrecks. By five P.M. the *Hiryu* was destroyed. Yamamoto tried to lure the American big ships into a desperate frontal engagement but to no avail. And the Japanese steamed away in flight. After 2 days of pursuit, Admiral Spruance, who took over the command after Admiral Fletcher's ship, the *Yorktown*, was disabled, sailed back with the recognition that Yamamoto, without his fleet carriers, was doomed to be on the defensive from then on.

As the English proverb puts it:

The first blow is half the battle.

JUNE 7

On this day in the year 1899, William James repeated his temperamental aversion against bigness to Mrs. Henry Whitman.

The professor was sick of its "inviolable molecular moral forces that work from individual to individual, stealing in through the crannies of the world like so many soft rootlets, or like the capillary oozing water, and yet rending the hardest monuments of man's pride, if you give them time. The bigger the unit you deal with, the hollower, the more brutal, the more mendacious is the life displayed." Rather than big organizations, big successes, and big results, especially those on a national scale, James favored "the eternal forces of truth which always work in the individual and immediately unsuccessful way, underdogs always, till history comes, after they are long dead, and puts them on top."

As the Georgian proverb puts it:

Better drink fresh water from the small spring than salt water from the great ocean.

JUNE 8

On this day in the year 1917, John J. Pershing arrived at Liverpool to assume command of the American Expeditionary Forces.

The General of the Armies was accompanied by a small group of officers as he stepped off the Cunarder *Baltic*. After the formal welcome by their British counterparts, one of the hosts pointed to the cadre and asked, "Is this your complete *personal* staff, General?" Pershing replied, "No, this is my complete *general* staff."

As the Italian proverb puts it:

Whosoever wishes to be ill served, let him have many servants.

JUNE 9

On this day in the year 1831, Alexis de Tocqueville analyzed the character of the American people for the benefit of his friend Chabral, following his latest trip to the United States.

The French statesman-writer saw a conglomerate society of all nations, "a society without roots, memories, prejudices, routines, common ideas, or national character." Private interest operates as the cohesive element holding them together. The common index of value is "How much money does it bring in?" Although this goal of getting rich may lead to an orderly community, the people themselves are caught up in its restless pursuit. The instability is pervasive: "In the course of his life an American will take up, give up, then take up again ten different occupations; he is continually changing his home and constantly starting new enterprises." The American is less reluctant than anyone else in the world to risk "a fortune once acquired, for he feels that he can easily gain another. Moreover, to him change is man's natural state and how could it be otherwise? Everything around him is constantly in motion: laws, opinions, public officials and fortunes; even the land itself here is daily changing in appearance. In the midst of this universal movement the American could not stay still."

As the Malayan proverb puts it:

As the drum beats, so goes the dance.

JUNE 10

On this day in the year 1962, Sanzo Nosaka called for the termination of American power in Japan.

"Scrap the United States-Japan Security Treaty," shouted the Communist leader in his election campaign. "See that the United States Forces go home." Yet when he had returned to Tokyo in January 1946, after a long absence in Russia and China, he moved his party along the path of "peaceful revolution." The "lovable Communist Party" cooperated with the United States Occupation Army. Nosaka was even criticized by the Comminform in 1950 as having "gone soft on capitalism." By sticking to his mode of adapting to the situational realities, he enlarged the Japanese Communist Party to 1 million members and 3 million votes by 1949. He himself rose progressively through the political ladder to become a member of the upper house of the Diet.

As the Chinese proverb puts it:

The bamboo bends with the blast.

JUNE 11

On this day in the year 1666, Michel de Ruyter faced the British navy in the Channel between Dunkirk and the Downs.

The long engagement left the English with 11 ships sunk and 11 more captured and with 2300 prisoners and 5000 killed and wounded. The Dutch lost only 6 ships and had 2000 killed and wounded. As the victorious fleet headed home with flags and streamers flying, de Ruyter was his own serene self aboard his flagship *Seven Provinces*. As noted in the logs by a fellow officer, "I have never seen him otherwise than even tempered, and when victory was certain he always said it is God who gives it to us. In any disorder and when loss seemed certain, he appeared to me to be thinking only of the misfortunes of his country, but always submissive to the will of God. It might be said that he has something of the freedom and the absence of courtliness of the patriarchs; and finally, the day after the victory, I found him sweeping out his room and feeding his chickens."

As the Sanskrit proverb puts it:

A good disposition gains all.

JUNE 12

On this day in the year 1966, Pablo Neruda explained to Robert Bly how it came about that, despite all the intense and dangerous political entanglements over decades, his poetry remained progressively more human and affectionate.

The Chilean poet put his finger on the nub of many influences. His fellow countrymen are a politically conscious people and provide considerable stimulus to his activities. "Practically all the writers in Chile are out to the left—there are almost no exceptions. We feel supported and understood by our own people. That gives us great security and the numbers of people who support us are very great. You see the elections in Chile are won by one side or the other by a few votes only. As poets we are really in touch with the people, which is very rare." Neruda himself reads his poems "everywhere in my country—every village, every town—for years and years, and I feel it is my duty to do it. It is a tiresome thing, but partly from that has come my attachment to politics. I have seen so much. The poverty I see—I cannot get away from it."

As the Hindi proverb puts it:

Great rivers, shady trees, medicinal plants, and virtuous people are not born for themselves.

JUNE 13

On this day in the year 1783, Pierre-Augustin Caron de Beaumarchais stood awaiting the opening of his play, *The Marriage of Figaro*.

Half an hour before curtain time, the King's messenger arrived with an order to the actors to refrain from going on stage "under pain if incurring His Majesty's wrath." At an earlier private showing the King had been angered by the playwright's irreverence. "Because you are a great lord, you believe you are a great genius! Nobility, fortune, rank, position, all that makes you so great! What have you done to enjoy so many advantages?" Thus did Beaumarchais' Almaviva insult the King's associates: "You have taken the trouble to be born—nothing more! . . . Pretend not to know what one knows and to know what one does not know . . . appear profound when one is empty and hollow . . . try to ennoble the poverty of means by the importance of objectives—that's all there is to politics." *Figaro* was finally permitted a public showing at the Comédie-Francaise about 6 months later. The audience loved it but the critics panned it. In the exchange, Beaumarchais affronted the King's brother. For that he was thrown into Saint-Lazare—the prison for juvenile delinquents, who are detained for one night for misdemeanors and given a spanking on their *fesses*. Beaumarchais was released red-faced.

As the Polish proverb puts it:

Whosoever blows into a hive will have a swollen face.

JUNE 14

On this day in the year 1940, André Gide expressed his sadness not so much at France's capitulation to Germany, as at the unrealism of the *flatus vocis* in the air.

"Despite everything, we shall shout very loud: 'Honor is

saved!' resembling that lackey in Malraux who says: 'I don't like people to show disrespect for me' while receiving a kick in the rear," wrote the French novelist in his journal. "Doubtless there is no shame in being conquered when the enemy forces are so superior, and I cannot feel any; but it is with an indescribable sorrow that I hear these phrases that exhibit all the shortcomings that have brought us to our ruin: vague and stupid idealism, ignorance of reality, improvidence, heedlessness, and absurd belief in the value of token remarks that have ceased to have credit save in the imagination of simpletons."

As the Tamil proverb puts it:

> *Even when kicked about and rolling in the dust, he boasts that his mustache had not touched the earth.*

JUNE 15

On this day in the year 1601, Matteo Ricci demonstrated the superiority of his calculations on the eclipse of the moon over that of the Board of Mathematics in Peking.

The Italian Jesuit had gone to China in 1582 to convert the Chinese. He followed the usual missionary approach of his order at mastering the thinking of the heathens and showing through devastating skill in disputing how all knowledge conforms to its sacred theology. Mathematics and astronomy were to serve as his principal salients. The Chinese had attached great importance to the calendar as a result of its astrological, as well as practical, implications. Dates for plowing, harvesting, moving, marrying, and other activities must be propitious. The Emperor's own program must be in harmony with the heavenly movements. When Ricci had predicted the eclipse of the moon and the sun with far greater accuracy than the Chinese on several occasions, his hopes of being invited to reform the Chinese calendar were raised. Through such an official relationship he would then be in a position to establish a firm foothold for Catholicism. But the request never came. Although he was highly respected, he never saw the Emperor. When he died in 1610 he made but few converts. There were just too many competing mathematicians, too many jealous eunuchs, too many Chinese to be converted. And there was only 1 Ricci.

As the Japanese proverb puts it:

One cannot dissipate the mist with a fan.

JUNE 16

On this day in the year 1902, Albert Einstein was appointed Technical Expert (Third Class) in the Swiss Patent Office.

After 2 years his salary was raised from 3500 francs to 3900; but his grade remained the same, since, in the words of the supervisor, "He is not yet fully accustomed to matters of mechanical engineering." It took yet another 2 years in 1906 before he was promoted to Class II, the director noting in his justification that Einstein had "acquired the title of Dr. Phil. from the University of Zurich." Despite the fact that Einstein had no associates within the office with whom to discuss his scientfic thoughts, he managed to publish several important papers on his own between 1902 and 1905. Then in the spring of 1950, he unveiled the ideas already outlined in a letter to his friend, Conrad Habicht: the first one "is on the radiation and energy of light, and it is very revolutionary as you will see for yourself . . . The second discusses the methods of measuring the real dimensions of atoms by studying the diffusion and internal friction of liquid solutions. The third shows that . . . bodies of the order of .001 mm in size when suspended in liquid undergo apparently random motions due to the thermal movements of the molecules . . . The fourth . . . changes the theory of space and time . . ." Modern physics has not been the same since.

As the Creole proverb puts it:

A good cock crows in any henhouse.

JUNE 17

On this day in the year 1952, Jacobo Arbenz Gúzman imposed sweeping land reforms in Guatemala.

The President decreed a redistribution of all absentee-owned property with compensation in 20-year bonds at 3% interest on declared tax values. Intensively cultivated land was exempted, although fallow and other uncultivated lands were also redistributed above a certain acreage. Since a large part of Guatemala's plantations belonged to the United Fruit

Company, the United States reacted quickly, having already stopped selling arms to Guatemala since 1948 and having confiscated a Swiss shipment in the interim. The United States pushed through a censuring motion in a 1954 meeting of the Foreign Ministers of the Organization of American States. Finally, it armed a rebel army from Honduras and Nicaragua, supported by 6 P-47s piloted by American volunteers, under a Guatemalan graduate of the United States Command and General Staff College at Fort Leavenworth, Kansas, by the name of Colonel Carlos Costillo Armas. Arbenz was deposed with ease.

As the Spanish proverb puts it:

Whether the pitcher hits the stone or the stone hits the pitcher, woe be to the pitcher.

JUNE 18

On this day in the year 1905, Lev Nikolaevich Tolstoy contemplated the far-reaching significance of the Japanese destruction of the Russian fleet.

The Russian author noted in his diary that the ramifications went beyond the destruction of the Russian military to that of the pseudo-Christian civilization. The process had begun long ago "in the struggle for money, the struggle for success in the so-called scientific and artistic fields of activity." Later in the year, he expanded on his views about where the movement was leading to the English newspaperman Henry W. Nevinson, who was his house guest at Yasnaya Polyana: "As you grow older you will find, as I have found, that day follows day, and there does not seem much change in you, till suddenly you hear people talking of you as an old man. It is the same with an age in history; day follows day, and there does not seem to be much change, till all of a sudden it turns out that the age has become old. It is finished; it is passé." The clashes between workers and soldiers the previous January in St. Petersburg and other social disturbances were not simply riots or even revolutions. As Tolstoy saw it, they represented "the end of an age."

As the Japanese proverb puts it:

With the fall of a single leaf, we know that autumn has come to the world.

JUNE 19

On this day in the year 1917, John Quinn wrote a qualification and rebuttal to George Russell, regarding the latter's views on "style."

To Russell, style was basically a concomitant of intellectual honesty and unselfconsciousness: "Style is truth telling at its root. It is saying exactly what one feels or thinks, and if one does that, adding nothing, exaggerating nothing or sophisticating nothing, if the thought, feeling or imagination is good the literary expression will be good. That is my gospel, briefly, and the folks who write learnedly and endlessly about style bore me." To this, his friend and patron of artists and writers replied: "Imitation, of course, will not make great art, nor fine writing make great art, nor taking thought as to style. Neither will truth telling produce great art. . . . At the same time, matter is not everything . . . It takes the miracle of style for a work of art to be really living, whether painting or poetry or prose. But that doesn't come by thinking overmuch of style."

As the Australian proverb puts it:

Printing of twaddle is a waste of time and money.

JUNE 20

On this day in the year 1921, Billy Mitchell began a series of tests to demonstrate that a direct hit is not necessary for an aerial bomb to sink a warship.

The American army officer had been championing the efficacy of air power against what he criticized as obstructionists on the General Staff. Secretary of the Navy Josephus Daniels joined the opposition, as he scoffingly said that he was prepared "to stand bareheaded on the deck of a battleship and let Brigadier General Mitchell take a crack at me with a bombing airplane." The War Department eventually gave in to public and congressional pressures and authorized a field test. Five abandoned naval vessels were provided. As the world looked on, the bombers flew first over an old submarine, then an obsolete battleship, a relatively new destroyer, a more modern cruiser, and finally the "unsinkable" German battleship *Ostfriesland*. Every single one went under. But Secretary of War John W. Weeks remained unmoved, stating that he was not going to be stampeded "by that circus performer." Despite restraining directives from his superiors, Mitchell persisted in his campaign and attracted greater attention than ever. This led to his court martial on October 28, 1925, for breaking discipline and damaging the morale of the army. He was convicted on December 17 and stripped of his general's star and command.

As the Egyptian proverb puts it:

The tongue is the neck's enemy.

JUNE 21

On this day in the year 1895, Charles A. Barber fell off the log he was driving on the Connecticut River at Summer's Falls in Vermont and drowned.

The body of the 19-year-old riverman was fished out of the water, left on the bank, and covered with a blanket. The paymaster than wired his father, who sped up from Cherryfield with a pair of fast horses. He collected the $300 back pay owed his dead son and took off without tending to the body. The fellow workers buried Charles beside the road, scratched his name on a stone, and placed it over the gravesite. Thus passed the life of another of the thousands of tough and nameless lumbermen among the tall trees in the New England forests, who provided the wood for the pretty houses and furnishings in the towns.

As the Ethiopian proverb puts it:

Those who wear pearls do not know how many times the divers have been bitten by the sharks.

JUNE 22

On this day in the year 1611, Henry Hudson was set adrift in Hudson Bay with his son and 7 others in a shallop with neither "food, drink, clothing, or other necessaries."

The English explorer had been searching for a northwest passage to Cathay. He drove his small *Discovery* against the turbulent seas, continually dodging icebergs and chipping ice off her frozen topsides. The men began to grumble against what appeared to them to be a foolhardy adventure. Hudson stubbornly pressed on. When they passed the Hudson Strait into a large body of water, he mistook the Hudson Bay for the Pacific Ocean and sailed due south. He soon found himself maneuvering among islands again. The men grew more anxious. Finally, the ship was locked by ice near the southern shore of James Bay. Supplies ran low. The crew became ill. Morale was shattered. By spring, the crew was homesick and starving. Hudson was suspected of hiding food for himself and close friends. The crew revolted, tossed them into the little boat, and turned home. They were later acquitted by an English court and Hudson was never heard from again.

As the Greek proverb puts it:

The bravest horse is the one that's blind.

JUNE 23

On this day in the year 1757, Robert Clive laid down the indemnity demands after his successful expedition against Siraj-ud-Daula.

When Siraj-ud-Daula took over from his grandfather as Nawab of Bengal in April 1756, he had visions of a greatly expanded domain. Under pretext of a disagreement with the East India Company, he marched against Calcutta. The British defenses caved in with the Governor fleeing ignominiously on June 19. Responding to an urgent appeal, Clive returned to India and recaptured Calcutta in one night. The Nawab was seized and assassinated. Compensation from Bengal amounted to 7.5 million silver rupees and another 4 million rupees. Nine hundred square miles south of Calcutta were annexed by the East India Company. For his own services, Clive was to receive 234,000 pounds from East India on the spot and 30,000 pounds a year for the rest of his life. He dispatched a letter forthwith to his father in Shropshire, asking him to fix up the family mansion and prepare the way for his entry into Parliament.

As the Japanese proverb puts it:

A fight between kingfisher and clam is profitable to the fisherman.

JUNE 24

On this day in the year 1894, Rose Piacintini was abruptly forced off the trolley in Coney Island, New York.

Mrs. Piacintini was on her way from Brooklyn to West Brighton with her 9-month-old infant in her arms. The baby had apparently stopped breathing at the stop in Unionville, but the mother had not noticed it. She suddenly discovered it at the Bridge Station and screamed. The conductor came hurrying over to inquire about the trouble. When he found out, he immediately ejected her, without solace or assistance, and clanged the street car speedily out of sight.

As the German proverb puts it:

It is a good world, but there are bad people in it.

JUNE 25

On this day in the year 1741, Maria Thérèsa knelt, kissed the cross, placed her hand on the Bible, and swore to uphold the laws of Hungary.

No one had foreseen to what detail the new Queen was to govern. One of her most famous schemes was the Chastity Commission of 1753. Public and private turpitude of lust was to be wiped out. Men entertaining "women of the opera" were arrested. So were women strolling the streets at night. Military officers were forbidden to visit houses of ill fame. Prostitutes were shipped off to southern Hungary. All complaints by spouses against each other were to be thoroughly tracked down and appropriate punishments meted out. The drive collapsed. Ladies of pleasure learned to ply their trade unmolested by walking with heads lowered and fingering their rosaries. Among the more organized offenders were members of the Brotherhood of Figleaf and the Order of Free Ladies, who met regularly, attired only in masks and pseudonyms. The Queen's own husband took on Princess Wilhelmina Auersperg as mistress.

As the English proverb puts it:

Nature will have its course.

JUNE 26

On this day in the year 1813, Napoleon Bonaparte argued for over 8 hours with Klemens von Metternich over the possibilities of war between their countries.

The French Emperor tried to intimidate the Austrian Prince: "So you, too, want war! You shall have it! I have beaten the Russians at Bautzen. Now you want your turn. So let it be." The latter was not cowed, feeling that Austria was a member of the coalition with the superior balance of power. He called attention to the potential repetition of 1812, which would now turn out to be a catastrophe for the entire French population, instead of only a small fraction as before. "Is not your army of today made up of the next generation? I have seen your soldiers. They are mere youngsters. Your Majesty has the feeling that you are essential for the country. But is not the country also essential for you? Should the adolescent army that you have raised only yesterday be wiped out, what then?" To which Napoleon snapped back in rage, according to the Prince's cleaned-up version: "You're no soldier, and you don't know what goes on in the mind of a soldier. I was brought up on the battlefield, and a man like me does not get worked up much over the lives of a million men."

As the Chinese proverb puts it:

A general's reputation is made by ten-thousand corpses.

JUNE 27

On this day in the year 1787, Edward Gibbon completed the last lines of his magnum opus, which he had started some 17 years before.

The 6-volume *History of the Decline and Fall of the Roman Empire* reflected the English historian's thesis that the dignity and nobility of man can only come with political and spiritual freedom. It began with an eloquent tribute to the Antonine emperors who tempered their power with civility and gentleness. Then it went on to show how after this line of conscientious and benevolent rulers, Lucius Commodus injected the virus of brutality into the body politic, which brought on a steady degeneration. The cruel and corrupt style of the emperors became emulated by the citizenry in its pursuit of selfish gains and passing pleasures. Within a century or so, the glory of Rome became a thing of the past.

As the Turkish proverb puts it:

Fish rots from the head.

JUNE 28

On this day in the year 1860, Thomas Henry Huxley delivered one of his most forceful defenses of Charles Darwin's theory of evolution.

The *Origin of Species* had appeared during November of the previous year. This not only split the theologians from the scientists, but also the scientists among themselves. The most outspoken antagonist was the Bishop of Oxford; the most committed supporter was the young biology professor. They met that day at a meeting of the British Association. Samuel Wilberforce was first to address the assembly, dropping the casual remark that "I shall like to ask Professor Huxley, who is sitting by me and is about to tear me to pieces when I have sat down, as to his belief in being descended from an ape. Is it on his grandfather's or his grandmother's side that the ape ancestry comes in?" The biologist then proceeded with a serious scientific presentation and concluded in answer to the critic's taunt: "I asserted—and I repeat—that a man has no reason to be ashamed of having an ape for his grandfather. If there were an ancestor whom I should feel shame in recalling it would rather to be a man—a man of restless and versatile intellect—who, not content with an equivocal success in his own sphere of activity plunges into scientific questions with which he has not real acquaintance, only to obscure them by an aimless rhetoric, and distract the attention of his bearers from the real point at issue by eloquent digressions and skilled appeals to religious prejudice."

As the English proverb puts it:

Better say nothing than not to the purpose.

JUNE 29

On this day in the year 1936, Haile Selassie again petitioned the League of Nations for help against Benito Mussolini's invasion of his country.

"What real assistance was given to Ethiopia by the 52 nations who had undertaken to prevent the triumph of the aggressor?" the Emperor challenged the conscience of the representatives in session. "Has each of the member states, as was its duty to do in virtue of its signature appended to Article XVI of the Covenant, considered the aggressor as having committed an act of war personally directed against itself? I had placed all my hopes in the execution of these undertakings. My confidence had been confirmed by the repeated declarations made in the Council to the effect that aggression must not be rewarded and that force would be compelled to bow before right." The League continued looking the other way.

As the Spanish proverb puts it:

Words should be weighed, not counted.

JUNE 30

On this day in the year 1628, Johannes Junius was again exhorted to confess his witchcraft.

At first, the Burgomaster of Hamburg refused to plead guilty. Thumbscrews were applied; he still refused. Legscrews followed; still he refused. Strappado next followed; still he refused. Under compulsion 6 of his former friends and acquaintances testified publicly against him, while begging his forgiveness in private. Finally, on July 5, he broke down. To avoid further torture he fabricated a story about meeting a lady witch in 1624, who changed into a goat and threatened him into recognizing the Devil as his God. He was named Krix and his paramour was called Vixen. Under orders to murder his son, Junius pretended to do so by killing his horse instead. The whole confession was written out and signed on August 6. As per protocol, he was burnt at the stake shortly thereafter.

As the English proverb puts it:

When arguing with a chicken, the cockroach is always wrong.

JULY 1

On this day in the year 1916, Joseph Joffre persuaded Douglas Haig to take the offensive against the Germans along the old Roman road from Alpert to Bapaume in the great plain of northern France.

From July to mid-November Sir Douglas saw his British army grinding away yard by yard in the Battle of the Somme along a 20-odd mile front. The Germans fell back some 7 miles. Bapaume, only 12 miles away, was never reached. But Marshal Joffre called the bloodiest battle in history a victory nonetheless. The overall price? Six-hundred-thousand casualties on each side. The purpose? It was never clear. The area was of minor significance militarily and the defensive lines were exceedingly strong at that point. Some said the reasons were political; others were not so sure.

As the Spanish proverb puts it:

Valor not founded on prudence is rashness.

JULY 2

On this day in the year 1844, Edgar Allan Poe voiced his lack of faith in the perfectibility of man in a letter to James Russell Lowell.

"I think that human exertion will have no appreciable effect upon humanity. Man is now only more active—not more happy—nor more wise, than he was 6000 years ago," the American writer concluded. "The result will never vary—and to suppose that it will, is to suppose that the foregone man has lived in vain—that the foregone time is but the rudiment of the future—that the myriads who have perished have not been with equal footing with ourselves—nor are we with our posterity."

As the Hausan proverb puts it:

The seed of the baobab does not grow into a tamarind.

JULY 3

On this day in the year 1608, Samuel de Champlain unfurled the fleur-de-lis at the point of Quebec on the St. Lawrence River and marked the birth of Canada as a nation.

The French explorer set peaceful coexistence with the local Montagnais as his first priority. Although he had assisted them in many ways, such as feeding the starving children when their mothers ran out of milk, he was aware that charity alone would not necessarily make anyone a dependable neighbor. He decided that he must help them in a more essential manner. The most dreaded danger facing them and the friendly Algonquins and Hurons upriver was the Iroquois Five Nations from the New York region. Champlain therefore joined the decisive battle the following spring on the shores of Lake Champlain. Two hundred Mohawk warriors slowly advanced from their barricades led by 3 chiefs. Moving to within 200 yards of them, the Montagnais and their allies called on Champlain to show his wares. Loading his harquebus with 4 bullets, he leveled a blast at the chiefs. All 3 went down. A second harquebus roared from the flanks. The Mohawks panicked with the Montagnais in chase. Victory was complete without a single casualty in the ranks of the defenders. From then on, the French enjoyed the finest of relations and trade with the local Indians.

As the Irish proverb puts it:

Go to a person in great difficulty and you get a bargain.

JULY 4

On this day in the year 1934, Joe Louis won his first professional boxing match by knocking out Jack Kracken from Chicago.

The 20-year-old black heavyweight had just been lifted from the amateur ranks through the skillful training of the veteran black fighter-turned-manager Jack Blackburn. Among the first things he passed on to the young poker-faced fighter was the reality of decision making in the arena. There is no use on the part of a black boxer to complain about unfair judgment by white judges and referees when the fight goes the distance. No argument arises about who has won, however, in the case of a knockout. Louis learned quickly and knocked out 10 of his first 12 opponents during the ensuing year.

As the German proverb puts it:

A handful of might is better than a sackful of right.

JULY 5

On this day in the year 1869, John Fiske expressed his great delight at being invited by Charles William Eliot to teach a course on Positivism at Harvard University.

It was the year of theological controversy with the publication of such books as Herbert Spencer's *First Principles* of evolution. To the entrenched school of philosophy, August Comte's Positivism represented the thinking of infidels. But the incoming President Eliot had decided to broaden the range of intellectual offerings to the students. "From the sentimental aspect it is worthy of notice that only 8 years ago I was threatened with dismissal from college if caught talking Comtism to any one," the young scholar wrote in the letter to his mother. "Now, without any solicitation on my part, I am asked to expound Comtism to the college, and defend or attack it as I like. This shows how vast is the revolution in feeling which has come over Harvard in 8 years, and which is shown among other things in the selection of such a President as Eliot."

As the French proverb puts it:

The clash of opinions brings sparks of light.

JULY 6

On this day in the year 1415, John Hus was burnt at the stake for heresy and his ashes thrown into the Rhine.

The Bohemian had defended the English reformer John Wycliffe, opposed the sale of indulgences by the Church on the streets of Prague, and questioned the absolute obedience to the Pontiff. He was excommunicated by the Vatican for these and other actions inimical to the interests of Rome. Although he could have remained in relative safety where he was living, he voluntarily chose to attend the Council of Constance in Germany in 1414, feeling that he was still secure under the protection of King Sigismund, the Holy Roman Emperor, who was to be in attendance. On Hus' arrival, however, he was arrested and placed on trial before the Council. When he refused to recant his views, his books were ordered burnt and he himself condemned to death.

As the Chuanan proverb puts it:

Never follow the beast into its lair.

JULY 7

On this day in the year 1683, Leopold I fled Vienna with his family, servants, riches, jewels, rugs, and everything that could be packed into the available coaches, leaving his people at the mercy of the advancing Turks.

In keeping with his treaty with Austria, King John Sobieski of Poland marched from Krakow, joined the Duke of Lorraine, and routed the besieging Turks on September 12. The rescuers entered the city the following day. The people were worshipfully grateful. Victory was celebrated with a mass in the Augustiner Church and a banquet in the palace of the Commander Count Starhemberg. When word of the liberation reached the Emperor, he immediately sent orders that no celebration was to take place until he arrived. "Otherwise the love of my subjects for me would be diminished, and their affection for others increase." On meeting Sobieski, who had lost half of his men in the campaign, outside Vienna at Schwechat, Leopold thanked him in a stiff and brief Latin speech. He treated his savior as a Hapsburg Emperor would ordinarily receive a mere elected king. He did not even bend one jot from the precise conventional protocol when Sobieski introduced his own son.

As the Greek proverb puts it:

Feed a wolf in the winter and he will bite you in the summer.

JULY 8

On this day in the year 1924, Milne Watson praised the goodwill of the trade union leaders in the gas industry in England.

The President of the National Gas Council took note of the restlessness that seemed to have been building up over several months. He referred to the advantages of short-term agreements, founded in "sweet reasonableness" and spoke warmly about the loyalty and faithfulness of the trade union representatives as well as pledged his own loyalty and faithfulness in facing the difficulties that were certain to rise in the near future. As to long-term contracts, he felt that "it was idle to try to prescribe wages conformable or conditions of service applicable to conditions obtaining in the distant future. Their object was to make such wage agreements as would be in harmony with the prevailing economic situation. It was futile to take the formalistic view that an agreement made years ago under different circumstances and to meet another situation was as inviolable and unalterable as the laws of the Medes and Persians. That did not mean that agreements were to be held in low esteem. The sanctity of agreement was, of course, beyond question or argument."

As the Chinese proverb puts it:

Great faithfulness is not bounded by covenants.

JULY 9

On this day in the year 1854, Matthew C. Perry anchored off the city or Uraga, 27 miles from Tokyo.

The town chief came aboard to discuss arrangements with the commodore's aide about the delivery of a letter from the President of the United States to the Emperor and an appropriate interview with a Japanese dignitary of the highest rank. He stated that Nagasaki was the official place for the conduct of foreign negotiations and the Americans will have to go there. "To which," according to Perry's records, "he was told that I had come purposely to Uraga, it being near to [Tokyo], and should not go [to Nagasaki], that I expected the letter to be duly and properly received where I then was, that my intentions were perfectly friendly, but I would allow no indignity. Nor should I permit the guard boats which were collecting about the ships to remain where they then were, and if they were not immediately removed I would disperse them by force." To this, the Japanese officials got up and waved the boats away. A few of them, however, chose to remain nearby. Perry then sent one of his own boats to motion them away and show their ready weapons at the same time. This "had the desired effect. All of them disappeared and we saw nothing more of them near the ships during the remainder of our stay. Here was the first important point gained."

As the Icelandic proverb puts it:

Keep your teeth in front of your tongue.

JULY 10

On this day in the year 1796, Karl Friedrich Gauss entered into his notebook: EYPHKA! num $= \triangle + \triangle + \triangle$.

Translated, the statement means "Eureka! Every positive integer is the sum of three triangular numbers." A triangular number is one of the sequence, 0, 1, 3, 6, 10, 15 . . . where each number after 0 is of the form ½ n ($n + 1$), n being any positive integer. The prince of mathematics was not yet 20 years of age, when he made such major discoveries as the double periodicity of certain elliptic functions and the regular polygon of 17 sides. Ideas gushed into his mind so rapidly that he often did not have sufficient time to elaborate any exposition. One hundred forty-six of these brilliant mathematical accomplishments, often cryptically given, were recorded in his secret journal, which was not made public until 43 years after his death. He had not bothered to publish his findings during his lifetime, because he had never felt the need for reputation and adulation. He was at peace with the world in just being free to express his own nature in his scientific work.

As the English proverb puts it:

Tranquility begins where ambition ends.

JULY 11

On this day in the year 1780, Axel Fersen arrived from France with Rochambeau's army at Newport.

Count Fersen was known as the handsomest Frenchman alive and one of the greatest lovers. He had risked death several times to save his royal mistress from the guillotine. The eyes of the Newport maidens were glued on the romantic and gallant hero as he strode up and down the avenues. After a survey of the field, he concentrated on Eliza Hunter, just 18. Fersen became a regular visitor to the Hunter household, which was quartering his friend, Duc de Lauzun. He taught Eliza French and Eliza taught him English. The nights grew longer as he spoke of his boyhood in the Swedish courts of Gustav III, where his father was a leading statesman, of the chivalrous tournaments, of the Count's own triumphs. He told of how the Queen of France made up to him in a masked ball, of how they sang the old Swedish folk ballad

"Reap, reap the oats!," of how they stayed long in a private room, of how they became the gossip of the town thereafter. Encouraged, the Count asked for Eliza's hand. She turned him down cold. The Hunter girls were not his kind. As Lauzun noted in his diary, "I never fell in love with the mademoiselles Hunter. But if they had been my sisters I could not have been fonder of them, especially the eldest [Eliza], one of the most charming persons I have ever met."

As the Chinese proverb puts it:

As long as the trunk is firm, worry not over the branches swaying in the wind.

JULY 12

On this day the year 1874, Richard Kyle Fox arrived in the hold of the *Turcarora* at New York from Belfast with his wife and less than $2 in his pocket.

Within 2 years he became the sole owner of the *Police Gazette*. By 1880 the circulation zoomed to 400,000 and Fox became rich. He decided to do something for the poor, who accounted for much of the material for his magazine and many of its readers. He bought and renovated a row of rat-infested slum houses on the Lower East Side. Modern conveniences were installed and the hallways were decorated with pictures and statues of the heavyweight champion, trapeze queen, and other celebrities of the day. Among the first tenants was the famous burglar Barney Blood, fresh out of Sing Sing Prison. On his way the "Piano Tuner" robbed a house in Yonkers. When the cops came to question him, his neighbors attacked them and the first of many riots followed suit. The police battered down Blood's door and hauled him and 7 others off to jail. As time went on, the bronze statues, plumbing fixtures, and other detachables were ripped off and peddled by the occupants. One of them even sold 2 flights of Vermont marble stairs, leaving some tenants marooned on the upper floors, who had to be rescued by the fire department. Fox finally gave up on the project and concentrated on the publishing business.

As the German proverb puts it:

The Devil likes to pour water where it is already damp.

JULY 13

On this day in the year 1865, Horace Greeley gave some advice to young civil servants dissatisfied with their low salaries in Washington, D.C.

"Washington is not a place to live in. The rents are high, the food is bad, the dust is disgusting and the morals are deplorable," the founder of the New York *Tribune* commented in an editorial. "Go West, young man, go West and grow up with the country."

As the Spanish proverb puts it:

A change of pasture makes fat calves.

JULY 14

On this day in the year 1959, Paul P. Schenck succeeded in pushing his bill on limiting exhaust fumes through a congressional subcommittee.

The legislation would require automobile manufacturers to restrict the amount of air pollution emanating from their cars. The Congressman from Ohio was envisioning early relief from the smog for his fellow citizens, as he saw his proposal hurdle the first obstacle on Capitol Hill. But 10 years later, the atmospheric contaminants remained as heavy as ever.

As the Greek proverb puts it:

The tree wants to blossom but the frost will not let it.

JULY 15

On this day in the year 1847, Vissarion Grigor'evich Belinskii found fault with Nikolai Vasilievich Gogol following the publication of his *The Inspector General*.

The literary critic disagreed with the novelist's ideas about the societal and spiritual problems of the times. The book was interpreted as blaming the ills of the people solely on their moral degeneration and not on the country's political, social, and economic system. "Hence you have failed to observe that Russia sees her salvation not in mysticism, not in asceticism, not in pietism, but in the achievements of civilization, enlightenment, and humanitarianism. . . . Even the government . . . knows full well what the landowners do to their peasants and how many of the former have their throats cut by the latter every year . . ." He censured Gogol for not paying due respect to the writer's responsibility as a leader for the nation's progress. "Living in that 'fair faraway retreat' of yours, you remain a total stranger to Russia and live by and in yourself, or in a single-minded coterie which shares your views and is unable to resist your influence."

As the Latin proverb puts it:

The greatest scholars are not the wisest people.

JULY 16

On this day in the year 1945, J. Robert Oppenheimer, Leslie Groves, and other leaders of the Manhattan Project witnessed the successful completion of their $2-billion experiment at Alamogordo, New Mexico.

In the words of one of them, they "embraced" each other "with shouts of glee." They had developed the most devastating and cruelest weapon imaginable by imaginative human beings up to that time. A single primitive prototype annihilated a large city and left 80,000 casualties several months later. An advanced version several decades later could destroy an entire country or kill 50 million people. The feat involved the most brilliant and largest team of professors, scientists, engineers, nobel laureates, and nobel laureates-to-be ever assembled in history. It has given humankind the atomic shivers ever since.

As the Chinese proverb puts it:

It is the clever offspring who ruins the family.

JULY 17

On this day in the year 1429, Charles was crowned King of France at Rheims.

For some time the country had been divided under 2 leaders, the Duke of Burgundy and the Dauphin Charles. The latter had been ruled out by the invading Henry V of England on the grounds of bastardy, although the French people, long used to the practice of father-to-son succession to the throne, did not quite go along. Nevertheless, uncertainty prevailed. On November 1, 1428, the Dauphin himself prayed to God in the privacy of his chambers for deliverance from his grave doubts. The divine guidance came 2 days after his arrival at Chinon in February 1429. A shepherdess had come to see him from Domrémy, one of the Dauphin's own fiefs north of the Loire. She spoke of the saints Catherine and Margaret speaking to her and passing on God's message that he was the King's son and heir to the throne and that she, Joan of Arc, was to save it for him. With that, all paralyzing hesitations concerning the legitimate king disappeared. No Christian could disregard the word of God, especially when buttressed with a few military successes. France was saved, and the people were united.

As the French proverb puts it:

The horse is his who mounts it.

JULY 18

On this day in the year 1939, Henry Miller sailed aboard the *Théophile Gautier* from Marseilles to visit Lawrence Durrell in Corfu, thereby ending his European exile.

The American author was approaching 50 years of age. His reflections over the previous year convinced him that a large part of his life had been wasted. His inept attempt at adapting to the world had been masked as an expression of creative writing. He now realized that he should have been paying greater attention to his inner harmony. "I should have been adapting myself to myself," he conceded in his letter on February 21, 1939, from Paris to Anaïs Nin. "Unconsciously I was, no doubt. With endless groping one finally becomes aware—the random shots in the dark are too striking to be ignored. Every deep realization of this sort is a real advance, a real consolidation in the hitherto blind grasp at the truth. Suddenly you perceive, that, if you listen properly the truth is always speaking to you. And then you become terribly quiet and contained. You cease trying to do more than you can do. You also never do less than you are able to do.

But you work and act from a new level which is like an inexhaustible reserve of strength and inspiration."

As the Chinese proverb puts it:

If a man is not enlightened within, what lamp shall he light?

JULY 19

On this day in the year 1848, Elizabeth Cady Stanton delivered the keynote address at the first women's rights convention in Seneca Falls, New York.

She rallied her fellow suffragettes "to protest against a form of government existing without the consent of the governed—to declare our right to be free as man is free, to be represented in the government which we are taxed to support, to have such disgraceful laws as give man the power to chastise and imprison his wife, to take the wages which she earns, the property which she inherits, and, in the case of separation, the children of her love; laws which make her the mere dependent of his bounty." She expected that against their banners "will beat the dark clouds of opposition from those who have entrenched themselves behind the stormy bulwarks of custom and authority, and who have fortified their position by every means, holy and unholy." But they will persevere. They will march forward. "Undauntedly, we will unfurl it to the gale, for we know that the storm cannot rend from it a shred, that the electric flash will but more clearly show to us the glorious words inscribed upon it, 'Equality of Rights.' " Cheers rose from the female audience and jeers from the male press.

As the French proverb puts it:

A deaf husband and a blind wife make the best couple.

JULY 20

On this day in the year 1922, Harold Newman called for a repeal of the Volstead Prohibition Law and for legalized prostitution in restricted districts in New Orleans, Louisiana.

"Contempt for the Volstead Law has led to contempt of other laws," the President of the New Orleans Association of

Commerce pleaded before the New Orleans Crime Commission. "The abolition of the restricted district has led to the spread of prostitution all over New Orleans." Because of this, working folks and women could not be protected from contamination by the prostitutes, who drift into the workers' residential areas. "This contempt for law is a canker that is serious and that is going to grow more serious," he emphasized. "Let's get back to safe and sane enforcement of law and not make law enforcement a farce as it is in many instances now."

As the Irish proverb puts it:

Trampling on dung only spreads it more.

JULY 21

On this day in the year 1960, Sukarno embarked on a policy of confrontation against Holland.

This meant undeclared war over "the liberation of West Irian." The President of Indonesia had begun to bolster his country's military strength by procuring small shipments of arms from the United States in 1950. By 1957 Djarkarta increased the request to $600 million worth of credit from the Pentagon. Supersonic fighters and landing crafts were desired. Washington declined to oblige. The Indonesians then turned to the Soviet Union. Eager to extend Soviet influence, the Kremlin immediately responded with a $250 million line of credit. In 1958 the Indonesians again requested the United States to reequip 20 battalions, as well as provide a continuing flow of arms, food, and other material. When Washington slowed down in 1960, Indonesia turned to Russia a second time. This resulted in a long-term military assistance program amounting to $1.4 billion. Items included a 19,000-ton cruiser, 26 submarines, scores of destroyers, tenders, and torpedo boats, 26 long-range bombers, 30 fighters, and helicopters. With a fully equipped 330,000-man army, a 50,000-man navy, a 30,000-man air force, and a large population reserve Indonesia felt ready to take on the Dutch.

As the Nigerian proverb puts it:

A canoe is paddled on both sides.

JULY 22

On this day in the year 1692, Don Carlos de Sigüena y Góngora described the fears over the possibility of Mexico City's being flooded by the swelling Lake Texoco.

The Creole poet-scholar observed how the hard-working Viceroy patiently went about trying out all the recommendations from the citizens. One suggested that "there was some opening into the lake through which the water was at present entering and who volunteered to point out its location. To cheer the Viceroy up he asserted that within a short time the whole lake would be dried up again." Another involved a priest, who proposed unplugging a drain in a nearby hill. The designated large tree was dug up and pulled out by the deep roots. Instead of a drain, a spring was found. The Viceroy appointed Sr. Doctor Juan de Excalante y Mendoza as Commissioner of the program, even though he knew nothing about the subject and all his schemes came to naught. The Viceroy apparently did this "in order that the meddling individual might not feel hurt, also in order that a failure to consider this scheme which, in the circumstances under which it was offered, was worthless might not later be construed as neglect on the Viceroy's part in what concerns the welfare of Mexico City."

As the Chinese proverb puts it:

Behave toward everyone as if you are attending a great guest.

JULY 23

On this day in the year 1846, William Henry Seward heard the death sentence pronounced for his client William Freeman.

Freeman was a poor black, who had murdered a family. When Seward visited the jail, he saw that the defendant was "deaf, deserted, ignorant," and his conduct was "unexplainable on any principle of sanity." Despite potential damage to his social and financial position, the former Whig governor of New York and leading citizen of the upstate town of Auburn, agreed to defend him. The strategy adopted was insanity based on the opinion of Lord Chief Justice Tindal in the

M'naghten case of 1843, "that at the time of the committing of the act, [he] was laboring under such a defect of reason, from disease of the mind, as not to know the nature and quality of the act he was doing; or, if he did know it, that he did not know he was doing what was wrong." After several weeks of trial, Seward's arguments remained unconvincing. "I rise from these fruitless labors," he dejectedly wrote his friend, "exhausted in mind and body, covered with public reproach, stunned with protests." His appeal to the Supreme Court, however, bore fruit. The conviction was set aside and a new trial ordered. But the decision came too late; Freeman had died in the meantime. Autopsy revealed an extensive lesion of insanity in the brain. As word of the finding spread, the criticisms evaporated. And Seward resumed his further rise to Senator and Secretary of State.

As the Tamashek proverb puts it:

Take the high road even if it twists and turns.

JULY 24

On this day in the year 1851, Cyrus Hall McCormick stood on a farm in England awaiting the first public competitive field trial of his own reaper and 2 others by an impartial judge.

After selling 3000 reapers in the United States the inventor wanted to expand into foreign markets. The London Exposition of 1851 provided a natural entrée and he placed a model in the American section. It was the ugly duckling of the trade fair, parodied by the leading British paper as "a cross between an Astley chariot, a wheelbarrow, and a flying machine." An Anglo-American John J. Mechi sponsored a comparative demonstration of the McCormick reaper, the Hussey model, and a third on his farm. Within 70 seconds the McCormick machine had cut 74 yards of grain, while the other 2 machines had broken down. The English market instantly became his for the asking. McCormick's reaper won a First Prize and a Council Medal at the Exposition. At the end of the fair, it was extolled by the same British newspaper as "the most valuable contribution from abroad to the stock of out previous knowledge, that we have yet discovered. It is worth the whole cost of the Exposition."

As the Welsh proverb puts it:

Better late singing than early singing.

JULY 25

On this day in the year 1926, Will Rogers was praised by the London *Times* as "America's Prime Minister of Mirth," whose presence on the English stage was "enchanted both in matter and manner."

Wherever he appeared and whatever he wrote, the humorist had always cheered people up. *The Cowboy Philosopher on Prohibition* typified Rogers' writings. In it, he thanked "the Writers of the Old and New Testaments for furnishing facts for some of my strongest arguments against Prohibition." He dreaded a future with Prohibition because he liked to talk to "an audience who have had a few nips, just enough so that they can see the joke and still sober enough to applaud it." He sympathized with congressmen who had voted for it, for nobody will listen to a congressman or senator "without a certain amount of liquor in him." Furthermore, "getting bit by a snake" would soon become a lost art, since "no man is going to let a snake bite him after liquor goes out." Actually, it doesn't "make any difference to me which side I am on. I get paid for getting laughs and I found out that the majority of the people would laugh more if I kidded the drys. But lots of people *laugh one way* and *vote another.* Look at Congress, it *voted dry* and *drinks wet.*"

As the Italian proverb puts it:

Laughter makes good blood.

JULY 26

On this day in the year 1892, Marcus Samuel saw his tanker *Murex* sail from West Hartlepool in England.

The ship incorporated the finest art of naval engineering. The deft design enabled it to proceed to Batum, fill its 4000-ton tanks with oil, pass through the Suez Canal, discharge two-thirds of the cargo at one of Samuel's terminals near Singapore, and with the lightened draught cross the bar to discharge the rest at another of Samuel's terminals at

Bangkok. Prior to the *Murex,* oil had been shipped in barrels and tins. With the newly developed tanker, competition was severely shaken. Standard Oil itself had recognized the value of shipment by bulk tenders early and had attempted to do so in 1890. But its ships had been refused passage through the Suez Canal on grounds of safety. The Samuel fleet, however, met all the rigid specifications, especially in the innovative cargo-handling compartments. By the end of 1895 the pioneering passage of a bulk carrier through the Canal had been followed by 68 others, all but 4 of which were either owned or chartered by Samuel. Having captured the Orient's oil market, he was well on the way to becoming the first Viscount Bearsted.

As the Yiddish proverb puts it:

A craft is a kingdom.

JULY 27

On this day in the year 1949, the Lord Chancellor of England said in the House of Lords that "whenever we debate this subject [rights of women peers] we get into the most frightful muddle."

The Upper House had just passed a motion by 45 votes to 27 regarding the admission of peeresses in their own rights to a seat in the House of Lords. As finally carried the motion by Lord Reading read: "That steps should be taken to obtain leave to introduce legislation as soon as may be praticable to confer upon women peers who under existing conditions are not qualified to take their seats in the House the same rights, duties and privileges that are now enjoyed by male peers having a seat, place and voice in this House." Everyone thought the statement was plain enough. But when attempts were made to interpret what was actually meant, a confused jumble ensued. As a Westminster reporter described the proceedings at that point, "As successive peers, including Lord Addison and Lord Chancellor, sought elucidation of its purpose, confusion was added to confusion, and it was left to Lord Cecil to advise the hot and embarassed assembly to take the motion as it stood and let interpretation take care of itself."

As the Sanskrit proverb puts it:

Better a doubtful condition, than a crushing defeat.

JULY 28

On this day in the year 1955, Manuel Odría announced that he planned to step down when his constitutional term of office ended a year later.

The dictator of Peru had felt that the country needed 10 to 15 years of internal peace and constructive social programs. He pointed to the tripling of national income in 6 years, doubling of mineral production, 50% increase in exports, 3000 miles of new roads, 31,000 hectares of new irrigated desert land, 34 new schools and colleges, 40 new hospitals, and so on. Peru was back on her economic feet and guided onto the path of far-reaching and major improvements in foreign and domestic affairs. Nevertheless, the people remained understandably skeptical of strong men proclaiming their intention to withdraw from power. When the time came, however, Odría surprised them all and voluntarily did do just that.

As the Chinese proverb puts it:

He who is content can never be ruined.

JULY 29

On this day in the year 1975, Casper Weinberger lifted the ban on research on living fetuses in the United States.

During the latter half of the twentieth century, biological scientists began to move into controversial realms of investigation at crosscurrents with traditional mores regarding the divine preserve of the creation of life, the privacy of sexual relations, and the like. Protests of antiabortion and other groups led to the imposition of a moratorium on fetal research by Congress. A National Commission on Protection of Human Subjects of Biomedical and Behavioral Research studied the situation and recommended to the Secretary of Health, Education, and Welfare that fetal research be continued if performed "respectfully and with dignity" and if it does not "offend community sensibilities." The Commission contended that the opposition's thesis of the "right to life" as an interpretation of ethics was not as relevant as respect and dignity. Weinberger accepted the Commission's position and decreed that research on fetuses is to go on. Approval by a national ethical advisory board, composed largely of scientists, is to be obtained in the case of experiments on artificial fertilization of human eggs in vitro toward the creation of test-tube babies. Value-free science had finally gained official acceptance of its own standard of ethics, to be interpreted by its own spokesmen, beyond the systems of religion and jurisprudence. But the public remained uneasy.

As the Spanish proverb puts it:

How can those be trusted who know not how to blush?

JULY 30

On this day in the year 1848, Terence McManus inspected the Irish Insurgent Army of 38 men, equipped with pikes, 20 guns with 1 charge apiece, and 80 men and women carrying stones at Ballingarry.

A Young Ireland Council of War had been held the night before. The majority wanted to go underground and resurface at a more propitious occasion. The Irish were not ready for open rebellion. When Father Kenyon was urged to toll his chapel bells, recruit his parishioners, and march at the head of his column to join William Smith O'Brien, he refused. He would fight if the people were also so prepared. But he would not engage in a "bootless struggle." O'Brien remained defiant: "I won't hide. I won't be a fugitive where my forefathers reigned. I will continue to appeal to the people as I have been doing, until we gather enough support to enable us to take the field." He and McManus forged ahead and took on the police. The brief skirmish ended with the rebel mob fleeing in disorder, O'Brien escaping on a police horse, and McManus bleeding behind.

As the German proverb puts it:

If you want to be strong, know your weakness.

JULY 31

On this day in the year 1944, George S. Patton readied the American Third Army for an attack on the German defenses the following morning.

"Forget this goddamed business about worrying about the flanks. We must guard our flanks, but not to the extent that we don't do anything else. Some goddamn fool once said that the flanks must be secured, and since then sons-of-bitches all over the world have been going crazy guarding their flanks. Flanks are something for the enemy to worry about, not us," the Lieutenant General admonished his staff. "Our basic plan of operation is to advance and to keep on advancing regardless of whether we have to go over, under or through the enemy. We have one motto, 'Audacious, audacious, always audacious.' Remember that. From here on out, until we win or die in the attempt, we will always be audacious."

As the French proverb puts it:

When the will is ready, the feet are light.

AUGUST 1

On this day in the year 1798, Horatio Nelson crushed the French navy at Abukir Bay in the Battle of the Nile.

During the close engagement the Admiral himself suffered what was feared to have been a fatal wound. He was taken below deck to the fleet surgeon for emergency attention. As he was being rushed ahead of everyone else, he noticed a seaman about to have his leg amputated without anesthesia. Nelson quietly stopped his attendants and said: "I will wait my turn with my brave fellows."

As the Japanese proverb puts it:

The great swordsman surpasses in decorum.

AUGUST 2

On this day in the year 1713, Duc du Maine was formally received by the French Parlement as Prince of the Blood, with right of royal succession.

The bluebloods ill-concealed their disgust over the King's elevation of his bastard son. They shuddered as he walked past. But they ceremoniously smiled and nodded nonetheless. "Hypocrisy was depicted on the countenances and in the whole bearing of M. du Maine, bending over his stick with studied humility, stopping at every step so that his bows . . . might be deeper; sometimes with a marked pause before he raised himself again," bemused Duc de St. Simon, as he observed the formalities. The mild gravity on du Maine's face "seemed to say *nom sum dignis* from the depths of his soul, but the joy which sparkled in his eyes as he darted furtive glances over the assembly gave the lie to his assumed humility. When he reached his place, he again bowed repeatedly before sitting down; and it was delightful to watch him during and after the proceedings."

As the Finnish proverb puts it:

The more the cat is stroked, the higher she lifts her tail.

AUGUST 3

On this day in the year 1492, Christopher Columbus set sail from the Harbor of Palos.

The Sovereign had promised 10,000 maravedis to the man who first sighted land. After 70 days out at sea at two in the morning one of the sailors on the *Pinta,* Rodrigo de Triano, yelled out: "Land! Land!" But the reward went to Columbus instead. It was stated that earlier that night he had seen a light used by natives passing from hut to hut. But Triano felt cheated. On his return to Europe he became a Muslim.

As the Russian proverb puts it:

The bear dances but the gypsy takes the money.

AUGUST 4

On this day in the year 1865, Robert E. Lee was offered the Presidency of Washington College of Lexington in Virginia.

The defeated general of the Confederate Army felt that his academic qualifications were not of sufficient stature for the post. He also raised questions about his still being "an object of censure to a portion of the country." This might well draw hostilities on the college. He did not, on that account, want to cause injury to the institution that he cherished so deeply. Believing that it is "the duty of every citizen, in the present condition of the country, to do all in his power to aid in the restoration of peace and harmony, and in no way oppose the policy of the State or General Government directed to that object," Lee declined the invitation. "It is particularly incumbent on those charged with the instruction of the young to set them an example of submission to authority, and I could not consent to be the cause of animadversion upon the college." The board of trustees was not discouraged by his letter and urged him a second time on August 31. Lee finally agreed to serve.

As the Punjabi proverb puts it:

Stretch your legs according to your sheet.

AUGUST 5

On this day in the year 1191, Saladin attacked Richard the Lion Hearted defending Jaffa.

The Sultan stood on the highground and followed the early sallies by his cavalry of 7000 and the counterattacks by the Christian side with 2000 soldiers and 15 mounted units. He was impressed by Richard's display of courage. When he saw Richard's horse killed from under him, Saladin sent a groom with 2 horses to his brave enemy in the middle of the continuing battle. At the end of the day, Saladin marched back with his troops to Jerusalem in good order and a new round of negotiations began the following morning.

As the Chinese proverb puts it:

His virtues exceed his talents—a superior man.

AUGUST 6

On this day in the year 1744, young Jean-Jacques Rousseau quarreled with Pierre de Montaigu.

As Secretary to the French Ambassador at Venice since September 4, 1743, Rousseau had been the second-ranking man in the Embassy. He was proud of the position and imagined much better things to come in light of the incompetence of his superior. Being a career officer, Count de Montaigu had been accustomed to responsive acquiescence to his every wish on the part of subordinates. This was not forthcoming from

Rousseau, who had sights on honors much higher than that of a mere diplomat. In retaliation for Rousseau's refusal to split visa fees with him, the Count began charging him for miscellaneous office expenses. Rousseau, in turn, began spreading increasingly disparaging remarks about him, at the same time praising his own contributions to the Venetians. Gradually, Rousseau's manners became more arrogant and exhibitionistic. He became enmeshed in an ancillary fracas with the assistant Domenico Vitali, whom Rousseau had humiliated in public. He finally submitted his resignation. The Ambassador was reluctant to lose his capable administrative aide and did not accept it. So Rousseau sent a letter to the Ambassador's brother detailing all his complaints. On receiving the brother's ensuing note, the Ambassador lost his temper and threatened to have his valets throw Rousseau out the window. Bolting the door, Rousseau, in turn, threatened to beat him up, then walked out for good.

As the Japanese proverb puts it:

A protruding stake will be hammered.

AUGUST 7

On this day in the year 1704, Eugene of Savoy and John Churchill Marlborough executed one of the greatest examples of combat coordination in the history of warfare.

After deceiving Duke Francois de N. de Villeroi into thinking he was staying near the Rhine, the Austrian prince marched rapidly eastward with 20,000 men to join the Earl of Marlborough with 36,000 men. Not knowing Eugene's whereabouts, Villeroi with his 60,000 men decided to stay near Strasbourg to protect Alsace. In the meantime, Marlborough rid his main force of the less competent Margrave Louis of Baden by sending him off to besiege Ingolstadt and marched westward. Eugene and Marlborough united on August 12 to engage the combined armies of Count Camille de Tallard with 30,000 and Count Ferdinand de Marsin and Elector Maximilian of Bavaria with 30,000. In the subsequent Battle of Blenheim, Eugene contained Marsin and Maximilian with an aggressive holding attack and slow advance with heavy fighting in accordance with plans. Marlborough carried the main attacking thrust at Tallard. Despite fierce resistance,

Marlborough did not slow down. He finally forced Tallard to commit his reserves. Marlborough then charged with his cavalry squadrons, which broke through Tallard's center after an hour. Tallard was captured; Marsin and Maximilian fled. The British lost heavily. But French power was destroyed.

As the English proverb puts it:

A lion's skin is never cheap.

AUGUST 8

On this day in the year 1700, Peter the Great decided to declare war on Sweden.

In the first major encounter at Narva the Swedish King Charles XII defeated him. But the Tsar refused to be discouraged. He instituted conscription, raised new armies, trained recruits, and improved his artillery. He strengthened the home front by imposing drastic measures: limiting the authority of the ecclesiastical hierarchy, replacing hereditary functionaries with meritorious candidates, and importing skilled craftsmen and technicians. He even modernized the long gowns and beards of his countrymen. At a state banquet, the Tsar's jester went around the table and snipped off the beards of the boyars, who had not yet come around to the approved fashion of the new order. Finally, he met Charles a second time at the decisive Battle of Poltava on June 27, 1709. Charles was put to flight, never to molest Russia again.

As the American proverb puts it:

Sweat and be saved.

AUGUST 9

On this day in the year 1784, Marie Antoinette heard a plea from Boehmer for a long overdue first installment on the purchase of a very costly diamond necklace, of which she had never heard before.

The court jeweler stammered that "an intimate friend of Your Majesty, the Countess of Valois, inspected the necklace" and told him that the Queen wanted to buy it. Then his Eminence Louis Cardinal de Rohan told him that "he was commissioned by the Queen to deliver the 1,600,000-livre necklace." Marie was furious at the unauthorized use of her name. She did not know the Countess and hated the Cardinal. Instead of requesting an official investigation, the Queen focused her anger on the latter and demanded of her husband Louis XVI that the Cardinal be publicly disgraced. Just as de Rohan, fully dressed in scarlet for a pontifical high mass in celebration of the Queen's name-day the following week, joined the waiting nobility in the King's anteroom, Baron de Breteuil signaled to the King's bodyguard: "Arrest Monsieur le Cardinal!" The Cardinal refused to beg for Royal Grace but demanded his right to trial by the Parlement of Paris. The hearings showed that the Cardinal himself had been deceived by the woman named Valois with a forged letter from the Queen. He was acquitted "without a stain upon his character," which was an undisguised condemnation of the Queen. The nobles were indignant over the high-handed treatment of a member of their privileged class. The crowds on the northern banks of the Seine cried: "Long live the Parlement! Long live the Cardinal!" There was no "Long live the Queen!"

As the Vai proverb puts it:

The catfish's hatred for the frog brought him ashore.

AUGUST 10

On this day in the year 1939, Alfred Naujocks was commanded by Reinhard Heydrich to attack a German radio station at Hohenlinde near the Polish border, making it appear that Poles were involved.

The SS major was told by the Chief of the Nazi Security Police that the dramatic incident was "needed for the foreign press, as well as for German purposes." Germany had intended to use the emerging news as a pretext for opening its planned attack on Poland within a few days. The 6-member team seized the German facility and held it long enough for 1 of them to broadcast a 4-minute speech in Polish. The speech called on the Poles to begin an immediate confrontation with the Germans and to kill any German who would resist. A concentration camp victim shot behind the head was left at the door. The raid took place on August 31 and war broke out on September 1.

As the German proverb puts it:

A bad cause requires many words.

AUGUST 11

On this day in the year 117, Publius Aelius Hadrianus was proclaimed Emperor of the Roman Empire.

Recognizing that Rome did not have sufficient soldiers and resources to defend her extended realm, Hadrianus took immediate steps to shrink the boundaries to securable proportions. It had stretched beyond the island of Britain to the northwest; Asia Minor, Armenia, and Arabia to the east; all of North Africa to the south; and all of the Iberian peninsula and Gaul to the west. Hadrianus therefore abandoned Mesopotamia and Assyria to the Parthians, appeased the dissident tribes on the frontiers with the designation of the Euphrates as the eastern boundary, and built a protective wall in Britain fron Tyne to Solway Firth.

As the English proverb puts it:

Grasp no more than thy hand will hold.

AUGUST 12

On this day in the year 1946, Moses Katane approved a strike by 50,000 miners in South Africa.

Two days after the go-ahead signal by the Secretary of the Communist party, 4000 of them marched on Johannesburg. The police drove the Bantu mob back to the mines and raided the offices of the Communist party and affiliated organizations. On the urging of the Communist party, the advisory Natives Representative Council demanded a promise from the government for a basic revision of the country's race legislation. When the Acting Minister Jan Hofmeyr refused, the Bantu professor Z. K. Matthew moved that the Council adjourn *sine die*. The motion passed. By thus being excluded from participation in government, the Bantus were pushed no longer to seek legislative reform but political equality. The incident further isolated the South African government from the white liberals and left little choice to the Bantu leaders other than aligning themselves with the Communist party, if they wanted to make a practical difference in their political struggle. Although the Party lost tactically in its fight for wage increases, it gained strategically in its broadened base of support.

As the Yiddish proverb puts it:

Whosoever cringes well creeps forward.

AUGUST 13

On this day in the year 1829, Thomas Skidmore published his *Rights of Man to Property*.

The first American self-taught, cracker-barrel Communist-unionist had just guided the New York carpenters, masons, and machinists in preventing the employers' plan to lengthen their newly won 10-hour day to 11 hours. Instead of calling a strike, he led a series of mass protest meetings attended by as many as 6000. The threat to the employers was clear enough. Unless they backed down, the movement would quickly grow into violent radicalism. They did back down and Skidmore won his immediate goal. However, his tactics were counterproductive in terms of longer-term consequences. He had denounced the employers as "aristocratic oppressors." Skidmore's publication implied that a revolution might be required to abolish the class distinctions as a result of maldistribution of land and wealth. The public's suspicion penetrated much deeper than justified. The label of "red and dangerous" stuck, which unnecessarily hampered the union's progress for many years to come.

As the Indian proverb puts it:

Kill the snake but do not break the stick.

AUGUST 14

On this day in the year 1867, Benito Juárez issued a *convocatoria* to election.

Having brought peace and democracy to the Mexicans after 57 years of internal dissensions and 2 foreign invasions, the President felt that he was so loved by his countrymen that he could press for more drastic reforms. In particular, he wanted a bicameral Congress giving the President a veto, subject to the concurrence of only a third of the legislators instead of a half. This was an action of his toward converting the constitutional form of government into a paternal presidentialism. By this time, however, the Constitution had become sacrosanct to the people. In attempting to modify it, Juárez overextended himself. Many were shocked by his naked grab for more power. The *convocatoria* was defeated. Juárez did not even poll a majority in the 1871 elections that followed.

As the Italian proverb puts it:

Once the most is done, it is best to do the least.

AUGUST 15

On this day in the year 778, Roland fell in battle against the Basques at the pass of Roncevaux in the Pyrenees.

The heroism of the Duke of Breton March inspired the French epic, *The Song of Roland*. *The Song* tells of how Charlemagne attacked the Saracens of Spain, how Roland and his rear guard of 20,000 were betrayed by the paladin Gamelon, how they fought valiantly as the 12 peers fell one by one, and how Charlemagne finally heard the urgent call of Roland's horn and returned—too late to save the hero but in time to destroy the enemy. Roland's confident pride in his own faith and prowess was destroyed by the unrelenting progression of disaster and death to his comrades in arms. His enlightenment opened the way to humility. With that transformation, Roland's soul was lifted into heaven as that of a saint.

As the Chinese proverb puts it:

To light a lamp before Buddha, first extinguish self.

AUGUST 16

On this day in the year 1972, Philip Alford Potter was elected General Secretary of the World Council of Churches at its international meeting in Utrecht.

The Methodist pastor from the British West Indies was the

first nonwhite person chosen to lead the society to which belonged some 25,000 Protestant, Anglican, and Orthodox churches throughout the world. In response to questions from reporters, he reminisced over some of his earlier encounters with violent forms of racial discrimination. The memory had by then receded into the background. "But it taught me one thing," he said. "And that is, when people do not recognize your humanity, they become inhuman themselves."

As the Spanish proverb puts it:

The cask smells of the wine it holds.

AUGUST 17

On this day in the year 1499, Amerigo Vespucci anchored off the bulge of Brazil.

The navigator from Florence landed a party of men, who tried to make contact with the natives. After several days they were able to barter for some much-needed water. Two of the sailors then obtained the Captain's permission to follow them inland to explore for riches. On the seventh day, native women began to appear. To overcome their shyness, the Portuguese crewmen returned to the ship, leaving 1 brave and agile mate to deal with them. Vespucci's account detailed what happened after that. "He went among the women, and they all began to touch and feel him, wondering at him exceedingly. Things being so, we saw a woman come down from the hill, carrying a huge stick in her hand. When she reached our Christian, she raised it and struck him with such a blow that he fell to the ground. The other women immediately grabbed him by the legs and dragged him toward the hill." The other sailors attempted to come to his rescue but were repulsed by a dense rain of arrows. Backaways the women were observed tearing the torso to pieces. "They made a large fire and roasted him before our eyes showing us the pieces and eating them. The men indicated by sign language that they had also killed and eaten the other two Christians."

As the Japanese proverb puts it:

Cross a shallow river as if it were deep.

AUGUST 18

On this day in the year 1871, Henry Meiggs received a contract of 1.6 million pounds to build a narrow gauge railway from Alajuela to Puerto Limón in Costa Rica.

Soon thereafter the builder of railroads in Chile and Peru handed over 100,000 pounds to the Dictator-President General Tomas Guardia. When the political opposition raised a storm in Congress, the General explained simply: "The contractor of the railway, Señor Henry Meiggs, without any prior agreement, and purely out of generosity, in accordance with customs in such negotiations, had placed at my disposal through Minister Manuel Alvarado the sum of 100,000 pounds. So that I should do with it in the way I thought best." Then he went on to say that he used it all in the service of the country.

As the Latin proverb puts it:

Fungus grows where the soil is rich.

AUGUST 19

On this day in the year 1576, Martin Frobisher climbed to the top of a hill on Baffin Island and saw, in the words of his sailing master Christopher Hall, "a number of small things fleeting in the Sea a farre off, whyche he supposed to be Porposes, or Ceales, or some kinds of strange fische."

The "strange fische" turned out to be Eskimos in kyaks. The English navigator returned to his ship and bartered for some furs, meat, and salmon. One of the Eskimos was engaged through sign language to lead the *Gabriel* through the strait by paddling ahead. Sir Martin then ordered a 5-member crew to take the Eskimo to a spot a good distance from his fellows and come back to the ship immediately. The crew followed the first half of his order, but not the second. They stopped on the way to do some trading on their own. After waiting several days without hearing from them, Frobisher ordered his men to capture several Eskimos as hostages for the return of the missing members. But the natives kept evading their lungings and clutchings, laughing contemptuously all the while. Frobisher then tried the blaring of trumpets and the firing of cannons to no avail. The Eskimos simply folded up their tiny tents and sledded off into the interior. He could do nothing else but sail home for England with his remaining 13 sailors, "so tyred and sik with laboure of their hard voyage."

As the Chinese proverb puts it:

In shallow waters, shrimps make fools of dragons.

AUGUST 20

On this day in the year 636, Khalid ibn al Waleed launched his attack against Theodorus in the Battle of Yarmouk, east of the Sea of Galilee.

A strong wind from the southeastern desert had started to blow the evening before and now reached full fury. The clouds of hot sand and dust swept from the direction of the charging bedouins. The defending Byzantines were completely disorganized by the strange and frightful storm, which scattered their tents, filled everything with grit, and burnt their faces. But the attacking Arabs were perfectly at home. Theodorus himself fell in the rout.

As the English proverb puts it:

Hoist your sail when the wind is fair.

AUGUST 21

On this day in the year 1886, Alexander of Battenberg was overthrown.

The bloodless coup went smoothly as a result of efficient covert intervention of Tsarist agents infiltrating the Bulgarian operations. A wave of convincing rumors was first generated concerning the imminence of war with Serbia. This caused the Prince to transfer his loyal first infantry division from the capital to the Serbian frontier. Russian agents and their Bulgarian co-conspirators then focused their attention on the second infantry division only 20 miles away at Struma. A quick march on the defenseless Alexander precipitated his abdication without much resistance.

As the Chinese proverb puts it:

Do not tear down the east wall to repair the west wall.

AUGUST 22

On this day in the year 1128, Roger II de Hauteville was invested with a triple dukedom by Honorius II.

As Roger rose from his knees, he became one of the most powerful of European rulers. Yet he had not quite acquired a peer status with the rest. He lacked an officially recognized crown. Two years later the opportunity presented itself. The irregular elections for a successor to the Pope had led to two claimants. Innocent II had the support of the continent; Anacletus II controlled Rome. Roger promised to recognize the latter, if he would in turn recognize Roger. The formal papal blessing was forthcoming and Roger became King with all the privileges appertaining thereunto.

As the Basque proverb puts it:

One gift awaits a better one.

AUGUST 23

On this day in the year 1875, Henry Morton Stanley again visited Mtesa.

The King of Uganda was in the midst of mobilization for a war against the rebellious Uvuma tribe, which had refused to pay tribute. He began his conversation by referring to the fine rifle that the English explorer had presented him on a previous visit. An old slave was brought in from the fields and the King addressed him as follows: "Look at this lightning spear, given to the Kabaka. The man said it can kill much faster than our own spears. Stand still. I would like to test it myself." After the convincing demonstration, the King sought to calm the horrified Stanley by saying that the fellow would have been killed in some future battle anyway and furthermore that "no one should be afraid of death." The topic of death provided an opening for Stanley to talk about God. He read the beginning of the Gospel of St. John. The King then returned to his advisors about whether they should follow the Christian, the Jewish, or the Muslim missionaries, especially in view of the fact that they had invited the Islamic representatives into the area not too many years before. Having witnessed the awesome gun display, they were unanimous: "The white man's book!" So Mtesa asked Stanley to send some Christian missionaries and, more importantly, instructions about how the Ugandans could produce the lightning spears themselves.

As the French proverb puts it:

Whosoever desires the ends desires the means.

AUGUST 24

On this day in the year 1572, Gaspard de Coligny was chopped down with a battle-ax in his room in Paris.

The murder of the French admiral and Huguenot leader triggered the massacre of St. Bartholomew. The Catholics in Paris and then in the provinces went on a killing and looting rampage against the Huguenots for several weeks until most of the Protestants were dead. Two who were spared were Henry of Navarre and Prince de Condé, who had been close friends of the King. They were summoned before Charles IX. Instead of the jesting companion of days gone by, the King was now stern. He came to the point quickly. Peace could prevail in his kingdom only if there were a single religion. Since Catholicism was his own, "I will suffer no other religion in my country. You must therefore give up your religion which was the cause of so much disturbance and you must attend mass. If not you must be ready to lose your lives and be treated as your associates."

As the English proverb puts it:

The king's favor is no inheritance.

AUGUST 25

On this day in the year 1667, 13-year-old K'ang-hsi-ti took over the reins of government from the 4 regents, who had ruled in his name since he was 7 years of age.

The young monarch had been observing their actions all along. He had seen how they had cheated the Chinese, proscribed the Christians, and condemned Father Adam Schall, a close friend of the former emperor, to death. Believing the trend was not good for the country, he asserted himself at the earliest feasible moment. After 2 years of familiarization, he investigated the former administration. One of the regents was sentenced to decapitation, later commuted to life imprisonment, and another demoted. Lands unjustly seized by the Manchus were restored to their rightful owners. Despite objections of the Confucian literati, he adopted the calendar proposed by the Belgian Jesuit Ferdinand Verbiest and bestowed appropriate favors on Christian savants. K'ang-hsi ruled for 60 years—one of the longest and most glorious reigns in the history of China.

As the Greek proverb puts it:

Nothing becomes a king so much as justice.

AUGUST 26

On this day in the year 1943, Hans Hemmen obtained the French government's consent to pay the cost of Nazi occupation.

Actually, the French had no alternative. The Chief of Nazi Armistice Delegation for Economic Affairs in occupied France had embarked on the systematic economic exploitation of the conquered country. On the same day the German government promulgated the following directive: "It is politically essential that orders placed for the execution of the war be fulfilled and the raw materials and capacity of the western territories should be assigned in such a way so as to do the most to support the German armament production and increase her combat effectiveness." By September 23, rationing was imposed with central regulation over the use of all raw materials. A comprehensive siphoning of resources into Germany followed.

As the Ukranian proverb puts it:

Whosoever owns the river banks owns the fish.

AUGUST 27

On this day in the year 410, Alaric ended the 3-day pillage of Rome, whose defenses he had pierced on August 24.

After being hailed as King of the Visigoths, he besieged the Eternal City on the Tiber. In the meantime the Roman Emperor Flavius Honorius had moved his Court to Ravenna, a powerful fortress on the Adriatic. When Alaric asked for an alliance, Honorius flatly refused, calling him "an impudent barbarian" in the process. Alaric was incensed and cut off Rome's food supply. When an envoy of the Roman Senate sought relief, he insisted that Honorius be deposed and Attalus be instated as his new replacement. The Senate followed suit and the flow of food and supplies resumed. After a while Attalus was not satisfied with merely being Alaric's puppet. He decided to rule on his own, whereupon Alaric stripped him of power. Disgusted with the Senate's inability to govern and angered by Honorius' plot to murder him, Alaric reentered Rome and sacked it.

As the French proverb puts it:

Where the goat is tethered, there she must graze.

AUGUST 28

On this day in the year 1526, Suleiman the Great decimated the Hungarian army at Mohacs.

The King, 8 bishops, many Magyar nobles, and 24,000 Hungarians perished from the original force of 100,000. When the body of the King was found, the invading Ottoman Sultan expressed public sorrow at the fate of his foe, who was about the same age: "May Allah be merciful to him, and punish those who misled his inexperience. I came indeed in arms against him; but it was not my wish that he should thus be cut off, while he had scarcely tasted the sweets of life and royalty." Similarly, sentimental respect had been made by him before when he had defeated the Knights of St. John at Malta in 1522. Suleiman had his interpreter relay his admiration for the Grand Master of Rhodes, Villiers De Lisle Adam, as follows: "It is not without regret that I force this brave man from his home in his old age."

As the English proverb puts it:

Bees with honey in their mouths have stings in their tails.

AUGUST 29

On this day in the year 1533, Atahualpa was given a Christian burial at Caxamarca, between Cuzco and Quito.

Under instruction from Charles V of Spain, Francisco Pizarro arrived the year before with 102 infantrymen and 62 horses. Atahualpa agreed to meet them in the town square. Pizarro's Chaplain Fray Vicente de Valverde then made a long speech about Charles V being the only true emperor and the Christian God being the only true God. When the Inca King demanded the authority that gave the Christian God precedence over his own god, the Sun, Valverde handed over a Bible. After a quick look Atahualpa tossed it to the ground. This gesture of sacrilegious disrespect was all the pretext that Pizarro needed. Pizarro's cannons and guns opened fire and a general slaughter resulted. Atahualpa was taken captive. He offered a huge ransom in gold and silver for his release. Pizarro agreed, provided the treasure could be delivered within 2 months. As soon as the 13,265 pounds of gold and 26,000 pounds of silver had been received, Pizarro leveled another charge at the Inca. Since Atahualpa had ordered his half-brother Huascar, who had been competing for the crown, killed, he was now accused of murder by the Spaniards and condemned to be burnt at the stakes. If he would accept Christianity, however, he would be strangled instead. Thus it came about that Atahualpa was converted into Christianity and welcomed into a Christian grave.

As the Russian proverb puts it:

If you want to find the Devil, look behind a cross.

AUGUST 30

On this day in the year 1930, A. D. Payne blew himself up with a small vial of nitroglycerin, which he had hidden around his neck, while awaiting trial in the Potter County jail in Amarillo, Texas.

The officials had suspected that he had murdered his wife but were unable to gather solid evidence. The wife had gone driving with their son one day. As related by the surviving son, he began to smell something like fuse powder burning under the hood. The mother remained unconcerned, saying that his father had advised her to drive a little faster should the engine smoke. She did so and the car blew up from the planted dynamite. A reporter finally dug up the motive. When confronted with it, Payne broke down and confessed. He had fallen in love with a secretary and had been visiting with her at various hotels.

As the Bulgarian proverb puts it:

A cock never has too many hens.

AUGUST 31

On this day in the year 1869, George Tichnor praised the approach used by the Province of Canterbury in controlling alcoholic intemperance as contrasted to that adopted by Massachusetts.

The British had followed the voluntary method. Over 1000 parishes and hamlets in Canterbury refrained from selling alcoholic beverages without the need of legislation. On the other hand, Massachusetts had relied on stringent laws to stop the sale of intoxicating liquor. "But no people, and especially no people living under such free institutions as ours can thus be driven," the American author noted in a letter to his English friend Sir Walter C. Trevelyan. "It is a moderate statement to say, that in Massachusetts the 'Liquor Law,' as it is called, is broken a hundred thousand times a day. In Boston I think any man can get what he wants, from a glass of wine to a glass of beer, whenever he likes and as often as he likes."

As the Sumerian proverb puts it:

That which is given in submission becomes a medium of defiance.

SEPTEMBER 1

On this day in the year 326, Constantine the Great circulated an edict compelling heretics to subject themselves to the bishops.

"Understand now by this present law, Novatians, Valentinians, Marcionites, Pavlinians, you who are called Cataphrygians . . . with what tissues of lies and vanities, with what destructive and venomous errors, your dogmas are inextricably entangled!" the autocratic Emperor of Rome sternly warned. They were prohibited to meet in assembly. The heretics' places of gathering and worship were confiscated and turned over to the Catholic Church. Yet when he had not been so all-powerful just 13 years earlier, the Emperor had joined with Licinius Augustus in the declaration that "we judged that the one thing above all others which we saw would be of benefit to most people was that relating to the laws surrounding the worship of God, that Christians and everyone else should be accorded the right to follow freely whatever religious belief they choose, in order that whatever god there is enthroned in Heaven would be well-disposed and propitious to all of us."

As the Hebrew proverb puts it:

Put not your trust in princes.

SEPTEMBER 2

On this day in the year 1766, David Hume told Richard Davenport about his low opinion of the latter's house guest.

The individual had been making scurrilous remarks about the Scottish philosopher and had threatened to publish them in his memoirs. Yet Hume was understanding of the good relations between the critic and Davenport. "When I say that he is a very dangerous man, I do not mean that he is likely to prove so to you. As you have been so happy as never to make yourself known to the public as an author, he is less likely to entertain any jealousy against you; and he may submit with the less repugnance to the great obligations, which he owes you."

As the Sudanese proverb puts it:

People throw stones at those they cannot overtake.

SEPTEMBER 3

On this day in the year 1886, Geronimo met with Nelson A. Miles outside Fort Bowie, Arizona, to discuss terms of surrender.

General Miles had gained the Apache leader's confidence and laid out attractive proposals. He gave assurance that all 3 Apache bands, with families and friends would be united within 5 days. He spoke of a land of clear waters and green woods, which would be given them to hold in guaranteed peace and prosperity. Geronimo accepted and the 498 Apaches were shipped off to Florida as prisoners and later transferred to the Mount Vernon Barracks in Alabama. The children and adolescents were sent to school at Carlisle. A fourth of them died within 3 years. By the time they were sent to Fort Sill in Oklahoma in 1896 they numbered 296. There they stayed never to return to their homeland. Geronimo himself died a prisoner in 1909. The curtain was finally drawn on the last of the Indian wars. The palefaces have completed their takeover of the green expanse.

As the Dutch proverb puts it:

He who would be a great dragon must first eat many little snakes.

SEPTEMBER 4

On this day in the year 1972, Ng Huan Lam and his wife Lo Fook Kuan, having been ordered to stop their acupuncture treatments, said goodbye to their patients in New York City's Chinatown.

"I've been to doctors, I've been to hospitals," said one of the patients suffering from arthritis. "Seven years I went, and they couldn't help. After the first visit here, I felt better than in all those years. Why is it when we find somebody who can help, they take him away?" The other 4 in the waiting room were equally irate. But the New York State Department of Health had decreed that the ancient Chinese art of acupuncture is the practice of medicine, that the Ngs were not licensed to practice in New York, and that therefore they must cease and desist forthwith.

As the Fulani proverb puts it:

What dog attends the hyena's mosque?

SEPTEMBER 5

On this day in the year 1917, William D. Haywood received word of simultaneous raids on the branch offices of his Industrial Workers of the World (IWW) by agents of the Justice Department and the local police.

After a survey of the situation the union leader decided that the papers confiscated can only serve to prove the innocence of the IWW against allegations of espionage. Two days later he notified his followers that "the situation . . . is not serious yet . . . No one is under arrest at the present time and we expect to have the office open for our usual transactions of business very soon." Unknown to him was the communique from the United States Attorney in Philadelphia to Attorney General Thomas Gregory in Washington, confirming that "our purpose being, as I understand it, very largely to put the IWW out of business." He was planning to use the Wobblies' own words, out of context and time relationships if needed, to prosecute the members for interfering with congressional acts and presidential proclamations on the war effort, conspiring to cause insubordination in the armed forces, and interfering with the constitutional rights of employers. On September 20 the Grand Jury indicted 166 of the union leaders.

As the Malayan proverb puts it:

Do not think there are no crocodiles just because the water is calm.

SEPTEMBER 6

On this day in the year 1909, Carl G. Jung arrived at Clark University in Massachusetts to receive an honorary Doctor of Laws degree and deliver a series of lectures.

"Our time is dreadfully crammed. The Americans are really masters at that; they hardly leave one time to catch one's breath," the Swiss psychiatrist wrote about the American compulsion for keeping busy in a letter to his wife Emma a couple of weeks later. "Right now I am rather worn out from all the fabulous things we have been through . . . My head is spinning. Last night at the awarding of the doctorate I had to deliver an impromptu talk before some 300 persons." Jung found himself "looking forward enormously to getting back to the sea again where the overstimulated psyche can recover in the presence of that infinite peace and spaciousness."

As the Bulgarian proverb puts it:

If you have a back, there are three hundred saddles for it.

SEPTEMBER 7

On this day in the year 1975, Manuel Orantes Corral won the United States Open Tennis Championship in Forest Hills, New York.

Officials, opponents, and fans the world over have come to admire and like the 26-year-old lefthander from Barcelona, Spain, as he defeated the leading tennis player of the year for the major title. Whether winning or losing, he was always cheerful, displaying an infectious smile. He applauded his opponent's good shots. He never argued with the referee about a bad call on him. "My business is to play tennis," he would say, "not argue about points." Above all, he was eminently gracious in his fairness. In the quarter finals of the tournament against a temperamental Roumanian, he purposely gave away a point at the beginning of the match and also the final point of the third set, because he felt that the opponent's shots had been unjustly called out by the officials.

As the Hindustani proverb puts it:

A good person finds the whole world friendly.

SEPTEMBER 8

On this day in the year 712, Jui-tsung abdicated.

The Emperor had been put on the T'ang throne by his son Li Lung-chi after the assassination of Empress Wu Tse-t'ien, who had poisoned her husband. Jui-tsung had always been a man of high moral character. After 6 years as chief of state, however, he recognized that he did not have the executive qualities necessary to cope with the domestic problems and the ravages of the Turks from Mongolia. Despite advice to the contrary, he insisted on giving way to someone who was fully equipped to do the job. This person, he felt, was his son, who had proven himself in overthrowing the Empress. The decision turned out to be a wise one, as his successor, Emperor Huan-tsung, ruled brilliantly and justly.

As the Dutch proverb puts it:

He who cannot build the dike should hand over the land.

SEPTEMBER 9

On this day in the year 1832, Ralph Waldo Emerson preached his last sermon as minister of the Congregational Unitarian Church in Boston.

For some time he had been uncomfortable with the rite of the Lord's Supper. After presenting a full exposition of his views, he ended the sermon by saying that while he had no objection to other members of the Church continuing to observe the sacrament, he himself will discontinue the ritual thenceforth. He was fired the following month.

As the Moorish proverb puts it:

If you see the town worshipping a calf, mow grass and feed it.

SEPTEMBER 10

On this day in the year 1919, William Morris Hughes moved in the Australian Parliament for a resolution of assent to the Treaty of Peace of World War I.

The recommended version, however, was not fashioned without strenuous objections to earlier drafts. One controversial issue involved his country's future influence in New Guinea. The Australian Prime Minister had been told by his British counterpart David Lloyd George that should Australia insist on hanging to the island, she could not count on the British navy. To this Hughes retorted angrily "with some burning words about men who, forgetful to the dignity of their high office, the great traditions of the British people and their heroic valour and immense sacrifice in the war, prostrated themselves in meek subservience before the representative of America—for whose people he was no longer entitled to speak." After exhausting his vituperative vocabulary in English, he resorted to his emotional and passionate Welsh. "My words poured out in a foaming cataract: they were highly personal, the kind of words even the most conventional of men would on occasion dearly love to use, but for what the trim and proper people all around them would think. To the members of the Cabinet staring at me open mouthed, they were words full of sound and fury without any definite meaning, but they hit Lloyd George between wind and water."

As the Chilean proverb puts it:

Ten persons who shout get more than ten who do not.

SEPTEMBER 11

On this day in the year 1778, 22-year-old Wolfgang Amadeus Mozart refused to follow his father's advice about taking a job at Salzburg.

In his letter from Paris the young composer expressed reservations about the Archbishop, who "has no faith in the intelligent and well-traveled people." Mozart felt that those who do not travel, especially those in the arts and sciences, "are pretty sorry creatures." He could not accept the position if the Archbishop would not allow him to travel at least every other year. "A person of ordinary talent will remain ordinary, whether or not he travels." But a person of extraordinary talent "(which I cannot deny myself to be without being impious) will degenerate if he stays in the same place."

As the Japanese proverb puts it:

Great fish do not live in brooks.

SEPTEMBER 12

On this day in the year 490 B.C., Miltiades faced Datis at Marathon.

Flushed from a series of triumphs, the Persians appeared invincible as they encamped on level ground so advantageous to their calvary. But Miltiades was not overawed. Instead of advancing at the usual slow pace of the Greek maneuvers of the day, he brought his 11,000 infantry spears at a run. They caught the Persians unprepared and engaged them in close action before the Persian calvary could mount any charge and before Datis could deploy his troops effectively. With their lighter weapons, wicker shields, and no body armor, the Persians reeled under the onslaught. The previously unbeatable horde fled, leaving 6400 dead. The Athenians lost 192 and their allies a comparably small number.

As the Pedi proverb puts it:

The experienced dog kills by pouncing suddenly.

SEPTEMBER 13

On this day in the year 1872, George Francis Train began his campaign for the presidency of the United States.

"I am that wonderful, eccentric, independent, extraordinary genius and political reformer of America, who is sweeping off all the politicians before him like a hurricane," he trumpeted to the American voters. "I am your modest, diffident, unassuming friend, the future President of America— George Francis Train!" Came election day, he got only a few votes.

As the Italian proverb puts it:

The ass who believes himself a deer discovers the truth when he tries to leap the ditch.

SEPTEMBER 14

On this day in the year 1918, Eugene V. Debs was found guilty in a Cleveland court for interfering with the enlistment process in World War I.

"I am thinking this morning of the men in the mills and factories; of the men in the mines and on the railroads," the socialist labor leader said to the judge before receiving sentence. "I am thinking of the women who for a paltry wage are compelled to work our their barren lives; of the little children who in this system we robbed of their childhood . . . their little lives broken and blasted because in this high noon of our twentieth-century Christian civilization money is still so much more important than flesh and blood of childhood. In very truth gold is god today and rules with pitiless sway in the affairs of men." But Debs and his 60 million socialists are patiently making "common cause." The time is approaching when "this emancipating gospel will spread among all the peoples, and when this minority will become the triumphant majority and, sweeping into power, inaugurate the greatest social and economic change in history." After his impassioned speech, the impassive judge sentenced him to 10 years in jail.

As the Ashanti proverb puts it:

When a poor person makes a proverb, it does not spread.

SEPTEMBER 15

On this day in the year 1810, Miguel de Hidalgo y Costilla rang his church bells in Querétaro and shouted the first cry for Mexican independence.

Under the banner of the Virgin of Guadalupe, Hidalgo's army of 50,000 peasants and Indians armed with practically nothing but farm tools advanced on other cities. The Old Creole priest was out to give the land back to the Indians, liberate the peons, and implement other reforms. But the uprising was short-lived. Four months later the rebels were decimated by the well-trained and well-armed Spanish regulars outside Guadalajara. Hidalgo was captured, defrocked, and executed.

As the French proverb puts it:

Don't show your teeth if you can't bite.

SEPTEMBER 16

On this day in the year 1963, P. M. O'Connor ordered the immediate release of Stanley Albert Randall from prison.

Randall had been put on probation at quarter sessions for 3 years on September 22, 1960, after being found guilty of housebreaking and theft. In August 1963, he was convicted by the local magistrate for a misdemeanor. He was to be bound over for 25 pounds on condition that he could find 2 sureties each in 10 pounds for his good behavior. The 40-year-old laborer of Queensmere, Essex, was unable to do so and was sent to prison for 6 months as a result. When the Recorder of Southland O'Connor heard about the action, he was furious. "It is an extraordinary case and it seems all wrong. I make no bones about it—I want to get him out of prison as fast as possible." Turning to the prosecutor, he asks: "Why is he in prison? He has almost completed his 3 years of probation and spoils it all by this 1 offense which is completely out of character."

As the English proverb puts it:

Much law but little justice.

SEPTEMBER 17

On this day in the year 1812, Meyer Rothschild dictated his last will.

The international banker bequeathed the control of his business completely into the hands of his sons, Kalmann and Salomon. The young Rothschilds, however, did not have their father's *savoir-vivre*, nor his ability to charm the courtiers. The young Rothschilds' forte was a kind of aggressive skill, which had been effective during the earlier emergency period but was no longer appreciated in the post-Napoleonic era. Welcomes by higher governmental functionaries gave way to evasions. The larger loans of Austria and France were now awarded to the more aristocratic bankers to handle. The cold shoulder continued until the 1818 issue of some 270 million francs for the liquidation of the French war indemnity. The final decision was to have been made at a conference with the victorious powers at Aix-la-Chapelle. Although ignored by salons and palaces through October, Kalmann and Salomon were no longer, came the morning of November 5. The French government had been noticing that their bonds from the 1817 loan were falling in value after a year's steady rise. The decline became steeper with time; financial institutions began to waver; a crash in the making. Why? The two brothers had been buying bonds with their immense reserves and abruptly dumping them. There was nothing for the once-haughty princes to do but bow the Rothschild clan back into the social whirl of European royalty. Overnight they became dignified as *The Rothschilds*.

As the Polish proverb puts it:

A golden key fits every door.

SEPTEMBER 18

On this day in the year 1773, Emilian Pugachev decided he was sufficiently powerful to take over the Cossacks in the region of Yaēk.

Declaring himself as none other than Tsar Peter III, who had escaped from his alleged death, the imposter from the Urals gathered a sizable following of Cossacks. Envisioning him as an effective tool against the boyars to reestablish their former position of authority, the leading Cossacks went along with his scheme and acknowledged him as Tsar. On that September day Pugachev demanded absolute allegiance. Those who refused would be tortured and killed. One of them was hung as a warning. The rest was compelled to march with him to take the fortress of Orenburg. This was to be a stepping-stone to the stronger town of Yaëk. But Pugachev was defeated at Tatisheva in the spring of 1774 and fled to Berda. The Cossacks began to intrigue about capturing and turning him over to the government, hoping to regain favor with the Tsar. Pugachev suspected their plans and stole away, leaving them to face the government troops in the battle ahead.

As the Welsh proverb puts it:

When you dine with the Devil, use a long spoon.

SEPTEMBER 19

On this day in the year 1418, Chu Ti received the Ambassador of Shādrukh Bahōdur.

The event was one of a long chain of diplomatic actions to restore friendly relations between China and Mongolia, which had been disrupted over the question of tribute. Initial attempts did not set well with either the Chinese or the Mongolian leader. Chu continued his claim of lord of the realms on the face of the earth and Shādrukh of the supremacy of Islam. The stalemate continued until the mutually deprecating nuances were gradually toned down. Finally, the Sultan was satisfied with Chu's reply of September 30, 1408. The Ming Emperor had struck a note of one ruler addressing another, instead of one speaking down to a vassal, and of one leader accepting gifts from another instead of tributes. Yet for home consumption, Chu had to retain an honorific elevation, which Shādrukh understood. At every mention, the Emperor's title extended slightly further into the margin of the text than the Sultan's.

As the Chinese proverb puts it:

Never take away a man's face.

SEPTEMBER 20

On this day in the year 1519, Ferdinand Magellan left Sanlúcar, Spain, with his 5 ships and 275 men.

Magellan's squadron circled the globe. But only 18 of his crew survived when the single ship *Victoria* reached Seville. The Portuguese navigator himself fell in a needless skirmish in the Philippines. Instead of concentrating on the navigational purpose of his trip, his missionary zeal had gotten the better of him. After arriving at the Island of Cebu, he talked the Chief into pledging allegiance to the King of Spain and embracing the Catholic faith. All the other island chiefs did the same, except the one on nearby Mactan. Magellan could not tolerate this dissent. Against the advice of his fellow officers, he landed 50 men to impose his wishes. They were met with a volley of javelins and arrows. Their armor protected the torsos, but the natives aimed low. As Magellan and his guard inched their way back toward the ships, a javelin struck his arm. Another spear slashed his leg. He pitched forward into the water. The mob pounced and hacked him to pieces, as the rest of his crew scurried back to safety and sailed away.

As the Danish proverb puts it:

If authority has no ears to listen, it has no head to govern.

SEPTEMBER 21

On this day in the year 1964, Robert N. Bavier, Jr., skippered the American *Constellation* in defense of the America's Cup against the British *Sovereign* off Newport, Rhode Island.

In preparation for the series, Bavier and his crew had developed a special maneuver, which up to then had been thought impossible with 12-meter sailboats. It was jibing with the spinnaker staysail set. The standard practice was to first lower the spinnaker staysail in order to swing the spinnaker pole through the fore-triangle. They devised a procedure of casting off the sheet and halyard just as the pole swung through. Besides not telegraphing one's intention ahead of time, the innovation saves 10 seconds of jibing time—an immense competitive advantage. Repeated rehearsals were conducted in secrecy to perfect this technique, ready to spring it on their rivals at the critical moment. As things turned out, it was never needed and never used. The *Constellation* won handily with conventional tactics in 4 straight races.

As the English proverb puts it:

Do not draw your dirk when a blow will do.

SEPTEMBER 22

On this day in the year 1945, Knut Hamsun appeared before the magistrate on charges of treason.

The date had been rescheduled after a few questions at a previous hearing on September 2, which had been postponed from May 26, when he and his wife were arrested for collaboration with the Nazi occupying authorities in Norway during World War II. After several questions, the September 22 session ended with yet another deferral to November 23. A couple more to May 1946, then September 1946, after which the Nobel Laureate in literature despaired in his memoirs: "My last postponement was until March 27, isn't that so? It is now March 1947 nearly April, but today I read that I have been put back until 'sometime during the summer'! I don't make any fuss over it, but only nod my head to show that I am aware of the situation. After 47 comes 48. A tame animal is tethered."

As the Czech proverb puts it:

Nothing kills so well as doing nothing.

SEPTEMBER 23

On this day in the year 1974, William B. Saxbe told the convention of the International Association of Chiefs of Police in Washington D.C., that prosecutors and the courts were responsible for the rising crime rates in America.

The United States Attorney General presented the results of a recent study in law enforcement showing that of 278 adults arrested in Atlanta, Georgia, for assault, 103 were indicted, 77 went to trial, 63 were convicted, and 23 were jailed. "What begins emerging here is the suspicion that many seriously dangerous offenders slip through the net of criminal justice, free to prey on society again," he said. Altogether too often, he continued, plea bargaining was used "by prosecutors to allow vast numbers of offenders at the state and local level to receive minimal punishment, if any at all."

As the English proverb puts it.

Mercy to the criminal may be cruelty to the people.

SEPTEMBER 24

On this day in the year 1814, Charles Maurice de Talley-rand-Périgord arrived in Vienna for an international meeting to reorganize Europe after 15 years of French hegemony.

Austria, Prussia, Russia, and Great Britain had agreed in the Treaty of Chaumont in March to present a solid front to Talleyrand. The Big Four were to take the initiative and submit their solutions to the assembled Congress of Vienna in September for ratification. But the French delegate proved too wily to be boxed out of power just because Paris had surrendered to the Allies 6 months earlier. He had convinced Tsar Alexander I, when the latter was his house guest after the capitulation of France, that Europe's peace and stability can only be assured by the return of Louis XVII as the Bourbon monarch. He had also taken note of the secret defense alliance of France, Russia, and Great Britain against Prussia. This would neutralize whatever urge Prussia had about going to war should the turn of events prove favorable to France. By playing on their dissension, he was able to manipulate the situation such that the Big Four had to invite France to join them as equal partners as the Big Five. The complicated territorial settlement was finally worked out and signed by all the European nations on June 9, 1815. In so doing Talley-rand was able to restore the front-rank status for France in European affairs surprisingly soon after her defeat.

As the Bulgarian proverb puts it:

When the stallions kick each other, the donkeys eat better hay.

SEPTEMBER 25

On this day in the year 1538, Kheyr-ed-Din, better known as Barbarossa, again challenged Andrea Doria in the Gulf of Arta.

The Algerian corsair with 122 galleys took on the greatest Christian admiral of the period with 166 galleys, 64 sailing vessels and 60,000 men. He sailed out from the Gulf and bombarded the becalmed *Galleon of Venice*, which had been ordered by Doria to fight. The battle went on all afternoon. As the galleon was preparing for what seemed to be its last stand, with the mast and upper deck shattered and the Lion Standard of St. Mark fallen, Barbarossa drew away to destroy several other Christian ships. Meantime, Doria did nothing to help, not even pulling up anchor for several hours. When he did so, he merely sailed back and forth as if attempting to draw Barbarossa farther out to deeper waters. The winds were in Doria's favor and he could have fought with advantage. To the dismay of the captains of the Papal and Venetian galleys, Doria turned away and headed for Corfu with his remaining ships without joining battle, leaving the Mohammedans masters of the Mediterranean for 30 years.

As the Russian proverb puts it:

To run away is not glorious but very healthy.

SEPTEMBER 26

On this day in the year 1789, Honoré Gabriel de Mirabeau rose a third time in the French Assembly to call for drastic measures to save the country from bankruptcy.

One of the proposals involved a 25% income tax. The opposition was on the verge of killing the bill, while the Count was out refining its language. Returning to the debate, he dared his fellow law-makers to look the disastrous threat in the face and agree that his list of 2000 wealthy men alone could make up the national deficit. He reasoned with them about giving up "a portion of one's income to save all of one's possessions." Unless they acted then and there, there would be universal ruin. "Vote, then, for this extraordinary subsidy; and it may be sufficient! Vote for it, if you have doubts on the means adopted, you have none as to its necessity or our inability to provide an immediate substitute. Vote, then, because public necessity admits no delay and we shall be held responsible for any delay that takes place. Beware of asking for more time! Misfortune never grants it!" Winding up his passionate speech, he said: "But today bankruptcy—hideous bankruptcy is here—it threatens to consume you, your properties, your honor! And yet you deliberate!"

As the Ewe proverb puts it:

When the snake is in the house, there is no need to discuss the matter at length.

SEPTEMBER 27

On this day in the year 1814, Charles Maurice de Talleyrand-Périgord arrived in Vienna for an international meeting to reorganize formation of the Society of Jesus.

While on their way to Rome during November 1537, Ignatius and his fellow Iniguists, Peter Faber and Diego Laynez, stopped by a little shrine at the intersection of the old Roman roads Claudia and Cassia. As he was praying a vision appeared. God the Father motioned to Christ carrying the cross, "I would that Thou take him for Thy servant." Then Christ looked to Ignatius and said, "I wish that you be My servant." The Father reassured Ignatius, "and I will be propitious to you at Rome." He had every reason to be optimistic about his request for a papal charter to their new religious order, submitted on the Feast of St. John the Baptist in 1539. But practical complications arose. Cardinal Ghinucci's objections negated the support of Cardinal Gaspar Contarini. The appointed arbiter Cardinal Bartolomeo Guidiccioni was negative. Ignatius and his associates had to rally overwhelming pressure. Through the friendly magistrates of Parma, the niece of the pope, Countess of Santa Fiora, was enlisted to contact Frederico del Prato, Charge d'Affairs for Parma at Rome; the Apostle of Sinna Paschase Broet called on Archbishop Bandini and the legate at Bologna Cardinal Ferreri; John III wrote the Pope himself. Francis I and others were also solicited to join the campaign. The resistance crumbled before this phalanx of influence and the Jesuits came into being.

As the Indian proverb puts it:

Call on God but row away from the rocks.

SEPTEMBER 28

On this day in the year 1859, Henri-Frederic Amiel went through a self-analysis with regard to his own sexual passion.

The 39-year-old Swiss professor of philosophy confessed in his diary that he was not as bashful about caresses, kisses, and bawdy stories as he used to be. "But practically I am not yet a man; I still belong to the fraternity of dreamers, seminarists, white monks," he wrote on. "Now this is a stupid position to occupy at my age; for if old maids are bores, old virgins of the male sex are perhaps laughable." He became determined therefore to "take the bull by the horns, no matter how great my repugnance, at first opportunity."

As the Irish proverb puts it:

Every hound's a pup until it hunts.

SEPTEMBER 29

On this day in the year 1919, Enrico Caruso sang in Mexico City for the first time in *L'Elisir d'Amore.*

Since his official debut in Naples in *L'Amico Francesco* on November 16, 1894, the Italian tenor had performed to great acclaim all over the world. Throughout his tours ending with his last appearance at the Metropolitan Opera House in New York City on December 24, 1920, in *La Juive,* he had always made it a point to be generous to the local people in ways other than sheer singing. Caruso would buy generously. When he did not have time for shopping, he would often send his personal secretary Bruno Zirato to donate some money for charity to the mayor or the president of the local chamber of commerce. On one occasion he purchased the entire stock of a little china shop in Niagara Falls. About why he acquired items he did not need, he simply smiled: "If I come to this city and ask the people to pay me $7000, I have to leave something to the merchants."

As the Mexican proverb puts it:

Do not refuse a wing to the person who gave you the whole chicken.

SEPTEMBER 30

On this day in the year 1903, Edward H. Harriman became a director of the Erie Railroad.

Throughout his executive career he had emphasized the delegation of responsibilities. During one of the meetings of the Executive Committee, approval was sought by the manager for $10,000 for the procurement of mules for the company's coal mines. "If the manager in charge cannot be trusted to buy mules without bringing the subject to the Executive Committee, a new manager should be selected," the transportation tycoon interrupted the debate. "My time is worth about a mule a minute and I can't stay to hear the rest of the discussion. I vote 'Aye' on the requisition."

As the Japanese proverb puts it:

Even the best hawk will not snare game unless let loose.

OCTOBER 1

On this day in the year 331 B.C., Alexander again defeated Darius and became the Great King of the former Persian Empire.

The Macedonian army was not large—only about 30,000 infantry and 7000 cavalry. But it was extremely well trained and organized. Alexander varied the tactics to fit the situation. The basic formation was a center-anchoring phalanx of 9000 heavily armed infantry. This was tightly structured, 3 feet between men in a mobile rectangle 18 or more men deep. On the right was the striking arm of the cavalry, with Alexander himself in their midst, and farther out the lancers, javelin men, and archers for flanking and skirmishing purposes. On the left were the other horsemen and light troops. One of the most effective tactics was for the left to hold firm, while Alexander on the right charged at the decisive moment and rolled the enemy onto the spears of the slowly advancing phalanx. Over and over, Alexander rehearsed the maneuver and variations in mock battles. Despite his much smaller army Alexander crushed Darius at the decisive confrontation at Gaugemela, east of the Tigris River.

As the Hausan proverb puts it:

To flay an elephant, the knife needs not be large but sharp.

OCTOBER 2

On this day in the year 1965, Fidel Castro reorganized the United Party of the Socialist Revolution into the Communist Party of Cuba and assumed the position of its First Secretary.

The Party's chief organizer was replaced in the process. So was the President of the National Institute for Agrarian Reform. Of the four official newspapers, two were combined into one and another abolished. Several years later 40 pro-Soviet members of the Party were purged. The head of the National Fruit Corporation and the Chairman of the Committee for the Defense of the Revolution were removed. Military commanders were continuously being reshuffled. By means of such incessant discontinuities in leaderships of key institutions, potential challengers to Castro never had a chance to grow to menacing proportions.

As the Japanese proverb puts it:

There is no being bored with precautions.

OCTOBER 3

On this day in the year 1930, Getúlio Vargas gave the signal for the coup against Júlio Prestes.

After the bitter and fraudulent presidential election of March 1, in which Prestes was declared the victor against Vargas, a revolutionary state of mind built up rapidly among the losers. When one of Vargas' political associates, the President of Pariaba João Pessoa, was murdered on July 26 at the hands of assassins hired by the government, subversive planning moved into high gear. Everything was ready in early September. But Vargas waited until firm assurances of support were received from the military commanders in Rio. By October 24, the Rio government was driven from office. A junta of two generals and an admiral formed an interim ruling body. After a week, they refused to relinquish power, having received the backing of the Chief of Police, Bertoldo Klinger, whereupon the junta was told by Vargas' friend Oswaldo Aranha that the revolutionary armies recognized only Vargas and would bury the 3 of them by bullets if necessary. They capitulated and Vargas took over on November 3.

As the Persian proverb puts it:

Keep the dogs near when you suppeth with the wolf.

OCTOBER 4

On this day in the year 1932, Samuel Insull was indicted for embezzlement by the Chicago Cook County Grand Jury.

He had set up the Insull Securities Company and other firms in the twenties to sell stocks to the new crop of Americans coming out of World War I. And sell them he did. During the first 8 months of 1929 the stock in Insull Utility Investments rose from $30 to $147 per share. Insull became the richest man in Chicago. On October 28, 1929, the stock market dropped precipitously. Companies began to fail. Insull tried to shore up his own corporations. It was to no avail. In April 1932 he was compelled to turn over his stocks, estate, and life insurance to creditors. Insull and his wife left quietly from Quebec for a trip to Europe and disappeared from sight. By September the investigators unearthed a series of irregularities. Against a background of losses to investors of the order of $700 million in Middle West Securities and $85 million in Corporation Securities, Insull had given illegal preferences to special creditors, transferred assets to pay questionable broker's fees, shifted collaterals among his companies, spread large profits among 1600 favored members, placed friends and relatives on the payroll in droves, and so on. He was finally tracked down and brought to trial on October 2, 1934.

As the Bantu proverb puts it:

Who learns how to steal must also learn how to run.

OCTOBER 5

On this day in the year 1918, Max von Baden called for an armistice based on an acceptance of Woodrow Wilson's "Fourteen Points."

Secret agreements among the Allies, however, were not quite consistent with the "Fourteen Points," as had been publicly declared before Congress on January 8 and understood by the German Prince. For example, it had been assumed by the French as early as 1916 that Germany would lose the Saar and the left bank of the Rhine. When the German representative Count von Brockdorff-Rantzau balked at the incompatibly severe terms, the Allies stated that the war would be resumed and the German land occupied. The Germans had no choice but to give in and the Versailles Treaty was signed on June 28, 1918. In the eyes of the German people the terms were so harsh that their envoys were referred to as "the November criminals" for many years thereafter.

As the French proverb puts it:

The beaten pays the fine.

OCTOBER 6

On this day in the year 1965, Arthur Gray pleaded not guilty to murdering his only child but guilty to manslaughter.

Accepting the pleas of the 44-year-old assistant foreman of Monmouthshire in Wales, Justice Streatfeild took note of the prosecutor's report: the father had been devoted to his partly paralyzed 12-year-old son, who was bedridden in constant pain with incurable cancer. Even the pressure of the bed clothes caused him agony. Gray decided to put an end to the suffering and, after giving the son some sleeping tablets, gassed him to death. "I am the last person in the world to think of punishing you for this offense, dreadful though it was," said the judge. "Your circumstances were quite intolerable and although it may be wrong ethically to take life, I can quite understand your motive in this case in that you felt positively driven to it. I can quite understand, too, that you felt you did the right thing. I am perfectly certain that there is not a single person in this court or outside of it who will feel you are in any sense a criminal. I am equally certain there is a forgiveness hereafter for you, just as there will be on earth." The father was sentenced to a 2-year probation, on condition of psychiatric treatment not to exceed 12 months.

As the Cairene proverb puts it:

Whenever a good person is needed, there he appears.

OCTOBER 7

On this day in the year 1337, Edward III of England claimed the added title of King of France and instructed the Bishop of Lincoln to pass the request to Philip VI to surrender his throne.

It seemed clear that to implement Edward's desires, England with a population of only 4 million would have to gain a quick military victory against France, with its 15 million people. If the French would avoid pitched battles and just hang on, sooner or later Edward would have to fold from exhaustion. When Philip forgot this elementary point and attacked the well-drilled English army with its tremendous firepower of archers near Crécy on August 26, 1346, the French left 10,000 dead on the field. The King himself had to flee. With the monarchy crumbling and the combat situation getting desperate, local defense units of peasants began to fill the void with some very capable leaders. From then on the French resistance, now under the command of Charles of Navarre, avoided all major stands. Material vacuums were created around the English wherever they went. The strategy proved costly for Edward, whose army finally arrived at the gates of Paris on March 31, 1360, exhausted and starving. He sued for peace.

As the Jabo proverb puts it:

Slowly, slowly will catch the monkey.

OCTOBER 8

On this day in the year 1629, René Descartes implored his friend Marin Marsenne not to address any more questions to him for a while.

The French philosopher explained to the Minim friar that he was absorbed in research on meteors and could not be diverted to thinking about other issues. "My mind is not sufficiently strong to dwell on several subjects at the same time," he brought out in his letter. "Since I can never discover anything except by a long sequence of consideration from various angles, I must immerse myself completely in one subject whenever I want to examine a facet of it."

As the Turkish proverb puts it:

The person who embraces much collects little.

OCTOBER 9

On this day in the year 1946, Eugene O'Neill saw his play *The Iceman Cometh* on Broadway hailed as "a superb drama of spendid and imposing stature which is at once powerful, moving, beautiful, eloquent and compassionate."

Some of the major characters in his masterpiece had been inspired by the people with whom O'Neill had lived two decades before. There he was in 1915—nearly penniless, out of a job, no hope of any money from playwriting. He was all alone, finding some solace in the company of the down-and-out habitués of a ramshackle saloon, called the Hell Hole, saturated with the smell of sour beer and talk of despairing woe. One of them by the name of "Happy" largely shaped the personality of Hickey. Another by the name of Terry Carlin became the one-time syndicalist-anarchist Larry Slade. Marie, a street girl rescued by Terry but later deserting him for a mountain retreat, became Anna Christie, who felt herself reborn on her father's barge and reflected: "It all seems like I'd been here before lots of times . . . why d'you s'pose I feel—so—like I'd found something I'd missed and been looking for . . . And I seem to have forgot—everything what's happened—like it didn't matter no more. And I can feel clean, somehow—like you feel just after you've took a bath. And I feel happy for once—yes, honest!—happier than I ever been anywhere before!"

As the Swiss proverb puts it:

The tree of knowledge is watered with tears.

OCTOBER 10

On this day in the year 1806, James Wilkinson sent a note to the Spanish Viceroy in Mexico City offering to reveal, for an immediate payment of $150,000 in gold, a pending plot injurious to Spanish rights in North America.

At the same time he dispatched another message to the American President, informing him of a move to dismember the West from American jurisdiction, stating his intent to protect the government's interest, and asking for instructions. Actually, Wilkinson himself had been half-heartedly collaborating with Aaron Burr to establish an independent empire in the West. Burr had sent him a letter saying that the plan had been set in motion. Wilkinson was given a series of directives with the promised reward that "Wilkinson will be second to Burr only." On receipt of the coded letter, the General detected gaping holes and foolhardy weaknesses throughout the approach. He therefore decided to save his own compromised skin by sacrificing his senior partner.

As the Bosnian proverb puts it:

Whoever lies for you will lie against you.

OCTOBER 11

On this day in the year 1633, Thomas Hooker was chosen pastor of the Newton congregation on the Charles River in Massachusetts.

The noblest of the New England Puritans had been a controversial nonconforming preacher in England. Hooker's unorthodox ideas were being repeated by the younger ministers in pulpits throughout the country, which incurred the anger of the ecclesiastics. "Our people's palate grow so out of tast, yt noe food contents them but of Mr. Hooker's dressing, the Vicar of Braintree protested to his superiors. "I have lived in Essex to see many changes, and have seene the people idolizing many new ministers and lecturers, but this surpasses them all for learning and some other considerable partes and . . . gains more and far greater followers than all beside him . . . If my Lord tender his owne future peace . . . let him connive at Mr. Hooker's departure." After narrowly escaping capture by the King's officers in England, Hooker sailed away on the *Griffin* in July for another land. The fugitive from religious persecution finally found the opportunity for service in America, which he had been pursuing for so long in England without success.

As the Chinese proverb puts it:

When there is no fish in one spot, cast your net in another.

OCTOBER 12

On this day in the year 1936, Miguel de Unamuno publicly defended the Spanish intellectual against the military.

Standing before a large portrait of Generalissimo Francisco Franco, General José Millan Astray addressed a convocation in the old Lecture Hall. He derided the Salamancan way of life, condemned the intellectuals, and rallied the new rightist disciples with the cry: "Long live death!" Astray's supporters in the audience burst out in thunderous approbation, whereupon the philosopher-poet and rector rose to deplore the sickness in the kind of philosophy with which Astray was attempting to saddle the Spanish people, ending with the cry: "Long live intelligence!" When dictator Franco heard about the challenge, he became determined to bring Spain's leading intellectual into line. "Shoot him, if necessary!" But that was not necessary. Unamuno died shortly thereafter on his own.

As the Spanish proverb puts it:

He who draws his sword with reason never lays it down without honor.

OCTOBER 13

On this day in the year 1974, Morinosuka Kajima said in Tokyo that he had organized a 14-month campaign to obtain the just-announced Nobel Peace Prize for Eisaku Sato.

The chairman of the construction firm Kajima Corporation and founder of the Kajima Peace Corporation stated that he "thought it was just about time to get the recognition for a Japanese, whose country has pursued peace under the no-war constitution rejecting nuclear arms." He obtained the cooperation of the Foreign Ministry, which instructed the Japanese diplomats throughout the world to promote the cause. Sato's speeches were translated, published, and distributed widely. The American Secretary of State sent aides to Japan to proofread the supporting documents. The former Japanese ambassador to the United Nations and then President of the

Kajima Peace Corporation, Toshikazu Kase, undertook a 10-month trip as a Foreign Ministry advisor, during which, he advanced Sato's nomination, especially before those former United Nations' representatives who were influential in the awarding of the prize. When Sato's award was proclaimed, most of the world was surprised. But his Japanese supporters were not—only expectantly pleased.

As the English proverb puts it:

Lay it on thick, some will stick.

OCTOBER 14

On this day in the year 1774, Philip Vickers Fithian became much agitated about the disorder on his face, although it did not interfere with his sleep or work.

"But my temper, I fear, in these respects is very phlegmatic; I find it unpleasing to myself, and it would be certainly unpleasant to anyone who was interested in my complaints," the Virginian schoolteacher recorded in his diary. "I am of so strange a constitution that very trifles make me utterly unhappy—a mere conceit, frivolous and unsubstantial often takes away my rest—This feeling I have possest from my infancy, I remember very well that a Cuff on my Ear would make me sullen for Several days when I was too young to go out to school; afterwards a disappointment of an hours play would make me disrelish for a long time both play-fellows and all Diversion! When I was at College one Blunder at recitation, or in any performance of my duty would make me dull, low-Spirited, and peevish; in fact any disappointment, even the most inconsiderable seems to have a general Effect on my Passions and mingle fear, and anger, and rage, together with many others which are excited by different and disagreeable modifications of our Bodies, and, tho' I am conscious of this frailty in myself, I have not yet brought it under so good subjection, as to make these humours give way intirely to Philosophy or Religion—It is, however, my constant study how I may accomplish this much wish'd for habit."

As the Nigerian proverb puts it:

A person must know not only how to ride but also how to fall.

OCTOBER 15

On this day in the year 1759, M. d'Affry turned down the Duc de Choiseul's request for assistance to Giacomo Casanova when he visited Holland.

Casanova's reputation for indiscretion, gambling, lusting, and bad company was known to d'Affry, who wanted no part of it. The case of Manon Balleti was not atypical. She had been seduced under repeated promise of marriage. This was solemnly pledged again by the Italian lover to her mother, who, before passing away, commended her daughter to his care. In his rendezvous with Manon on the eve of his departure for Holland, he swore that he would marry her—very soon. Manon finally came to her senses after he left town. On Christmas day Casanova received a package of his picture and letters. "Please return me my picture and if you have retained any of my letters, please burn them," the accompanying note from Manon came to the point. "I count on your honesty. Forget me! Duty compels me to do everything I can to forget you, because at this hour tomorrow I shall be the wife of Monsieur Blondel, the Architect to the King and Member of his Academy. You will do me the favor of pretending not to recognize me should you ever run into me when you come back to Paris."

As the English proverb puts it:

When a man keeps repeating his promise, he means to fail you.

OCTOBER 16

On this day in the year 1968, H.E. Sargant warned against the loss of public liberties.

In his inaugural address, the President of the Law Society of England reminded his fellow solicitors that the law is what the government of the day imposes. "Sometimes this is for the benefit of the majority, sometimes solely for the benefit of a minority," Sargant continued. "But frequently, whether for the benefit of the majority or the minority, the liberty of the individual becomes further curtailed." He exhorted them to maintain their independence from the government—not for selfish purposes, but to insure that the private citizen, how-

ever humble, would not be left without a champion to fight
for his freedom.

As the Kenyan proverb puts it:

Speak up, lest tomorrow you be prevented.

OCTOBER 17

On this day in the year 1904, A. P. Giannini said to his young
teller: "Vic, you may now open the front door."

The front door led, 5 decades later, to the largest bank in
the world. It began in the year 1953 with assets of $8,201,-
689,369.88, with 538 branches in 317 Californian cities and
towns. The giant concern catered especially to the little fellow. The deposits were distributed among 5,136,285 separate
accounts, averaging $873 for savings and $1567 for checking
balances, in the Bank of America.

As the Chinese proverb puts it:

The great river does not refuse the waters of tiny streams.

OCTOBER 18

On this day in the year 1604, Dmitri captured his first town
of Moravsk as he crossed the Dnieper from Poland to depose
Boris Godunov.

The Pretender to the Russian throne had claimed that the
Tsarevich had not been murdered by agents of the Tsar Boris
as had been believed by the populace. Another child had
been killed in his place. He Dmitri was the true living son of
Ivan IV and heir to the Russian throne. As his army advanced on to Moscow, the powerful boyar Vasili Shuiski appeared before the restless people at the Kremlin to bolster up
their morale. He swore on the cross that the true Tsarevich
was indeed dead: "I laid his body in the grave at Uglich with
my own hands. The man who uses the Tsarevich's name is an
imposter, who is actually an unfrocked fugitive monk in
league with the Devil and has been sentenced to death for his
crimes." But Dmitri was unstoppable. His messengers demanded surrender by Boris' son, Tsar Feodor, announced
pardon for those who had been misled, and summoned the
boyars, dyaks, and commanders to meet with Dmitri at Tula.
The crowd again asked Shuiski to speak the truth about the

Tsarevich. He expediently reversed himself: "Boris had sent an assassin to Uglich to murder the Tsarevich. But the son of a priest was substituted and the Tsarevich was saved." Dmitri was crowned Tsar on July 30, 1605, and Shuiski was pardoned.

As the French proverb puts it:

Dissimulation is a coward's virtue.

OCTOBER 19

On this day in the year 1846, Heinrich Heine mailed off another one of his characteristic letters to Heinrich Laube.

"I am glad you are coming," the lyric poet welcomed the news of his friend's visit. "Do not delay too long. Although my illness is a chronic affair, a sudden change may take place. If so you would arrive too late to argue with me about immortality, Fatherland, and other important questions. As a matter of fact, you might even find me singularly silent. I shall be at Faubourg Poissonière, No. 41 at least for the winter. If you do not find me here, then look for me in the Montmarte Cemetery, not at Père Lachaise—it's too noisy there for me." His continuous pain did not dull his delightful sense of humor, as he matter-of-factly took his coming death in stride.

As the English proverb puts it:

I owe God a death.

OCTOBER 20

On this day in the year 1952, Jomo Kenyatta was arrested by the British government in Kenya.

He had aroused his fellow Africans to a feverish pitch with a long-drawn blood-curdling cry of "Eeeeeeee." 3 months before at a meeting of the Kenya African Union. "God said this is our land," he sounded the call for unity of the natives. "Land in which we are to flourish as a people. We are not worried that other races are here with us in our country, but we insist that we are the leaders here, and what we want we get. We want our cattle to get fat on our land so that our children grow up in prosperity; we do not want that fat removed to feed others." When a Christian Kikuyu and British civil servant was subsequently murdered, the Governor declared a state of emergency. Before long 1400 British soldiers, white settlers, Mau-Mau terrorists, and natives were dead. Kenyatta was found guilty of sedition. After a decade of imprisonment, he had to be released to take over from the British. The latter simply could not win the fight in a milieu of people that were Kenyatta's.

As the Ronga proverb puts it:

The strength of the crocodile is water.

OCTOBER 21

On this day in the year 1788, Sun Shih-i crossed into Vietnam to restore the Le dynasty to the throne.

The Chinese expeditionary force of 15,000 men chased the rebel Nguyen Hue out of Hanoi and reinvested Emperor Le in about a month. Having achieved its purpose the Chinese Grand Council disapproved Sun's plans to move south to capture Nguyen in Quangnam and ordered him home. The campaign would have required over 53 additional stations along the way and another 100,000 men, which the Council could ill afford. Furthermore, the Chinese were not accustomed to the local climate and might well succumb to diseases and other stresses when the rains came. But Sun was driven by the desire for complete victory and pressed on. He was caught by surprise by Nguyen and driven back in disarray. Less than half of his army returned alive.

As the Greek proverb puts it:

Passions make good servants but bad masters.

OCTOBER 22

On this day in the year 1906, J. C. Thresh presided over a meeting of the Incorporated Institute of Hygiene in London to resolve the scare produced by the so-called revelations about canned foods.

Sixty million tins of canned salmon alone were being consumed annually in England and the population was becoming concerned about the safety of all canned foods. Managers of large institutions were asking health officials about the potential hazards of supplying them to their residents. Retail dealers were seeking inspection of their stocks with the issuance of certificates for continued sale. Many individuals were pressing for some reliable home method for ascertaining the wholesomeness of such commodities. "The recent scare had resulted in the less thoughtful class being filled with disgust," reported a London newspaper. "They believed all that they saw in print, and were incapable of perceiving that the statements might have the flimsiest foundation on facts, that everything might have been grossly exaggerated, and that the so-called revelations, which they were led to believe were made solely in the interests of public health, might have been made for an entirely different purpose."

As the Chinese proverb puts it:

One dog barks at the shadow; a hundred dogs bark at its bark.

OCTOBER 23

On this day in the year 1454, Thomas Devon surrounded the manor of Nicholas Radford with 100 henchmen.

The son of the Earl of Courtenay had seen his father humiliated by Lord Bonville during the War of the Roses. He sought revenge by striking at Sir Nicholas, who was Bonville's close friend. How to gain entry was the immediate problem. So young Devon swore on his "faith and truth" as a "true knight and gentleman" that Sir Nicholas would "suffer no bodily harm" and the property would not be damaged. Once let in, however, his men stripped the chapel, cleared out the stable, looted the house, and even pilfered the very bedsheets on which sick Lady Radford was lying. The elderly and feeble Sir Nicholas was kidnapped and hauled away. Less than a stone's throw from the door, one of Devon's servants hacked at his head until the brains spilled out, another slit his throat, and a third stabbed his heart, as Devon rode off yelling, "Farewell, Radford!"

As the Greek proverb puts it:

Remember to distrust.

OCTOBER 24

On this day in the year 1955, Jean-Pierre Hallet stood in a dugout canoe dynamiting fish off the eastern shore of Lake Tanganyika.

The Belgian argonomist-sociologist, who had spent his life in the Congo, had received word that 1000 families in South Mosso were facing starvation because of a severe drought. He sped to the area and augmented the natives' food supply by lighting sticks of dynamite and tossing them into schools of fish for days. In the process, a 2-stick charge with a defective fuse suddenly blew up in his right hand. The Hôpital Rodhain in Usumbura was some 200 winding miles farther north, after a 12-mile trip canoeing, hiking, and driving from Mwekarago Cove to Nyanza Lac. When he finally arrived in blood and pain, a medical aide hurriedly wheeled a litter forward. —"Something in me had rebelled at the thought of being carried into the hospital," Hallet recalled later. "I wanted to finish my trip the way I'd started it, the way I'd been forced to continue it for 8 terrible hours; and under my own power." He pushed his way through the swinging door, lurched toward a high metal bed, climbed up unassisted, and passed out for 48 hours.

As the Pedi proverb puts it:

The sweat of a brave person is blood.

OCTOBER 25

On this day in the year 1940, John L. Lewis made a slashing attack over nationwide radio to an estimated 30 million Americans against the President's campaign for a third term.

The powerful labor leader had opposed the third term as a "national evil of the first magnitude." He had objected to American intervention in Europe and was angered with the 8-year failure to solve many of the pressing domestic problems. Flushed with the feeling that he personally represented not only the CIO but all workers in America and with the belief that their loyalty to him was overwhelmingly greater than even that to the popular President, Lewis vowed that if the President were reelected again, "It will mean that the members of the Congress of Industrial Organizations have rejected my advice and recommendations. I will accept the results as being the equivalent of a vote of no confidence, and will retire as President of the Congress of Industrial Organizations, at its convention in November." The President won handily and Lewis stepped down.

As the English proverb puts it:

Make not thy sail too big for thy ballost.

OCTOBER 26

On this day in the year 1911, J. L. Garvin explained his reasons for not challenging the leadership of the Unionist party in England in a letter to Moreton Frewen.

There had been much grumbling within the ranks over the effectiveness of Arthur James Balfour. The Editor of the *Observer* himself despaired over Balfour's capacity to improve. Nevertheless, he bent every effort to prevent an intraparty feud. "The point about A. J. B. is rather a more difficult one since a leader's main business is not to subtilize but to mobilize," he wrote the member of Parliament from North-east Cork. "However, I hate all public squabbles. The greatest self-restraint is being shown by men who have been much provoked and, I hope, the quiet conversations going on will result, in a few weeks, in restoring the most complete fighting unity that our party has known for years."

As the Chinese proverb puts it:

When brothers split, outsiders enter the breach.

OCTOBBER 27

On this day in the year 1921, Feodor Ivanovich Chaliapin mailed off a letter of disappointment from New York City to his daughter Irina.

After triumphant performances at the Drury Lane Theater in London, the Russian basso had just landed for his American tour. Although he was very happy about the applauses in England, he was saddened by the number of exploiters hanging onto his coattails and actually cheating him on several occasions. Nevertheless, he was glad to have received more than 1000 pounds for famine relief in Russia, as well as many expressions of sympathy. After a few days in America he became disenchanted with it as well. He was required by the immigration officials "to state that my own contracts forbid me to give any concerts that would help these poor starving people at home." He was nauseated by the whole affair. "Oh my Irina, if only you knew the rascals and swindlers one comes across in Europe and America. They shelter under the respectable title of 'businessmen.' If one of them grabs something, he calls it 'business,' a splendid term. It doesn't sound as bad as plain robbery, though charmingly retains the same meaning."

As the English proverb puts it:

Much and money go together.

OCTOBER 28

On this day in the year 1937, Hino Ashihei wrote in his diary about the many talismans carried by his fellow Japanese soldiers in the Battle of Shanghai.

The most popular was the "belt of 1000 stitches," which was supposed to protect the wearer from wounds. It contained 1000 stitches of red threads sewn by well-wishes, given to the soldiers leaving for the war zone. One of the men, however, was constantly ridiculing the superstition. After all, he reminded his buddies, the Chinese troops also have amulets of their own. What kind of war is it, then, if they actually worked and nobody gets killed? "Of course, this was true and the men knew it," Ashihei recorded his annoyance. "Even so they do have faith in their charms. He seemed so cruel and heartless. If he himself does not want to believe in them, that is quite all right. But why should he go around shaking the confidence of the simple souls who did?" The cynic fell off the ship into the water on the way home and had to be rescued. As he was being pulled dripping wet into the lifeboat, lo and behold, tightly clutched in his hands was his own "belt of 1000 stitches."

As the Bengali proverb puts it:

The sieve says to the needle, "You have a large hole in your tail."

OCTOBER 29

On this day in the year 1970, John Weber began his forty-fourth year in the Chillicothe Correctional Institute in Ohio.

At age 95, Weber was the oldest known prisoner in the United States at the time. He was not the longest-serving prisoner. That record belonged to John Van Kyke Grigsby, who was discharged from Indiana State Prison in December 1974 at age 90, after serving 66 years and 127 days. Long as their life sentences were, however, they were nowhere near the one given to 2 confidence tricksters in Iran on June 15, 1969. That was 7109 years.

As the English proverb puts it:

In a thousand pounds of law there is not an ounce of love.

OCTOBER 30

On this day in the year 1503, Giuliano Della Rovere was given betting odds of 60% by the banks in Rome of being elected pope.

By the next day the odds shot up to 90%. To enter the conclave with sufficient votes in his pocket, the impetuous nephew of Sixtus IV had to make bargains, some of which were mutually exclusive. To Caesar Borgia, whose delegation was essential, the Cardinal promised the return of the state of Romagna, the position of Gonfalonier of the Church, and the use of Ostia for his personal safety. The Duke was so taken by these inducements that he forgot that the Cardinal had spent 10 years in self-exile out of dislike for the very name of Borgia. But when Rovere won on the first ballot and became Pope Julius II, he did not forget the past: Romagna was not given back; the Duke was not appointed Gonfalonier; he was not accorded guarantees of safe conduct by the Florentines as he went to Ostia to take ship. Niccolò Machiavelli had earlier surmised just as much from his diplomatic observation post in Rome: "The Duke allows himself to be carried away by his brave confidence, and believes that other people's words are more to be relied upon than his own."

As the Italian proverb puts it:

Trust not a reconciled enemy.

OCTOBER 31

On this day in the year 1517, Martin Luther nailed his Ninety-Five Theses on the door of the church at Wittenberg, which housed 4 hairs from the Virgin Mary, a strand of Christ's beard, a nail from the cross, 19,013 sacred bones, and other relics, which, if properly venerated and accompanied by an appropriate monetary contribution, would reduce 1,902,202 years and 270 days from one's sentence in Purgatory.

It took the Vatican bureaucracy until January 9, 1520, to institute proceedings against Luther. Not until June 15 was the papal bull of condemnation ready to go to press. In the meantime Luther himself had formulated the basic framework of his own thinking in clear terms and distributed his ideas widely to the German people. By the time the Diet of Worms was assembled on April 18, 1521, he had already gained such footing that he staked his position unflinchingly to the young emperor: "I cannot and I will not recant anything, for to go against conscience is neither right nor safe. God help me. Amen. Here I stand. I cannot do otherwise." The momentum of Lutheranism could not be stopped. The Medici Curia was too late and the corruption too widespread.

As the Chinese proverb puts it:

Prepare for calamity not yet in the bud.

NOVEMBER 1

On this day in the year 1929, Albert B. Fall was sentenced to a year in jail and a fine of $100,000.

The Secretary of Interior had accepted a bribe from Edward L. Doheny and approved the leasing of the Elks Hills naval oil reserve to private entrepreneurs.

As the Italian proverb puts it:

A greased mouth cannot say no.

NOVEMBER 2

On this day in the year 1907, John Pierpont Morgan called a meeting of the captains of the financial world of New York City to calm the panic of collapsing companies and trusts.

The bankers and financiers were ushered into the East Room of his marble library. From them he wanted $25 million to rescue Tennessee Coal and Iron, and Moore and Schley. The trust officials were led into the West Room. From them he asked for another $25 million to rescue the besieged Trust Company of America. Morgan stationed himself in the small Librarian's Room, just inside the entrance, as he talked to one chief executive after another about their commitments. When Benjamin Strong of Bankers Trust completed his private discussion with Morgan and started to leave, he found the door locked with the key in Morgan's pocket. He had to go back to the lounge in the East Room and wait until the session broke up at five fifteen in the morning. Morgan obtained the necessary assurances. With the approval of the federal government, the plan was put into effect and the financial crisis was abated.

As the Chinese proverb puts it:

For a swift arrow, pull hard on the string.

NOVEMBER 3

On this day in the year 1896, Mark Hanna wired William McKinley on his election as President: "God's in His Heaven, all's right with the world!"

The business-turned, political strategist had rebuilt the Republican party, controlled the regional bosses, and ushered in the golden years of the business-man's government. The Ohio coal and iron magnate had come into politics late in life. But he needed no tutoring. He knew well the ways of power from the jungle of industrial competition. He knew the uses of money and the avenues for more money and forged a close alliance between corporate tycoons and political bosses. High tariff, gold standard, bankers in key Washington posts, protection against hostile legislation, mergers . . . that was the Age of McKinley-Hanna.

As the French proverb puts it:

The dealer in onions is a good judge of leeks.

NOVEMBER 4

On this day in the year 1958, Angelo Roncalli was elected John XXIII.

Among the many cherished contributions he made to the Church of Rome during his short reign was the infusion of warmth and humor into the Vatican. When he paid a visit to the Regina Coeli Prison, he endeared himself to the inmates with the greeting: "You couldn't come to see me, so I came to see you." In his informal chat he mentioned how he first came to realize the difficulties of prison life when one of his cousins was sent to jail for poaching—a reference that was deleted in the later official releases in the Vatican papers. He smilingly stopped one of the priests in the midst of following the custom of 3 genuflections on entering the Pope's room: "Have you got the St. Vitus dance? Once is enough! Don't you think I believe you the first time?"

As the Bosnian proverb puts it:

Good humor is man's wings.

NOVEMBER 5

On this day in the year 1556, Akbar the Great slew Himu on the field of Panipot and founded the Mogul Empire of Northern India.

Although Akbar ruled effectively until his death in 1605, he was frequently plagued by family intrigues. Particularly distressing was the misconduct of his favorite son Prince Salim, who succeeded him as Jahangir, Conqueror of the World. Jahangir himself faced a rebellion led by his own son, Shah Jahan, who became emperor in 1628. Shah Jahan, in turn, was deposed by his son in 1658.

As the Swahili proverb puts it:

The louse that bites is in the inner shirt.

NOVEMBER 6

On this day in the year 1897, Wilhelm II received word of the "splendid opportunity" for profitable German action against China. A local group of residents in the village of Chu Yeh Hsien in southwestern Shantung had killed 2 of

Bishop Johann Anzer's missionaries in a drive to discourage their activities. With the tacit concurrence of Tsar Nicholas, the Kaiser sent his squadron of 3 ships from Wusung. Landing 700 men, Admiral Otto von Diedrichs occupied Chiao Chou Bay, hoisted the German flag on November 14, and proclaimed himself Governor. Subsequent negotiations ended with Germany receiving a long-term lease of Chiao Chou Bay, the right to operate railroads in Shantung province, and mining privileges along the route.

As the English proverb puts it:

Let not your will roar when your power can but whisper.

NOVEMBER 7

On this day in the year 1923, Birkenhead delivered the Rectorial Address at Glasgow University, Scotland.

Speaking on "Idealism in International Politics," the former Lord High Chancellor of Great Britain revealed his restlessness and cynicism, which had become increasingly evident as he passed his fifty-second birthday. "Yet nothing is more apparent than that politically, economically, and philosophically the motive of self-interest not only is, but must be, and ought to be, the mainspring of human conduct," he struck the keynote without equivocation. "The world continues to offer glittering prizes to those who have stout hearts and sharp words."

As the Slovenian proverb puts it:

Big thieves hang little thieves.

NOVEMBER 8

On this day in the year 1976, Gary Mark Gilmore was denied his wish for death before a firing squad as soon as possible.

The 35-year-old parolee had been sentenced in Provo, Utah, to die on October 7 for murder. But the court-appointed lawyer, whom he had repudiated, asked for a stay, which the court granted. Gilmore then mocked the court for not having the courage of its conviction, whereupon the court

reversed itself on November 10 and set the date of execution
for November 15. The Utah governor stepped in on the next
day, however, and again stayed the execution pending a review by the Utah Board of Pardons. In frustration, Gilmore
attempted suicide by taking an overdose of barbiturates on
November 16. The doctors would not let him die his own
way and pumped him out. He went on a hunger strike, while
the Pardons Board flipped and flopped. It finally granted his
death plea, setting the new date of execution as December 6.
In the meantime, the lawyers of the American Civil Liberties
Union (ACLU) became involved. Working with his mother,
they obtained a delay ordered by the United States Supreme
Court on December 3, which asked Utah to furnish proof
that the convicted slayer had been of sound mind when he
waived his right of appealing the death sentence. After receiving the state's reply, the Supreme Court voted on December
13 to vacate the stay. On December 15, the Utah District
Court finally set the execution for January 17, 1977. After
calling the judge a "moral coward" for not ordering an earlier
date, Gilmore made a second attempt at suicide. But again,
the doctors would not let him die when he wanted. The
ACLU lawyers yet again obtained a 10-day restraining order,
this time from the United States District Court at 1:05 A.M.
of the day on which Gilmore was to have been shot at dawn.
The Utah attorney general flew to Denver and obtained a reversal from the Circuit Court of Appeals, while the ACLU
lawyers appealed directly to the Supreme Court in Washington. The latter finally handed down a rejection just 3 minutes
before Gilmore was shot—after all the lawyers had had their
say in the gruesome ordeal. Gilmore had none.

As the English proverb puts it:

*If laws could speak, they would first complain about law-
yers.*

NOVEMBER 9

On this day in the year 1933, Harry Hopkins pushed through
a Presidential Executive Order establishing the Civil Works
Administration.

The purpose of the economic recovery progam with an initial working capital of $480 million was to create immediate jobs for 4 million people. The Administrator was a strong proponent of passing money as directly as possible to the poor. When one editor deprecated some of his projects as "boondoggles," he snorted: "They are damned good projects. You know, dumb people criticize something they do not understand, and that is what is going on up there. God damn it! Here are a lot of people broke and we are putting them to work making researches of one kind or another where the whole material costs 3%, and practically all the money goes for relief . . . I believe every one of these research projects are good projects. We don't need any apologies!" To a congressional appropriations committee member who made reference to a long-term view, Hopkins snapped back: "People don't eat in the long run, Senator. They eat every day."

As the Chinese proverb puts it:

What does a fine horseman know of aching feet?

NOVEMBER 10

On this day in the year 1630, Armand Jean de Richilieu upset the Queen Mother's plot to depose him.

As Prime Minister to Louis XIII the Cardinal had greatly increased the power of the throne. Authority was siphoned away from the nobles and centralized in the King. Local fortresses were destroyed. The lords' absolute control over the peasants was broken. Many of these reforms went against the wishes of the Queen Mother. After she and the Queen had nursed the King back to health from grave illness, the Queen Mother asked for the Cardinal's dismissal as reward. She repeated her demand in her own Luxembourg Palace and offered the Keeper of the Seals Michel de Marillac as successor. Soon thereafter the Cardinal suddenly entered unannounced through a secret passage and confronted the Queen Mother. She arrogantly stated that the King was given a choice between her and Richilieu. One or the other must go. As the shaken King withdrew alone to contemplate the painful decision in his hunting lodge, the nobles congratulated her on the expected victory. But the King sent for the Cardinal instead, reaffirmed his confidence in him, and signed an order for Marillac's arrest. The Queen Mother fled to Flanders.

As the Roman proverb puts it:

The old fox is not to be caught with a trap.

NOVEMBER 11

On this day in the year 1914, Rupert Brooke marched through Antwerp with his fellow British soldiers.

"Hundreds of thousands of refugees, their goods on barrows and handcarts and perambulators and wagons, moving with infinite slowness out into the night, two unending lines of them, the old men mostly weeping, the women with hard white drawn faces, the children playing or crying or sleeping," wrote the young English poet to his friend. Three civilians were being killed for every soldier in Belgium. Half of the youths were being "blown through pain to nothingness in the incessant mechanical slaughter of these modern battles." Brooke himself was soon to be among them.

As the Kenyan proverb puts it:

War has no eyes.

NOVEMBER 12

On this day in the year 1971, Richard M. Nixon announced the end of the American military intervention in Vietnam.

In the President's State of the World Address, he referred to the Vietnam War as America's "most anguishing problem." Despite the great pride in their military might and early predictions of success by their military civilian leaders, the American people saw no end in sight. After 12 years, 53,000 of their relatives and friends were killed. Even with vastly superior firepower, absolute domination of the air and sea, as well as superiority in numbers of men, the most powerful nation in history was unable to bring a fourth-rate power to her knees. The most intensive bombings ever carried out by man and the most innovative search-and-destroy tactics ever devised could not dislodge the North Vietnamese and Viet Cong troops from the jungles and highlands of South Vietnam. The lesson was clearly brought home that the power of a nation to impose its will on another has defined limits. As the Japanese proverb puts it:

Though the whip is long, it does not reach the horse's belly.

NOVEMBER 13

On this day in the year 1608, Edward Coke and his judicial associates were summoned by the King on the matter of encroaching on his royal prerogatives.

All the judges except the Lord Chief Justice of the Common Pleas nodded to the proposition that they are only agents of the King and whatever the agent may do the King may also do. Coke voiced his opinion that a defendant is to be tried only by a court of justice. The King countered: "My lords, I have always thought, and by my soul I have often heard the boast that your English law was founded upon reason. If that be so, why have not I and others reason as well as you, the judges?" Sir Edward remained steadfast: "True it is that God has endowed Your Majesty with excellent science, and great endowments of nature, but Your Majesty is not learned in the laws of your realm of England, and causes which concern the life, or inheritance, or goods, or fortune of your subjects, are not to be decided by natural reason, but by the artificial reason and judgment of law, which law is an art which requires long study and experience before that a man can attain to the cognizance of it. The law is the golden met-wand and measure to try the causes of Your Majesty's subjects, and it is by that law that Your Majesty is protected in safety and peace." The King fell into a rage: "Then I am to be *under* the law—which is treason to affirm." But Coke persisted: "Thus wrote Bracton: The King ought not be under any man but under God and the law."

As the English proverb puts it:

Use soft words and hard arguments.

NOVEMBER 14

On this day in the year 1938, George C. Marshall attended a meeting in the White House on the presidential program for building 10,000 warplanes in order to check the Nazi power in the event the United States was dragged into the European conflict.

Besides the President, the Secretary of Treasury, WPA Administrator, Solicitor General, Army Chief of Staff, and other high-ranking officials were present. As Deputy Chief of Staff of the Army, Major General Marshall was one of the junior attendants sitting off to the side. The President outlined his plans for building the stipulated number of planes, although he would ask Congress for twice the number. He did not think that a very much expanded ground force was necessary to deter the Germans, nor did he give much weight to the requirement of a large number of pilots to back up the planes. Most of the conferees agreed with the President; the others were soothing in their reservations. But when the President finally came around with a "Don't you think so, George?" Marshall dissented. "I am sorry, Mr. President. But I don't agree with that at all." According to his memorandum on the meeting, "That ended the conference. The President gave me a . . . startled look and when I went out they all bade me good-bye and said that my tour in Washington was over." But the reverse was to be the case. The President promoted him to be Chief of Staff of the Army on April 27, 1939.

As the Chinese proverb puts it:

Clear conscience fears not the midnight knock.

NOVEMBER 15

On this day in the year 1957, Boris Pasternak published *Dr. Zhivago* in Italy, having been denied permission to do so in the Soviet Union.

In dealing with "a thinking man in search of truth, with a creative and artistic bent," the novel disavowed the thesis of sacrificing the individual for "the good of the social collective." It evoked a prerevolutionary literary spirit, a deeper subconscious religious sentiment, and a hopeful view of a new Russian future. "The proclamations, the tumult, the excitement, are over," he had said to a Western journalist around that time. "Now something else is growing, something new. It is growing imperceptively and quietly, as the grass grows. It is growing as fruit does, and it is growing in the young. The essential thing in this epoch is that a new freedom is being born." For voicing such political dissonances, Pasternak was forced to turn down the Nobel Prize in literature, subjected to continual harassment, and kept isolated as a source of dangerous infection to the Russian people.

As the Russian proverb puts it:

If it cannot be done by washing, it must be done by mangling.

NOVEMBER 16

On this day in the year 1913, Pancho Villa surprised the federal garrison at Ciudad Juárez and took the city before daybreak.

After being stalled with heavy losses in the fighting for several days at Chihuahua, the Mexican revolutionary and 2000 men slipped around the city to the north, ambushed a train, loaded his troops into the boxcars, faked a series of telegrams to the Juárez commander, and bravely rode into the heart of the city at midnight. When the American Mayor E. C. Kelly of El Paso across the river met him at the International Bridge after the battle, Villa expressed regret that an American taxicab driver waiting for his fare in Juárez had been killed in the confused street fighting and promised that he would engage the government troops in the expected counterattack farther away from El Paso so that no Americans would be killed by stray bullets. When the shooting started a week later, Villa kept his word and confronted the federal contingent at Tierra Blanca, some 26 miles to the south.

As the Japanese proverb puts it:

The noble samurai knows compassion.

NOVEMBER 17

On this day in the year 1938, Nikos Kazantzakis paid tribute to "the Flame" in a letter to Lesh Levin Dunkelblum.

In the midst of these "fearfully heavy" times of "wars, shadows, pogroms" and "a few magnificent, fiery hearts," the Greek mystic wrote from Aegina, "what is our duty?" He had spent his life searching for "something in the human heart that can never be extinguished." Our duty, he emphasized, is "to remain faithful to the Flame. At present, it remains hidden, infirm, diffident. But the time will come when it shall rule again upon this awesome, marvellous earth." Once when he was extremely sick in Paris and everyone but he had given up hope, he dictated a short passage to his wife Helen, which he later put into the mouth of the Franciscan saint: "I turned to the almond tree and said: 'Brother, tell me about God.' And the almond tree blossomed."

As the Chinese proverb puts it:

A peace of mind not quite perfect deepens its awareness.

NOVEMBER 18

On this day in the year 1872, Susan B. Anthony was arrested by a deputy United States marshall for voting on November 5.

The pioneer for women suffrage had intended to sue the election inspectors for not counting her vote, only to find that she herself had violated an 1870 statute, which prohibits voting by anyone without the legal right to do so. Bail was set at $500. Her counsel Henry B. Selden refused to pay and applied for a writ of habeas corpus. The writ was denied and bail was raised to $1000. Anthony still refused but Selden could not bear seeing her in jail and insisted that she pay the bail, which she finally did. On leaving the courtroom, the two bumped into their associate John van Voorhis and told him what had happened. Voorhis burst out in exasperation: "You've lost your chance to present your case before the Supreme Court by writ of habeas corpus!" She dashed back into the courtroom to withdraw her payment, but too late. Althought Anthony appreciated the essential help of Selden, she never forgave his substitution of well-intentioned chivalry for legal sagacity.

As the Creole proverb puts it:

It is because of a good heart that the crab has no head.

NOVEMBER 19

On this day in the year 1919, William Edgar Borah led the congressional fight against the United States' entry into the League of Nations.

"How can you keep from meddling in the affairs of Europe or keep Europe from meddling in the affairs of America?" inquired the Senator from Idaho, persuasive in his speech on the floor. "It is in conflict with the right of our people to govern themselves free from all restraint legal or moral, of foreign powers . . . Peace upon any other basis than national independence, peace purchased at the cost of any part of our national integrity, is fit only for slaves, and even when purchased at such a price it is a delusion, for it cannot last."

As the American proverb puts it:

It's always best for every man to chew his own tobacco.

NOVEMBER 20

On this day in the year 1851, Richard Wagner told Franz Liszt how he finally worked out the structure for the *Ring of the Nibelung*.

The German composer initially thought of Siegfried's death. Half of the words had been written and the preliminary music had been put down. Somehow the result did not feel right. It gave the feeling of the last chapter of a myth being presented to the audience without a leading-in of some kind. So Wagner thought of beginning his story somewhat earlier during Siegfried's youth. He experimented with the forest scene. The music just flowed and he was very pleased with it. When he later took a fresh look, it became clear that the plot of Sigmund and Sieglinde, Wotan's problems, and Brünhilde's disobedience, in turn, called for a further stepping back into history. The Walküre just had to be. With that, the 4-opera cycle naturally came into being. The *Ring* must begin at the beginning—with the primeval happening, the first curse, the original state of the gods. And that beginning was the Rhine.

As the Chinese proverb puts it:

When one drinks water, he should think of the spring.

NOVEMBER 21

On this day in the year 1952, Louis Hoffner was released from life imprisonment in Dannemora Prison for a saloon payroll holdup.

When the destitute Brooklyn ex-clerk was convicted, a reporter from the *New York World-Telegram and Sun*, Edward J. Mowery, felt that he was innocent. Mowery studied the trial judge's charge to the jury, spoke to the former jurors, and consulted with legal experts on the proceedings. He uncovered evidence of perjury, illegal coercion by police, suppression of evidence that favored the defendant by the prosecutor, and uncertainty of identification of the alleged killer by a key witness. After publishing 70 articles over 5 years and using up most of his spare time, Mowery was finally able to get Hoffner exonerated.

As the French proverb puts it:

With the trowel of patience, we dig out the roots of truth.

NOVEMBER 22

On this day in the year 1848, Charlotte Brönte complained about her sister Emily's refusal to accept medical counsel from the doctor.

"Would that my sister added to her many qualities the humble one of tractability. I have again and again incurred her displeasure by urging the necessity of seeking advice, and I fear I must yet incur it again and again," Charlotte wrote in another letter two weeks later. Only a year before, she had warned Emily about her fraudulent publisher, who did not even correct the typographical errors shown on the proofs in order to save money. Charlotte urged Emily to switch to an honest one—but to no avail. She repeated the suggestion, when the publisher made false claims ascribing Charlotte's *Jane Eyre* and Anne's *Agnes Grey* to Emily in order to increase the sales of Emily's *Wuthering Heights* but again to no avail. It had been this way for years and it remained so until Emily passed away on December 19.

As the American proverb puts it:

Advice is something wise people don't need and fools won't take.

NOVEMBER 23

On this day in the year 1654, Blaise Pascal awakened from his night watch on the theme of man's misery without God with a "Joy, joy, joy, tears of joy!"

The French philosopher-mathematician had been exposed to the intellectual ferment of the period since early youth. The Academie Francaise had been organized in 1635. Free thinking was popular in Paris. Pascal himself had conducted a series of scientific studies on the vacuum during the latter part of 1646. His work on conic sections received the praise of the great mathematician Gottfried von Leibnitz. But his scientific preoccupations could not allay his restlessness. A sense of loneliness gradually crept over him. He became tormented by "the eternal silence of these infinite spaces." Suddenly, everything became clear that night. Lower orders of material concerns can never account for the uniqueness of the supernatural orders of love. Only from the higher vantage ground can one make sense of the lower. Pascal, the man of genius, became one with Pascal, the man of holiness. With the fusion of truth and charity came "Certitude. Feeling. Joy. Peace."

As the Chinese proverb puts it:

Seeing through wealth and fame gains little rest; seeing through life and death gains a big rest.

NOVEMBER 24

On this day in the year 1910, Arnold Bennett spoke glowingly of W. H. Hudson.

"I suppose that there are . . . few among the living more likely to be regarded, a hundred years hence, as having produced 'literature,' " Bennett declared in his article in the *New Age* under the pseudonym Jacob Tonson. Hudson's views on animals were especially lauded. "He seldom omits to describe the individualities of the wild beasts of his acquaintance. For him, a mole is not any mole, but a particular mole. He will tell you about a mole that did not dig like other moles but had a method of its own, and he will give you the reason why this singular mole lived in a great age."

As the Bihari proverb puts it:

Can the bark of one tree fit another?

NOVEMBER 25

On this day in the year 1812, Jean Lafitte strolled through the iron gates of the main square of New Orleans.

The night before a man by the name of Williams had arrived in the city by way of Cuba and spread a tale of blood and horror. The American merchantman *Independence,* on which he had been a crewman, had been attacked by pirates outside Havana. The ship was plundered. Everyone but he was murdered. He miraculously managed to escape and was picked up by a French vessel. The local people were fascinated by the news. Among themselves they whispered, "Lafitte, of course!" But the pirate kept walking along unmolested. He had powerful friends in City Hall. He was lionized by the men and idolized by the women. Eyelashes flickered and bosoms heaved among the quadroon mothers at the sight of him, as they gently nudged their maiden daughters: "Now, there's a man for you!" After Lafitte left town, the district attorney filed a brief report about an American ship carrying an illicit cargo of slaves being attacked by pirates in Mexican Gulf. A short item appeared in the newspapers. Within a week Williams and his story dropped out of sight and out of mind.

As the Hausan proverb puts it:

The friend of a chief is a chief.

NOVEMBER 26

On this day in the year 1834, Felix Mendelssohn wrote his actor-friend Edward Devrient about quitting his post as Conductor of the Düsseldorf Opera House.

"The hell with it!" said the German composer, after the reception accorded the première of his "model performances," which he had been trying to introduce to the community. It was *Don Giovanni*. A noisy row burst out in the middle of the music. Yells of "Money back!" filled the air. Newspapers were thrown on the stage with whistling and howling. During the first act alone, the curtain had to be rung down 3 times to quiet the tumult. It turned out that the fracas was instigated by a low-ranking city official who hated Mendelssohn.

As the Irish proverb puts it:

Keep the bad person on your side.

NOVEMBER 27

On this day in the year 1956, Yuri Zhukov discussed the worsening relations between the United States and the Soviet Union with C. L. Sulzberger.

As reported by the columnist of the *New York Times*, the advisor to the Soviet Foreign Minister spoke about both sides continually making mistakes, insulting and reinsulting each other. He was especially sensitive about Hungary. Russia, he emphasized, would not mind if American interest in that country remains just part of the Cold War propaganda. But he went on ominously: "If you want to take Hungary out of the Soviet camp, there will be war."

As the Latin proverb puts it:

If you want peace, prepare for peace.

NOVEMBER 28

On this day in the year 1953, Henri Navarre made light of his subordinate's alarm at the strength being built up by the Vietminh at Dienbienphu.

Major General René Dogny proposed the staging of immediate raids from his delta base in order to disrupt the enemy's lines of communication and the engaging of part of his battle corps to turn them back. But the French Commander-in-Chief in Indochina perceived otherwise. He did not judge the columns moving into the area to be divisions but much smaller units. Even so, when the time comes, his air force would destroy them as they approached and render their logistic resupply nearly impossible. Furthermore, he felt that their commander General Vo Nguyen Giap was inept in the handling of regimental size units in the kind of engagement that was shaping up. By enticing the hitherto elusive Vietminh into massing themselves, instead of dispersing in guerrilla elements, Navarre would then be able to deliver a fatal blow. By the time the smoke of combat cleared away, there was indeed a fatal blow, with 10,000 prisoners. It turned out to be that dealt the French.

As the Gandan proverb puts it:

If you wait until the whole animal appears, you will spear only the tail.

NOVEMBER 29

On this day in the year 1942, Antoine de Saint-Exupéry broadcasted "An Open Letter to Frenchmen Everywhere" over Canadian radio after the Germans had engulfed France.

"France is nothing more than silence. She is lost somewhere in the night, all light extinguished, like a ship. Her consciousness and her spiritual life are gathered together in her depths. We do not know even the names of the hostages Germany will shoot tomorrow." Then the author of *The Little Prince* counseled his fellow Frenchmen not to "play the part of braggarts." Rather let the 40 million brethren there "digest their slavery" and resolve their problems in their own way. "None of our verbiage in sociology, politics, or even art will carry any weight against their thinking. They will not read our books. They will not listen to our speeches. They may spit on our ideas. Let us be infinitely modest. Our political discussions are the discussions of the ghosts, and our ambitions are comic."

As the German proverb puts it:

Fair words do not butter cabbage.

NOVEMBER 30

On this day in the year 1945, e. e. cummings was approached for contributions to Ezra Pound's medical and psychiatric care.

The poet-painter fingered the check for $1000 he had just received that morning for a large canvas and looked at his wife. She nodded. He then endorsed it and handed it over to Pound's attorney. Years later, his friend Charles Norman let us in on the extent of the sacrifice on behalf of a fellow poet:

"I happened to know he had no other money. It was before any of those national awards which made his life easier, as did the Charles Eliot Norton professorship at Harvard and the publication of *Poems 1923-1954*."

As the Chinese proverb puts it:

With virtue you cannot be completely poor; without virtue you cannot be really rich.

DECEMBER 1

On this day in the year 1943, Franklin Roosevelt, Joseph Stalin, and Winston Churchill issued their high-sounding joint communique about the "elimination of tyranny and slavery" in ending the Teheran Conference.

Secretly, however, the three leaders had agreed to dismember Germany. While appearing rather indifferent to the deliberations and letting Roosevelt and Churchill do most of the talking, Stalin kept adding a Soviet bite to more territory now and then. He ended up with annexing the eastern half of Poland, as well as the ice-free ports of Koenigsberg and Memel on the Baltic and some territory of East Prussia. As a Russian satellite, Poland would move west by annexing the eastern parts of Germany. These and other terms rapidly built up the strength of an exhausted ally of the United States into that of an adversary of military parity 3 decades later.

As the Ethiopian proverb puts it:

A powerful friend becomes a powerful enemy.

DECEMBER 2

On this day in the year 1899, Bartlett Tripp concluded a treaty with his German and British counterparts to bring peace to Samoa for the sake of the Samoan people—so stated their proclamation.

When the native King Malietoa died in 1898, the Anglo-Americans supported his relative Manu as successor, while the Germans backed his enemy Chief Mataafa. Anchored in the Napia Harbor were 3 American warships, 2 British, and 1 German. Following a brief intervention by the American Admiral Albert Kautz, the 3 Western powers negotiated a settlement. The American Commissioner Tripp enthusiastically communicated their achievement: "The chiefs and warriors have returned to their homes. The smoke is now ascending from the native cabins and plantations in every portion of the islands. The war song is discontinued, the war camp abandoned, and the happy joyous nature of this unrevengeful people manifests itself in the ready forgiveness of their enemies and their glad welcome of returning peace." What was the magic formula? Upolo and Savaii were given to Germany; Tongo Islands, part of the Solomons, and other territorial bits to Britain; Tutulia with the prized anchorage of Pago Pago and several smaller islands to the United States. And what were given to the natives? The source of their frictions was eliminated, so that they could live in peace forever; their monarchy was abolished and their arms confiscated.

As the Basque proverb puts it:

When the foxes begin to preach look to your hens.

DECEMBER 3

On this day in the year 1597, Miguel de Cervantes Saavedra completed the first step that led him to literary immortality.

He was leaving the prison in Seville, in which he had spent several months for deficiencies in settling his money accounts. His cell mate had been a high official of the Treasury by the name of Mateo Alemán. As a bon vivant, Alemán was wise in the ways of the Court, tough in the gutters, and delightful as a raconteur. After they became friends, Alemán began to read to Cervantes from a manuscript he had finished, entitled *The Panorama of Human Life, Adventures and Life of the Rogue Gusmán de Afarache.* Cervantes soaked in every word with relish and inspiration. Don Quixote was thereby born and shaped in his mind. That imprisonment turned out to be his most fruitful summer.

As the Spanish proverb puts it:

Do not speak ill of the day until it is passed.

DECEMBER 4

On this day in the year 1902, Charles Wardell Stiles presented a paper on preventive medicine at a medical convention in Washington, D.C.

As Chief of the Division of Zoology of the Public Health Service, he droned on with *Ancyclostoma duodenale*, *Uncinaria americana*, and other technical facets of his program. Much to his annoyance, he noticed a member of the audience dozing away just below the lectern. But Stiles was determined to keep his composure as he went into the details of his hookworm project. He described how the disease induces a tired feeling in patients and how many of the poor in the South were so infected. Suddenly, the man snapped out of his snooze and began jotting down notes feverishly. Stiles ended his presentation on a note of high satisfaction over the renewed interest on the part of the listener. The next morning, as Stiles was casually scanning the newspapers, the headline leaped at him: "GERM OF LAZINESS FOUND"—by Dr. Charles Wardell Stiles! It was this amazing discovery that so dramatically jolted the reporter from the New York *Sun* out of his slumbers at the lecture the day before.

As the Latin proverb puts it:

What is not understood is always marvelous.

DECEMBER 5

On this day in the year 1955, Martin Luther King led the bus boycott by blacks in Montgomery, Alabama.

The minister-leader of the newly established Montgomery Improvement Association stood before his 4000 brethren that evening outside the Holt Street Church. He recalled the triggering incident of December 1 when black Mrs. Rosa Parks was told by the bus driver to move toward the back to make room for white passengers. When she refused, she was arrested, jailed, and fined $10. By evening, the black community was aroused to make a stand at this point in history. By the next day mimeographed notices of the boycott reached every black in Montgomery. He then ticked off the long list of injustices by the bus company with the audience responding in crescendos of Amens. "But there comes a time when people

get tired," King finally incited his fellow blacks to action.
"We are here this evening to say to those who have mis-
treated us so long that we are tired—tired of being segregated
and humiliated, tired of being kicked about by the brutal feet
of oppression. We have no alternative but to protest. For
many years we have shown amazing patience. We have sometimes given our white brothers the feeling that we liked the
way we were being treated. But we come here to be saved
from that patience that makes us patient with anything less
than freedom and justice."

As the Canaan proverb puts it:

*If ants are smitten, they will bite the hand that smites
them.*

DECEMBER 6

On this day in the year 1908, Frank G. Scammel of New Jersey announced plans to test the theory that the electric chair
does not kill.

Several New York physicians had claimed that the electric
chair only stuns the patient and that it had been the patholo-
gist's knife at autopsy or the quicklime in which the bodies
were buried that did the killing. To prove or disprove the
contention, the County Physician stated that he would assume
control of the body of the next convicted criminal sentenced
to be electrocuted the following December 21 immediately
after the shock. He would then apply every technique at re-
suscitation known to medical science. Then only would he be
satisfied that the letter of the law of death by the electric
chair had indeed been carried out. The condemned man expressed no views on the controversy.

As the German proverb puts it:

No tree suits the thief as far as hanging is concerned.

DECEMBER 7

On this day in the year 1830, Victor Hugo received a heart-
rending letter from Charles Augustin Sainte-Beuve.

The 2 French authors had been very close friends. But
both were in love with the same Adéle. She was Hugo's wife,

whom Sainte-Beuve used to comfort when Hugo was too occupied with his work. Hugo never had reason to feel suspicious of the attentions of his friend. The emotional
attachment between Sainte-Beuve and Adéle increased by the
day. When Hugo finally woke up, he first pleaded with
Sainte-Beuve to renounce his love, which was breaking up
their friendship. Then he broached the idea of letting Adéle
choose between them—the famous father of her 4 children
and a person who could hardly support himself. What could
Sainte-Beuve say? "There is despair in me and rage," Sainte-
Beuve's letter carried on. "At moments I could gladly kill
you, murder you—and for those horrible thoughts you must
extend to me your forgiveness. But do you, whose mind
teams with so many thoughts, just think for an instant how a
man must feel in whom a friendship such as ours has left so
vast an emptiness. Lost to one another for ever?" Seeing that
he could no longer sit in Hugo and Adéle's presence, he
wrote that the "only thing for me to do is withdraw." Even
so, Hugo rendered genuine sympathy for his pain and encouraged him to let time heal the wounds.

As the French proverb puts it:

If your friend is one-eyed, look at him in profile.

DECEMBER 8

On this day in the year 1886, Samuel Gompers was elected
the first President of the American Federation of Labor at its
charter meeting in Columbus, Ohio.

Gompers immediately allayed the fears of the member
unions of being swallowed by the amalgamation. He was convinced that previous failures at the unification of labor groups
was due to the "nonrecognition on the part of all who have
hitherto attempted it of the principle of autonomy, or the
right of several bodies composing the organization of self-
government. The American Federation of Labor avoids the
fatal rock upon which all previous attempts to affect the
unity of the working class have split, by leaving to each body
or affiliated organization the complete management of its own
affairs, especially its own particular trade affairs." The subsequent success of the AFL was due, in no small measure, to
this ability to attract support from the constituent members

through means compatible with their problems and character. Those who have been independent for some time cannot be asked to shed their freedoms overnight.

As the Chinese proverb puts it:

Give the bird room to fly.

DECEMBER 9

On this day in the year 1824, Antonio José de Sucre liberated Peru by defeating the Spanish in the Battle of Ayacucho.

Within a few years he was involved in organizing and heading another newly sovereign state, Bolivia. By 1828, however, mounting discontent over domestic problems and invasion by Peruvian troops moved Sucre to step down as President and give way to a constitutional congress. In his address to the Bolivian people, he reasserted his faith in compassion: "No widow or orphan mourns because of me. I have spared many condemned men from punishment and my administration has been characterized by clemency, tolerance, and kindness." And in gentleness: "It may be said that this moderation is the cause of my wounds; but I am glad of them if my successors with equal kindness will lead the Bolivians to obey the law without the need for bayonets threatening life and snares obstructing freedom. I shall look at my scars in my retirement and shall never regret them, for they will remind me that in order to establish Bolivia I preferred the rule of law to the tyranny of the sword."

As the Irish proverb puts it:

Greatness knows gentleness.

DECEMBER 10

On this day in the year 969, Theophano played the key role in the assassination of her husband Nicephorus Phocas.

After a late chat with the Byzantine emperor in their apartment, she said she had to say goodnight to some Bulgarian women guests of theirs and asked that he leave the door to their bedchamber unlocked so she could return without awakening him. After he fell asleep, she and her collaborators hoisted John Tzimisces over the walls. They entered the room and split his head open with a sword. Theophano had been in love with Tzimisces, who was Nicephorus' nephew, and had hoped to marry him and rule with him after his coronation. The prelate Polyeuctes of the Great Church of St. Sophia, however, refused to crown Tzimisces until the murderers had been punished, whereupon Tzimisces denied that he had anything to do with the plot, blamed Theophano, and exiled her to a convent.

As the English proverb puts it:

Clever people are the tools of knaves.

DECEMBER 11

On this day in the year 1825, Aleksandr Sergeevich Pushkin impulsively decided to leave Mikhailovskoye and join his friends in St. Petersburg without the permission of the Tsar.

As the young poet went to Trigorskoye to take leave of the Wulf-Osipov family, a rabbit crossed his path—an unlucky sign. Another rabbit did the same on his way home. On return, he found the servant who was to accompany him lying sick in bed. He picked a substitute and drove his carriage along the snowy road. Yet still another ill omen crossed his path—a priest in black. That was the limit. So he turned back. Furious with the turn of events and wondering about his friends, whose company he was missing so much, he tried to settle down to some reading. But his mind was not to be quieted. Several days later the cook returned from the capital and told him about an uprising that had been broken up with the capture of 121 youths from the nobility. The names of Pushkin's friends were among them. Two were hung and the rest deported to Siberia. Pushkin too would have been there, had he not finally heeded the insistent series of warning portents.

As the Greek proverb puts it:

Fate leads the willing, drags the unwilling.

DECEMBER 12

On this day in the year 639, Amr ibn al Assi crossed from Arabia into Egypt at El Arish.

The Arabian Commander had been wanting to invade Egypt and take the fortress of Babylon for some time. The Caliph Umar ibn al Khattab was more cautious. After vacillating back and forth, he reluctantly provided a force of 3500 men. Amr left Jerusalem, proceeded down the coastal plain by Gaza, and reached Rafah, when a messenger caught up with a note from the Caliph. The Commander did not open it immediately but kept going for another day until he reached El Arish. There he unsealed the envelope and read the dispatch. It directed that should the order reach him while he was still in Palestine, he should abandon the offensive and return. Should it reach him in Egypt, he should continue. With a straight face, he asked those around him whether he was in Egypt or in Palestine. Egypt, it was, of course. So he went on with the operation and captured Babylon on April 9, 641.

As the Danish proverb puts it:

Good advice is no better than bad, unless taken at the right time.

DECEMBER 13

On this day in the year 1291, Celestine V abdicated after only 4 months.

The saintly hermit did not relish the jousting for power surrounding the Papacy. One of the most disturbing at the time was the heated issue regarding the Pope's authority over the Orders. It was brought to a head on May 12, 1285, with the election of Munio of Zamora as Master-General of the Dominicans. The storm broke in 1290. Just as Celestine's predecessor Nicholas had come to the conclusion that Munio must be relieved for the good of the Order, he died. With Celestine, however, Munio reasserted himself with impunity. When Boniface VIII, who regarded Munio as a "pernicious example, odious in the sight of the Lord, full of abomination, worthy of condemnation, hostile to canon law," took over as Pope, he sent an order to Munio, with a copy to the Archbishop of Toledo, to appear at Rome within 3 months. Munio refused. Boniface then deprived the Archbishop of the right of extending confirmation, benefices, and other ecclesiastical powers and ordered him to present himself and Munio to Rome within 4 months with an explanation of his prior failure or face being deposed. They both showed up. The Archbishop was forgiven and Munio spent the rest of his life prisoner-like in the convent of St. Sabina.

As the Dualan proverb puts it:

Even if the elephant is thin, he is still king of the forest.

DECEMBER 14

On this day in the year 1852, William Cullen Bryant was more astonished than ever, while passing through Paris, at certain traits of the French people.

They seemed perfectly satisfied with the political and social situation. As long as the authorities do not interfere with their amusements they do not mind too much and they conform readily to the changes that occur. The American poet-journalist's letter from Marseilles quoted a German lady: "What a people! Three or four thousand unoffending and unresisting people—men, women, and children—were shot in the streets, at their doors, at their windows, or sitting in their apartments, a year ago, when Louis Napoleon abolished the French constitution. In a few weeks all recollection of the dreadful event seemed to have passed away. What a people, that such things should have been done, and that, after a few days, nothing should be said of them; that they should have been forgotten and pardoned!"

As the English proverb puts it:

A wonder lasts but nine days.

DECEMBER 15

On this day in the year 1668, Louis XIV, as Chairman of the Board of Directors of the new French East India Company, hosted a grand meeting of the disgruntled shareholders at the Tuileries.

Instead of sending the fleet to India for merchandise, as they had thought, the Sun-King had ordered it to Madagascar to expand his empire for colonial glory. The King's minister Jean Baptiste Colbert tried to mollify them by promising a departure from past promises and a concentration of future economic returns. When it came time for the King to speak, he said nothing of the sort but reminded them of their obligations to pay up on their pledges. After the session things went from bad to worse. The goods brought no profit. The ships got into difficulties with accidents and pirates, while Dutch employees cheated their French employers. By 1675 the French East India Company folded with the investors losing everything.

As the Arabic proverb puts it:

If the ass is invited to the wedding, it is only to carry wood.

DECEMBER 16

On this day in the year 1891, Moses and Warner Davis returned on the steamship *Dania* from Liberia with their 2 families totaling 11—all scrawny, tattered, and nearly naked.

Up to the previous May the 2 black brothers had been well-to-do farmers in Gainesville, Georgia. They had heard the spreading rumors about the wonderful opportunities for members of their race in the young country of Liberia. So they sold everything they owned and packed their families off to Monrovia. The rest of the story was a tale of woe. Everything they had heard turned out to be pure myth. There was nothing there for them—no future, no present. There was only misery. Their money dwindled away; their clothes shredded off. In their starving desperation, they appealed to their friends. The latter responded and sent boat fare. When asked in New York about their plans, they said they were going back to Georgia and start all over.

As the English proverb puts it:

Never quit certainty for hope.

DECEMBER 17

On this day in the year 1398, Mahmud Shah and Mallu Khan marched out of the gates of Delhi and engaged the Mongol force of Timur-i-leng.

The Indian army of 10,000 horsemen and 40,000 foot soldiers was spearheaded by a herd of much-dreaded warrior elephants. Clanking forward in heavy armor, tusks tipped with long swords, fortified turrets on top with archers, crossbowmen, and rocket launchers, the elephants projected the specter of invincibility. Tamberlaine, however, was creatively resilient. His ramparts were staked with 3-branch metal spikes. His cavalry was equipped with devices with 4 sharp prongs, one of which always pointed upward. These were scattered on the ground after luring the elephants in pursuit. Large bundles of dried grass were tied to camels and buffaloes, which were driven against the advancing elephants, and set on fire at the last moment. The tactics raised terror and havoc among the giant beasts, which trampled their own men to death. Before the day was over, Mahmud and Mallu had to flee.

As the Bantu proverb puts it:

He who is stronger hits you with the stick you carry.

DECEMBER 18

On this day in the year 1792, Thomas Erskine defended Tom Paine in his trial *in absentia* in London for libeling the royal family and Parliament in *The Rights of Man*.

The British trial lawyer traced Paine's thesis on the rights of man and the necessity of the will of a whole people to change or affect the rule by which a nation is to be governed. He ended his appeal to the jury with Lucian's story: "Jupiter and a countryman were walking together, conversing with great freedom and familiarity upon the subject of heaven and earth. The countryman listened with attention and acquiescence, while Jupiter strove only to convince him—but happening to hint a doubt, Jupiter turned hastily around and threatened him with his thunder. 'Ah! Ah!' says the countryman, 'Now, Jupiter, I know that you are wrong; you are always wrong when you appeal to your thunder.' " Erskine drew an analogy to the situation at hand: "I can reason with the people of England but I cannot fight against the thunder of authority." As the attorney general rose to reply, the foreman of the jury also rose. "My Lord," he declared, "your reply will be unnecessary, unless you want to make it. The jury has already reached its verdict without any need for argument. The verdict is guilty."

As the Japanese proverb puts it:

When force pushes on, reason draws back.

DECEMBER 19

On this day in the year 1732, Benjamin Franklin published his *Poor Richard's Almanac*.

For the next 2 centuries, the wit and wisdom of the Philadelphian savant were widely quoted throughout America—but with dubious impact on the mores of the American people. "A stitch in time saves nine," so one quotation went; yet the American way continues to be crisis-paced. "A penny saved is a penny earned," so another quotation went; yet the American way continues to be deficit-based. "He is a fool that cannot conceal his wisdom," so a third quotation went; yet the American way continues to be publicity-faced, and so on and on.

As the Russian proverb puts it:

An old proverb is uttered to the winds.

DECEMBER 20

On this day in the year 1830, Charles Lamb reflected over the consequences of the poor cogitating over their own condition.

The farmers had never bothered before to think about things any more than his horse did. "Now the biped carries a box of phosphorus in his leather-breeches; and in the dead of night the half-illuminated beast steals his magic potion into a cleft in a barn, and half a country is grinning with new fires," the English writer pondered in his letter to George Dyer. "What a power to intoxicate his crude brains, just muddingly awake, to perceive that something is wrong in the social system!—what a hellish faculty above gunpowder." It was not a mere matter of revenge, but one of mischief to boot. "Think of a disrespectful clod that was trod into the earth, that was nothing, on a sudden by damned arts refined into an exterminating angel, devouring the fruits of the earth and their growers in a mass of fire! What a new existence!—what a temptation above Lucifer!"

As the Irish proverb puts it:

A ploughman is taller on his feet than a lord on his knees.

DECEMBER 21

On this day in the eighteenth century B.C., the legendary T'ang initiated the Chinese royal tradition of praying in the Temple of Heaven at the winter solstice.

Since the Emperor ruled by a Mandate from Heaven, he was permitted to continue only insofar as Heaven was pleased. Minor misfortunes represented timely admonitions. Famines and droughts were considered severe warnings to him to mend his ways. His dynasty passed to another when Heaven gave up on his tenure. Accordingly, on that day T'ang begged forgiveness for the sins of his people and himself, but accepted full responsibility for all. "If someone is to be punished," the Emperor touched his head on the floor 3 times, "let it be I."

As the French proverb puts it:

Nobility imposes obligations.

DECEMBER 22

On this day in the year 1839, Fëdor Mikhailovich Dostoevsky was about to face a firing squad on Semonovsky Square in St. Petersburg, Russia.

The young novelist had been arrested with a group of companions for spreading socialistic ideas of emancipating the serfs, abolishing censorship, and reforming other established practices. The 6 of them were tried at the Fortress of Peter-Paul and condemned to be shot. After being given the cross to kiss, the first group of 3 was marched up before the palisade for execution. Dostoevsky waited in the second group. He did not have many minutes to live. He embraced his comrades to the right and left. Then he thought of his elder brother Michael, whom he loved deeply. As the soldiers were preparing to fire, a messenger suddenly interrupted the proceedings. Retreat was sounded. The message was read. His

Imperial Majesty had commuted the death sentences. Dostoevsky was to serve 4 years of imprisonment at Omsk instead.

As the Russian proverb puts it:

Between life and death is less than a flea's hop.

DECEMBER 23

On this day in the year 1938, Meade "Lux" Lewis and Albert Ammons sat at their pianos in Carnegie Hall in New York City and introduced boogie-woogie to the concert-going public.

As the duo swung into "Beat Me Daddy, Eight to the Bar" and other boogie classics, the listeners heard something they had never sensed before—the absorbing, powerful, rhythmic contrast and the hyponotic repeated rolling figure. They nodded their heads and tapped their feet to the characteristic beat of eight-to-the-bar. This was the latest expression of the black emotional experience in their slow two-century transformation from slavery into the mainstream of American society. The African chants and litanies of the newly arrived slaves bewailing their lot in the work fields since 1651, followed by the blues of the disheartened generations, then the jazz of the spirited yearning around the turn of the twentieth century, and now the transformation of the symbolic piano of the upper-class living room into an instrument of their own language. Step by step the black man's music had been asserting his rightful place in America. Note by note he was being heard.

As the English proverb puts it:

Musicians are magicians.

DECEMBER 24

On this day in the year 1890, Emin Pasha in Central Africa entered in his daily record: "Despite any amount of hard work I can't shake off the feeling of approaching evil."

The Mohammedan explorer's sight had already begun to fail a year before; he had to lift his food to within an inch of his face to recognize what he was eating. Yet when the German Imperial government invited him to head an expedition to bring the native chiefs between Lake Tanganyika and Lake Victoria under its jurisdiction, he readily accepted. He reached the southern shore of Lake Victoria by September 1890, averaging less than 4 hours of sleep a night. By that time, his physical strength had declined to a low level. His Wambuba guides bolted soon thereafter; his bearers began to melt away. Within another year, the remaining bearers became so hungry and sick that they could barely keep up. They refused to go farther and Emin had to turn back. The next month was a succession of calamities: lightning just missing his hut, torrential rains, earthquakes. On December 6 he had to stop making meteorological calculations because of increasing blindness. On December 7, 13 cases of smallpox broke out. On December 24, 1891 his diary read: "Everybody drunk again. Little to eat. Plenty to drink; women as well . . . Hyenas are digging up our dead. Several vultures hovering about." So it went, until he was killed in Ipoto by a trader by the name of Kinena on October 23, 1892.

As the Arabian proverb puts it:

Think of coming out before going in.

DECEMBER 25

On this day in the year 1933, George Santayana expressed disappointment over the lecture of T. S. Eliot.

"What you say about Eliot's lectures is exactly what I felt," the poet-philosopher wrote about his former pupil and later Nobel Laureate to Daniel Cory. "He wasn't inspired. He didn't make the subject personal enough. If he had explained why . . . he himself would prefer illiterate public for his poetry; it might have been enlightening; and he would have had plenty of occasions to show how this newly discovered essence of living poetry, which had been running underground . . . was suppressed or possibly occasionally burst out unintentionally even in the interval. But Eliot is entangled in his own coils."

As the Hindi proverb puts it:

Write like the learned; speak like the masses.

DECEMBER 26

On this day in the year 1831, Stephen Girard lay stone cold as his will was being read.

The Philadelphian millionaire had been feared, envied, and hated throughout his life. Ruthless in business, he massed a fortune from shipping and banking, owning large tracts of land and shares in railroad and river navigation companies. He lived as a crusty, solitary miser in his old age and immersed himself in the works of Denis Diderot and others in his 4-story house. He scoffed at the churchmen and ignored the charities. People sneered behind his back. But when the provisions of his last testament were revealed, what a surprise! The city received $500,000 for civic improvements. Another $300,000 went to fixing the canals of Pennsylvania. A large sum of $6,000,000 endowed a college for orphans. New Orleans received a valuable estate. Each relative was bequeathed something; each apprentice got $500; each old servant annuities. A thousand others were remembered in cash. Overnight, Girard was glorified to the skies. Praises were lavished on him throughout the country. Even his clothes were preserved for posthumous reverence.

As the Turkish proverb puts it:

Buy the respect of the insolent.

DECEMBER 27

On this day in the year 1927, Jerome Kern heard the opening of his *Show Boat* in the Ziegfeld Theater in New York City.

The novel on which the musical was based had been written by Edna Ferber. When the composer read it, he fell in love with it and wrote the author for permission to convert it into a musical. She was adamant against the idea. On meeting Alexander Wolcott in the lobby of a theater between acts one evening, he prevailed on Wolcott for an introduction to his date, who happened to be Miss Ferber. With the aid of Wolcott, Kern spoke fast and earnestly. She then agreed, although with considerable reluctance. To eliminate the last traces of her reservations, Kern would visit her week after week with the developing music, singing the lyrics by Oscar Hammerstein. Finally came the day when he brought "Ol' Man River." Ferber treasured the moment in her memoirs:

"the music mounted, mounted, and I give you my word my hair stood on end, the tears came to my eyes. I breathed like a heroine in a melodrama. That was music that would outlast Jerome Kern's day and mine."

As the Japanese proverb puts it:

Fallen blossoms leave their fragrance behind.

DECEMBER 28

On this day in the year 1879, Arthur Sullivan finished the full score for *The Pirates of Penzance,* which he and William Schwenck Gilbert were to present on December 31 at the Fifth Avenue Theater in New York City.

That, however, was only one of the many close calls that he and his librettist had to overcome. The most serious was the threatened strike of the orchestra for higher pay. The players had decided that *The Pirates* was an opera and not an ordinary operetta. Accordingly, they asked for compensation at a higher rate. The English composer said that he was complimented by the judgment but begged to differ with it nonetheless and refused to grant the raise. Furthermore, he said that if the Americans would not perform, he knew that the Covent Garden Orchestra in England happened to be free at the moment and would be most happy to pick up the engagement. In the meantime, he would go on with himself at the piano and his friend at the harmonium. Sullivan was then "interviewed" by a local reporter, to whom he was quite free with his opinions. The musicians gave in and everything went smoothly thereafter. Little did they realize that the facts of the situation had been very much in their favor. "Of course," as Sullivan later owned up, "the idea of getting the Covent Garden band over was hardly less absurd than the ludicrous idea of using the pianoforte and harmonium in a big theater, but, fortunately, public opinion was with me, and my one game of bluff was successful."

As the Italian proverb puts it:

Keep an open contenance but a secret thought.

DECEMBER 29

On this day in the year 1777, George Washington asked his chef to devise some way of raising the morale of his troops at Valley Forge.

The winter was bitterly cold. Food was scarce. The General's ingenious camp cook managed to scrounge up a large quantity of tripe, a few vegetables, and some peppercorns. From that combination of ingredients, he invented the now well-known "Philadelphia Pepper Pot." The welcomed dish filled the empty stomachs and warmed the cold bodies, thereby helping immeasurably to stave off the down-drifting of spirit into open desertion.

As the Chinese proverb puts it:

A full stomach is heaven; the rest is luxury.

DECEMBER 30

On this day in the year 1898, Cora Crane reprimanded Alice Creelman for the way the latter responded to her appeal for contributions for the support of the 3 youngest children of Harold Frederic.

With the death of the American novelist, Mrs. Stephen Crane had been caring for Frederic's and Kate Lyon's babies for 5 months in her own home. Having run low on funds she was forced to solicit financial assistance from her friends and acquaintances. One of them was James Creelman of the *New York Journal* in London. In his absence, Mrs. Creelman opened the letter and sent back the refusal of a virtuous lady outraged at the "unfortunate scandal." Cora Crane fired a blast about those nasty gossipmongers with "blood soured by lack of true charity." Referring to the "example of Christ's loving kindness to sinners," she went on: "And how can any creature knowing itself mortal lose an opportunity to be charitable in the true sense? . . . the supreme egotism of women who never having been tempted, and so knowing nothing of the temptation of another's soul, set themselves upon their pedestals of self-conceit and conscious virtue, judging their unfortunate sisters guilty alike, is the hardest thing in life."

As the Yiddish proverb puts it:

Do good and ask not for whom.

DECEMBER 31

On this day in the year 1900, Walter Reed composed a letter to his wife about his experiment concluded on December 20, demonstrating that mosquitoes are the carriers of yellow fever.

It was 10 minutes to midnight in Quemados, Cuba. The American military doctor had been reading material written by La Roche on yellow fever, dated 1853. Now Reed was looking back on his own efforts with deep satisfaction. He wrote: "Forty-seven years later it has been permitted to me and my associates to lift the impenetrable evil that has surrounded the causation of this most dreadful pest of humanity and to put it on a rational and scientific basis. I thank God that this has been accomplished during the latter days of the old century. May its cure be wrought in the early days of the new! The prayer that has been mine for 20 years, that I might be permitted in some way or at some time to do something to alleviate human suffering has been granted! A thousand Happy New Years!"

As the Singhalese proverb puts it:

Wipe the tears off him who comes weeping.

2.

100 MANAGEMENT PROVERBS

The cumulative wisdom over the ages has been encapsulated in hundreds of thousands of proverbs. Many of these proverbs relate to various facets of leadership and executive functions. A selected 100 are presented in this appendix.

ON MASTERSHIP:

Fish rots from the head.

To be a person of principle, be first a person of courage.

When an anvil, bear; when a hammer, strike.

Nothing becomes a king so much as justice.

There are no bad soldiers under a good general.

The person with no bread has no authority.

Apply yourself too much to little things and you become incapable of great ones.

He who plows and plows but never sows does not reap.

The eagle does not stop to catch flies.

A large tree provides a large shade.

ON GOALS:

He who would be a great dragon must first eat many little snakes.

The clever rat does not eat the grain near its hole.

He is a fool who kisses the maid when he may kiss the mistress.

Asses sing badly because they pitch their voices too high.

Better weak beer than strong lemonade.
Better having a horse than knowing how to ride.
Better turning back than getting lost.
Hope of ill-gotten gains is the beginning of losses.
Peace without truth is poison.
Dead songbirds make a sad meal.

ON PERSONNEL:

Not teaching a person capable of learning is a waste of a human being; trying to teach one incapable of learning is a waste of words.
Put the saddle on the right horse.
He who has diarrhea cannot support him who vomits.
A flawed diamond is preferable to a perfect stone.
An honest person is none the worse because a dog barks at him.
A fisherman is wise in the morning, a shepherd in the evening.
An old ox makes a straight furrow.
The jackals that live in the wilds of Mazanderan can only be caught by the hounds of Mazanderan.
All are not hunters that blow the horn.
When the blind person carries the lame, both go forward.

ON PLANS:

Think of coming out before going in.
The shrike hunting the locust is unaware of the hawk hunting him.
People who would enjoy the fruit must not spoil the blossom.
One must walk a long time behind a wild duck before picking up an ostrich feather.
Do not try to catch two frogs with one hand.
The mouse with but one hole is easily taken.
It is not they who plow nearest the hedge who are the richest.
Do not throw out dirty water until you have clean.

An irrigation ditch running in the direction of the wind brings copious water.

Pick up the hen and you gather all her chickens.

ON OPERATIONS:

Set not your loaf in till the oven is hot.

Shift your sails with the wind.

One "no" averts seventy evils.

Do not make a stitch without tying a knot.

Fleece your lambs all right, but do not go beyond their tender skins.

It is better to struggle with a sick jackass than carry the wood yourself.

Numerous instructions confuse the dog.

Do not throw stone at mouse and break precious vase.

When the road bends sharply, take short steps.

Don't get shipwrecked on entering port.

ON PUBLIC RELATIONS:

If you bow at all, bow low.

He who knows not how to flatter knows not how to reign.

Care not how many you please, but whom.

Do not insult the crocodile until you have crossed the river.

Preach the sermon according to the congregation.

A bashful beggar has an empty purse.

Who will sell a blind horse praises the feet.

Goods exhibited much lose their color.

Do not throw dirt into the fountain from which you drink.

Leave a good name behind in case you return.

ON EVALUATIONS:

The end of fishing is not angling but catching.

It is not fish until it is on the shore.

He who moves not forward goes backward.

The camel is drowning and the donkey asks how deep is the water.

Counting your sheep won't keep the wolves away.

Profit is better than fame.

He pays too high a price for honey who licks it off thorns.

To lose can be to win.

Of what use is a silver cup if it is filled with tears?

A little late is much too late.

ON REWARD:

If you wish the dog to follow you, feed it.

The crow does not delouse the buffalo to cleanse him but to feed himself.

Pay peanuts and you get monkeys.

Be just before being generous.

Do not refuse a wing to the person who gave you the whole chicken.

Give a grateful person more than he asks.

Never pay with the skin when you may pay with the wool.

He doubles his gift who gives in time.

Praise makes good men better and bad men worse.

A hundred plowings do not equal one manuring.

ON PUNISHMENT:

Never spur a willing horse.

Do not beat the ox for not giving milk.

The crab bit you and you hit the water.

Whoso cannot build the dike should hand over the land.

Mercy to the criminal may be cruelty to the people.

Learn the master's name before striking the dog.

We generally rescue the drowning child out of the water before spanking him.

Much goading teaches donkey to rear.

Foolish falcon, what have you gained by taking from the little bird its nest?

Who rules by cruelty must sleep lightly.

ON EXECUTIVE PHILOSOPHY:

Govern a large country as you would fry a tiny fish.

Whosoever sacrifices conscience to ambition burns a picture to obtain the ashes.

Arrange matters such that the wolf is satisfied and the lamb yet lives.

Do not crush the flower to smell it.

One person weeping keeps the entire village from sleeping.

If you give a person a fish, he will eat once; if you teach him how to fish, he will eat the rest of his life.

Keep your friendships in constant repair.

Don't wrestle with pigs; you get dirty and they enjoy it.

Who wins when my right hand defeats my left?

The hare is not the elephant's slave, for the forest has brought them together.

NAME INDEX

Adams, Abigail S., 138
Adams, Samuel, 125
Addison, Joseph, 168
Addison, Lord, 228
Agamemnon, 7
Aguinaldo, Emilio, 188
Akbar the Great, 285
Alaric, 245
Alcibiades, 50
Alemán, Mateo, 301
Alexander, 113
Alexander I, 261
Alexander VI, 114
Alexander of Battenberg, 242
Alexander the Great, 265
Alfonso X, 86
Ali, Mohammed, 101
Allègre, 142
Allen, Fred, 161
Allende, Salvador, 6
Alsop, Stewart, 32
Alvarado, Manuel, 241
Amenhotep III, 72
Amiel, Henri-Frederic, 264
Ammons, Albert, 313
Anacletus II, 243
Anderson, Marian, 166
Andrews, C. F., 197
Anne, 148
Anthony, Susan B., 293
Antigone, 7
Antoinette, Marie, 235

Anzer, Johann, 286
Apollo, 7
Apominga, 186
Aquinas, Thomas, 45
Aranha, Oswaldo, 267
Aristotle, 16
Armas, Carlos C., 205
Ashihei, Hino, 281
Astor, John J., 123
Astray, José M., 272
Atahualpa, 246–47
Aton, 72
Attalus, 246
Auden, W. H., 33
Auersperg, Wilhelmina, 209
Augustine, 86
Augustus, Licinius, 249
Aurangzeb, 53
Avery, Benjamin, 160

Bacon, Francis, 179
Baden, Max von, 267
Baker, T. H., 144
Bakunin, Mikhail, 99
Baldridge, J. Victor, 76
Balfour, Arthur J., 280
Balleti, Manon, 274
Balzac, Honoré de, 184
Bandini, 263
Barbarossa, 262
Barber, Charles A., 207
Barton, Randolph G., 41

325

SUBJECT INDEX